WORKER PARTICIPATION

WORKER PARTICIPATION

SOUTH AFRICAN OPTIONS AND EXPERIENCES

Proceedings of the 1989 Conference on Worker Participation

Edited by
MARK ANSTEY

Director of the Industrial Relations Unit,
University of Port Elizabeth

1990
JUTA & CO, LTD

ISBN 0 7021 2440 0

Printed and bound by Eduprint, Hillstar Road, Wetton.

PREFACE

The primary purpose of this book is to open debate on the question of worker participation in South Africa. The readings comprise papers presented at the 1989 Conference on Worker Participation organised by the Industrial Relations Unit at the University of Port Elizabeth.

Worker participation is a term used to denote many concepts and practices, but unitary approaches of a technical or ideological nature have served to blunt debate and limit flexibility. The conference aimed to provide its delegates with a conceptual framework which might encompass the full range of forms of worker participation, and thence to gather together a collection of speakers with expertise in particular approaches to share their perspectives and experience within this framework. Academic and practice-based experts were approached, and two international speakers provided inputs on developments in their industrial relations systems. As with the conference, this book has the objective of opening rather than closing debate. As a consequence no concluding chapter with a prescriptive unitary approach based on the inputs of the authors or list of techniques has been attempted, and no attempt is made to have a definitive ideological 'last word' on the subject. I have confined myself to opening the discussion in chapter one with a conceptual framework which introduces the other chapters in a way that allows them to hang together in a meaningful whole for the reader, and asked the other authors to develop ideas in particular areas. This is not an uncritical approach—a critique lies not only in the first chapter but also in the range of views and approaches presented by the authors who certainly do not share an ideological stable.

It seems more than likely that South Africa will have a mixed economy based on market principles for the foreseeable future, regardless of the political dispensation to emerge from negotiations between the government, the ANC and other interest groupings. The future South Africa is not likely to have a political economy which is either rigorously worker controlled or free enterprise in character. This recognition must surely caution both utopian socialists and laissez-faire capitalists in their advocacy of particular unitary solutions for a South African economic or industrial relations system. Likewise owners of capital, managers, workers and trade unions will require a flexibility of approach in tackling issues of industrial democracy, productivity, unemployment, education and training, wealth distribution and welfare. If a mixed economy in a multiparty democracy is to emerge as a powerful and efficient remedy to the dimension of problems facing a new South Africa, then new forms of relations between labour and management will be required which move beyond the adversarial. State, private, and cooperative sectors will have to develop in an integrated fashion. A variety of forms of worker participation will be required, including a viable collective bargaining system to deal with the inherent conflict in labour–management relations but which goes beyond to also explore the potentials of cooperative endeavour at all levels of the economy. In a mixed economy a range of worker participation efforts will be required. This book is an attempt to open the debate on future alternatives as complementary rather than exclusive approaches.

Structure of the book

The book comprises two sections: the first part deals with conceptual, theoretical and practical issues, and gives attention to some international trends of influence; the second describes a selection of South African initiatives in worker participation. The work does not pretend to be either definitive or exhaustive in its scope. I am aware that there are many other initiatives in evidence in the country which deserve exploration, and trends and exploratory efforts in economies other than those described here. Hopefully follow-up texts will expand coverage.

Finally while there is some trade union work represented in this book, there is clearly not enough. This is not because there is inadequate recognition of the critically important role unions have in the introduction and implementation of participatory drives, either by way of support or resistance. Apart from the union perspectives presented here, two of the largest trade unions in the country were asked to share perspectives in the conference, particularly on their experiences of employer initiatives. In the event, one declined the opportunity at the eleventh hour, and the speaker from the other was unable to attend owing to a wave of industrial action in the industry concerned which saw thousands of union members dismissed and demanding that he be involved in negotiations for their reinstatement—a sobering background for a conference on worker participation! Again I have resisted the temptation to attempt another chapter on my own to fill the gap of the union critique—hopefully it will find expression from a trade unionist in a follow up.

With these constraints in mind I shall introduce the book with a short discussion of the contents of each chapter.

In *chapter one* concepts and issues are discussed. Various forms of worker participation are canvassed within a conceptual framework which gives consideration to the extent of participation, the level at which it is expressed, and its scope, i.e. whether it is task centred or power centred in nature. The centrality of collective bargaining in South Africa's industrial relations systems is acknowledged, but it is argued that a focus on adversarialism alone may not be sufficient for a future South Africa. Options beyond collective bargaining are then briefly explored, including bilateralism and social policy options; worker directors and works councils; worker controlled enterprises; employee shareholding schemes and shopfloor participation. After a brief debate on the merits, issues and dilemmas of each of these forms, attention is given to some requirements for a move beyond adversarialism— new vision on the part of both labour and management, appropriate organisation and a capacity for risk taking. This chapter serves as an introduction to more thorough debate in each of the areas mentioned later in the work, and attempts to supply a framework for what might otherwise have appeared to be a loose spread of papers without a direct bearing on each others' content.

In *chapter two*, Charles Nupen shares some thoughts on the problems and potentials of collective bargaining as the basic labour–management relations system pertaining in the country. In recognising the radical and often polarised nature of negotiation, he suggests a forum beyond the immediacy of the shopfloor where the parties might discuss issues of broader political significance in an attempt to locate a more cooperative drive against apartheid and human rights infringements. This theme is taken up more fully by Douwes Dekker in chapter six. Nupen proceeds to identify some of the major obstacles to an effective negotiation process in South Africa including problems associated with positional bargaining, lack of information disclosure, poor motivations, linkages and trade-offs. He suggests that a new understanding is required if the parties are to break the malaise— the concepts of good faith bargaining must be given practical expression, constituencies should give their representatives more flexibility in order to strike deals where settlement is close at hand, viable procedures must be developed and 'lived out' and serious attention must be given to the evolution of acceptable collective bargaining structures. He concludes by noting that parties need to bargain with an understanding that the country as a whole is entering a new political era, and suggests a long-term vision rather than a focus solely on immediate power plays.

Chapters three, four and five explore some international trends which have influenced current thinking on worker participation forms in South Africa. Brian Robinson provides an insight into the workings of the West German codetermination system of industrial relations, giving particular attention to structures within VWAG. The influences of this highly regulated but very participative system are evidenced to some extent in the holistic approach to industrial relations evolved by VWSA which is discussed by Brian Smith in chapter nine. Perhaps the most notable feature of the West German system is that it has succeeded in separating its adversarial and cooperative features in a way that seems acceptable to both labour and management interests. Robinson completes the chapter with some interesting perspectives on current and future developments in the West German system, including management representation, new technology, financial participation, and work reorganisation, as well as implications of Europa 1992 for the co-determination approach.

Don Power outlines some of the trends in industrial relations in the USA which have shifted parties to an active exploration of the merits and workings of cooperative endeavour. The bulk of his contribution, however, focuses on the practical aspects of establishing and maintaining effective workplace employee involvement programmes based on his extensive experience of this process. Some important lessons are shared for those parties interested in the pursuit of shop-floor approaches, not least the necessary preconditions for the process, the central involvement of top management and the union, and the importance of realistic expectations and time spans. The emphasis on training at all levels is clearly a key element of workable initiatives, and Power voices strong resistance to 'whitewash' and 'faddist' approaches. This chapter provides an interesting contrast in approach from that reflected in Robinson's chapter on the West German system, illustrating the distinction between worker participation and employee involvement.

Frank Horwitz discusses some international trends in financial participation. He proposes that a proper understanding of comparative patterns is confused by terminology and points to the need for a valid and reliable conceptual framework. Beyond this attention should be directed at both the processes which lend legitimation to schemes and to their content and structure. As with other industrial relations trends, financial participation has to be understood in the context of a country's unique history and economic developments, shifts in union power and collective bargaining arrangements. Horwitz debates the objectives of schemes, giving particular attention to managerial style issues and trade union concerns—in other words their ideological as well as mechanical aspects. He concludes with some consideration of factors which might promote cooperative coexistence between labour and management and promote the evolution of acceptable and viable participative initiatives.

In *chapter six* Loet Douwes Dekker addresses the issue of labour–management participation beyond the workplace—a joint engagement on matters of social policy. He distinguishes between political and industrial citizenship, and highlights some of the 'tough choices' which organised employer and employee groupings must make in order to influence economic and social issue at a national level. Douwes Dekker proposes that effective influence at this level requires a multi-tiered collective bargaining system with the national level acting to provide industrial relations guidelines for the other tiers, negotiate trade-offs on matters of national interest, and influence government on these issues. The evolution of an effective bilateralism might in due course see the emergence of an acceptable tripartism involving the state as an acceptable third player in the industrial relations system. The current unacceptability of the state should not preclude labour and management from attempting to tackle tasks of joint concern beyond the workplace in an effort to build a credible social democracy which would not be dependent on state actions.

Chapter seven explores the emergence, problems and potentials of worker cooperatives. Georgina Jaffee relates steps in the development of cooperatives both internationally and in south Africa, noting the diversity in their structure and organisation. She defines cooperatives as enterprises which are collectively and democratically controlled by those who work in them, and points out that they are not simply 'another way of doing business', but a vehicle for social and political change as well. Jaffe distinguishes between cooperatives and employee share ownership schemes on the basis of the issue of control. Acknowledging the limitations of cooperatives, she observes that they may be either reformist or transformative in nature. She argues that the former are directed at the economic liberation of disadvantaged people, and designed to incorporate them into the mainstream of the socio-economic system. These will have serious shortcomings in serving the interests of the majority of people in the country. She suggests that only the transformative cooperatives of the union movement can really be of major benefit, serving defensively to maintain working class unity in difficult times, and offensively to provide workers and their unions with experience in worker control and democracy. Jaffee concludes with an honest evaluation of the difficulties facing the devel-

opment of cooperatives in a hostile environment, but points
out that current initiatives are important for learning purposes and that soundly based worker controlled enterprises
are very much items for a future political and economic
agenda.

Part One of the book then, attempts to provide the reader
with a range of perspectives on worker participation and a
conceptual framework within which to organise these perspectives. Options are spread along a continuum stretching
from shopfloor initiatives to alliances beyond the workplace
on matters of social policy. Each of the options faces its own
problems of structure and implementation, and its own ideological debates. An alternative form of organising work
relations in the form of worker controlled enterprises is also
presented as an important option for a future South African
political economy. If a market-based, mixed economy is to
prevail, then it is suggested here that the full spread of options
needs to be explored, not as exclusive, but as complementary
vehicles for a just and viable dispensation. The key to effective
systems is very basic—worker participation requires genuine
joint action at whatever level it occurs and a genuine desire
on the part of the parties to shift their relations beyond the
safety of adversarialism into cooperative endeavour. A close
reading of the texts in Part One reveals no shortage of obstacles to any of the options emerging as viable.

Part Two of the book focuses on a few (too few) selected
examples of worker participation initiatives in South Africa.
These initiatives were not loosely chosen but identified as
being examples of the more theoretical options presented in
part one of this work. Thus a trade union initiative with a
cooperative is discussed linking to some of the issues and
concerns raised by Jaffee; a large employee shareholding
scheme is presented in relation to Horwitz's contribution on
approaches to financial participation; two motor manufac-

turers describe their approaches to worker participation, one clearly influenced by Japanese and American approaches (Toyota), and the other by aspects of the West German system (VWSA). The roots of these influences can be found in the chapters by Robinson and Power in Part One. Finally two specific forms of participation are discussed—a pension scheme, and health and safety measures.

In *chapter eight* Glen Cormack discusses the background to the SACTWU initiative, a trade union cooperative which emerged in response to a threatened retrenchment. Cormack outlines the debate leading up to the establishment of the cooperative before describing the details of how it was manned and structured, and pointing out some of the obstacles it has faced and will face. Some important lessons emerge from the SACTWU experience for similar initiatives in the future and for thinkers on economic options for the future.

In *chapter nine* Brian Smith describes VWSA's holistic approach to worker participation. This system attempts to cater for both individual and collective interests, and to enhance cooperative potentials without denying any of the adversarialism inherent in the relationship. Its components are evidenced from the shopfloor to high-level exchanges in the company, including quarterly strategic meetings with the union on the state of the business. The range of participative mechanisms introduced and the attempt to separate adversarial from cooperative relations are a clear reflection of the company's West German roots.

Steve Dewar's description of Toyota's total worker involvement programme in *chapter ten* reflects a different influence in its reference to Japanese concepts which the company has tried to adapt for South African conditions. Dewar gives particular attention to two aspects of Toyota's approach— quality circles and siyacabanga, discussing the essential ele-

ments for their effective implementation as well as their philosophical underpinnings. The shopfloor emphasis of the
Toyota approach has clear links with the labour–management
cooperation process outlined by Power in chapter four.

In *chapter eleven* Clive Fletcher provides an explanation of
the background to the Anglo-American employee shareholding scheme. He clarifies the corporation's thinking behind the
scheme in the context of employee stakeholding and involvement in the wealth creation process, and in relation to complementary processes of employee involvement. Apart from
describing the workings of the scheme, and the steps Anglo
took for its implementation, Fletcher also responds to its
critics and elucidates its objectives.

Chapter twelve by Rob Birt analyses the evolution of AECI's
Employees' Pension Fund from its beginnings in 1972, against
the company's philosophy of employee involvement and
participation. Birt discusses the structure and function of
participatory committees outlining the developing extent of
worker representation in management of the fund, decisions
on apportionment of benefits, interviewing spouses, contact-
ing family members of deceased persons, and changing rules
of the fund. Differences between traditional funds and the
AECI Employee's Pension Fund are addressed and Birt responds to trade union concerns about pension funds in his
conclusion.

Gopalang Sekobe of the Urban Training Project, a trade
union service body, reviews the question of worker participation in health and safety matters in the *final chapter* of the book.
He addresses questions as to the role of legislation, appropriate workplace structures, cost–benefit arguments, and cultural factors, and provides checklists on three important areas:
functions of safety shop stewards, joint union–management
safety committees, and safety policy.

ACKNOWLEDGEMENTS

This book represents a work of considerable communal effort. The gap between a conference presentation and a chapter for a book is considerable, and I am indebted to all the authors for their enthusiasm and sustained interest in the project. Very special appreciation must go to Cynthia Hopkins who typed and retyped so many of the papers, sometimes by way of transcripts off taped addresses. This arduous task cannot be undervalued, and her cheery response to having many hours of producing other peoples' work scribbled on and returned for reworking continues to amaze me. I am also very grateful for the patience, support and assistance of my family, and the staff of the Industrial Relations Unit at the University of Port Elizabeth, particularly Judy Parfitt and Martheanne Finnemore.

Gavin Stanford of Juta and Joy Wrench who wrestled with the cover design eased the agony of producing the work in final form, with consistently supportive efficiency and a high quality of workmanship.

LIST OF AUTHORS

MARK ANSTEY is Director of the Industrial Relations Unit of the University of Port Elizabeth.

CHARLES NUPEN is Director of the Independent Mediation Service of South Africa (IMSSA).

BRIAN ROBINSON is Head of International Personnel Operations, Volkswagen (AG), and is responsible for co-ordinating human resource activities throughout Volkswagen internationally.

DON POWER is a Commissioner of the Federal Mediation Service in the USA. He has over fifteen years of experience as a professional mediator. In recent times he has been active in initiating employee involvement programmes as employers and trade unions have sought to respond to shifts in the US economic and labour systems.

FRANK HORWITZ is Professor of Human Resources Management at the Graduate School of Business at the University of Cape Town.

LOET DOUWES DEKKER is Associate Professor of Industrial Relations at the Graduate School of Business at the University of the Witwatersrand.

GEORGINA JAFFEE is employed by Co-operative Planning and Education (COPE), a development organisation giving advice and assistance to organisations wishing to establish cooperatives.

GLEN CORMACK is the General Manager of Zenzeleni, the SACTWU cooperative.

BRIAN SMITH is Director of Human Resources at Volkswagen (SA).

STEVE DEWAR is Group Industrial Relations Consultant for Toyota (SA).

CLIVE FLETCHER is Manager of the Anglo American Group's Employee Shareholding Scheme.

ROB BIRT is Factory Personnel Manager of AECI's Modderfontein factory.

GOPALANG SEKOBE was employed by the Urban Training Project, a trade union resource organisation, and is a specialist on health and safety matters. He is currently furthering his education in the United Kingdom.

CONTENTS

1

Mark Anstey

WORKER PARTICIPATION: CONCEPTS AND ISSUES

INTRODUCTION

Worker participation is a widespread phenomenon internationally, appearing in various forms in the political economies of most industrialised nations. Cordova (1982) points out that while such schemes were in many instances conceived in times of economic growth for purposes of wealth redistribution, they were steeled in times of recession when tougher questions of cooperative endeavour for purposes of organisational survival and job security had to be addressed. Far-reaching changes have been required on the part of both managements and trade unions as new authority structures, decision-making levels and responsibilities have been introduced. While it is now clear that workers' participation 'is not just a passing vogue but a lasting and deeply rooted movement' (Cordova, 1982, p 126), its development has not been a systematic one, but characterised rather by a diversity of drives and initiatives across nations. This diversity has served both to invigorate and confuse the South African debate. The experiences of other countries provide a rich base of models, experiences and approaches to collective bargaining and worker participation from which to learn and local practitioners and academics have investigated many of these in the search for a South African 'model'. Not surprisingly, the learning has pulled in a variety of directions—trade unionists and socialist-leaning academics have looked to Yugoslavia's system of worker self-management, to the Mondragon experience in Spain and to the social democracies of Scandinavia for guidance. Employers and more business-based academics have found inspiration in the drives evidenced in the United Kingdom, the USA and Japan—quality circles, labour–management cooperation programmes and employee share ownership schemes, for example. What is most evident perhaps in these searches is that they are rooted primarily in the ideologies and interests of the search parties—not surprisingly each looks for models and examples which are least disruptive to its own world view. Ensuing debate is, as a consequence, often a sterile exchange wherein favoured international models are pitted against each other in a 'yours or mine/either-or' manner, often rooted in a capitalism-socialism argument in which each party argues from the sanctity of its conceptual base while attacking the practical failings and moral flaws of the other. There is of course no shortage of ammunition for such an exchange.

Many discussions ignore an area of major importance—*processes*. A focus on current systems in any country conceals the fact that they are all products of historical compromises, revolutions, economic crises, experiments and power exchanges and that none of them is in final form but really only in a stage of its own ongoing transition. Sisson (1987) points out that industrial relations systems are seldom the product of a systematic conceptual or legislative masterplan, but are rather the product of prolonged historical power exchanges and compromises between organised labour, employers and the state in the context of their evolving political economies. As a result no two systems are the same—each has been forged by unique forces within its own history.

South African labour relations are in the same sense a product of unique historical, social, political and economic forces. It is suggested here that while collective bargaining has been the method of worker participation which has developed most, other forms require attention into the future. The purpose of this book is to attempt to refine the debate on worker participation in South Africa by providing a more organised conceptualisation of its forms, and reviewing the initiatives of some companies and unions in the South African context. To this end a group of academics and local and overseas industrial relations practitioners share their perspectives and experiences on the subject in this work. The book makes no pretense of being definitive—it seeks in a cautious way to open the debate.

It is the purpose of this chapter to open the discussion, to attempt to provide a conceptual framework within which the contributions of these experts might be organised, and to provide introductory comment on the issues, directions and dilemmas which characterise the worker participation debate.

FORMS OF WORKER PARTICIPATION

In an attempt to clarify the debate Salamon (1987) proposes that the term worker 'participation' does not have a universally accepted meaning and is in fact capable of three quite different interpretations:

1   As a *socio-political concept or philosophy of industrial organisation* generally reflecting an approach which in its ultimate form would see a form of employee self-management prevail in organisations either owned by employees or the state. The managerial function is exercised through a group of elected representatives which has responsibility for organisational decision-making including the allocation of profits or surplus value. Major changes in economic and authority relations in organisations and the wider society would be required to achieve the 'vision' of this approach on a wide front.

2   As a *generic term to encompass all processes and institutions of employee influence* within organisations ranging from simple managerial information giving through joint consultation to collective bargaining, works councils and forms of worker control.

3   As a *term denoting a phase in the evolutionary development of traditional joint regulation process* envisaging a move beyond traditional collective bargaining, and certainly mere information giving and consultation ('pseudo-participation') to new levels of shared responsibility and shared decision-making ('real participation').

Salamon (1987) suggests that employee participation may be defined as:

> 'a philosophy or style of organisational management which recognises both the need and the right of employees, individually or collectively, to be involved with management in areas of the organisation's decision-making beyond that normally covered by collective bargaining' (p 296)

From this perspective systems of participation are an extension of the relationship, complementary to rather than a replacement of traditional adversarial collective bargaining.

Cordova (1982) proposes that at least four forms of worker participation are widely in evidence: shop-floor participation, works councils, collective bargaining and representation on company boards. However, beyond these a wide range of specialised participative systems have arisen to deal with such matters as health and safety (Roustang, 1983; Singleton, 1983) productivity, job classification and pension funds. Two areas of specialised participation are addressed in this volume—in Sekobe's chapter on health and safety (Chapter 13) and Birt's on AECI's pension fund (Chapter 12). Cordova states:

> 'A modern typology of workers participation should thus be based on different criteria and include various levels, forms and functions' (1982, p 127).

Similarly to Cordova (1982), Salamon (1987) proposes that an understanding of the various forms of employee participation might be promoted by differentiating between three constituent elements:

- *the method or extent of participation*—*direct* forms reflecting active individual involvement in decision-making processes, and *indirect* forms in which participation takes place through elected representatives;
- *the level in the organisation*—work station to board levels of participation.
- *the scope of participation*—lower level, direct forms of participation tend to be *task-centred* in orientation ie primarily concerned with the operational work situation; higher level, indirect forms of participation, on the other hand, tend to be *power centred* ie focused on managerial authority and decisions which determine the framework or environment within which operational decisions have to be made.

With some liberal modifications and extensions of Salamon's basic model to include processes beyond the workplace as well as within it, the following conceptual framework (figure 1.1) is proposed as a means of organising the worker participation debate in South Africa. Two directions may be discerned in worker participation initiatives: ascending forms and descending forms (Salamon, 1987; Blunt, 1978).

Before moving to an introductory comment on each of the forms of worker participation, some observations are necessary on the history and prospects of collective bargaining in South Africa.

Collective bargaining

Collective bargaining is the form of worker participation most in evidence internationally. Cordova (1982) observes:

'It may be carried on under different circumstances and by different means, and even under certain restrictions, but it remains one of the few

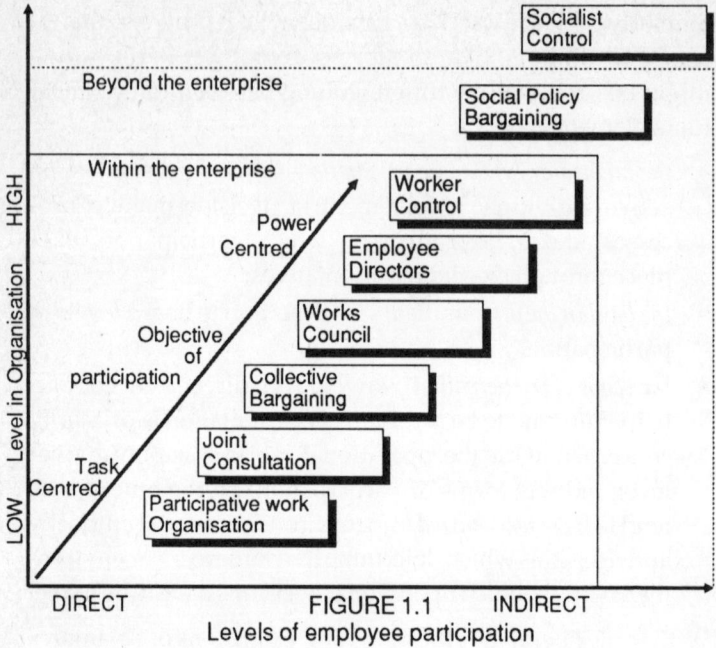

FIGURE 1.1
Levels of employee participation

forms of worker participation which cuts across ideological and national boundaries and can be found almost anywhere in the world' (p 128).

It is functional, flexible and, I believe, resilient, owing to the security of role its adversarial character provides for employers and trade unions alike.

Despite major obstacles it is certainly in this area that the major developments in South African labour–management relations have taken place. The first Industrial Conciliation Act of 1924 coupled with a vigorous programme of racial protectionism and upliftment effectively tamed the militancy of the white labour force producing a lasting labour peace in respect of this group. However, the deliberate exclusion of black workers limited industrial democracy (as with political democracy) to a minority of the country's workforce. The militancy of black workers was dealt with via acts of suppression rather than negotiation.

Since the reforms of 1979 and 1981 which followed the Wiehahn Commission a fiercely independent trade union movement has arisen, wary of co-optation by what it perceives as a traditional white state, white labour, white capital alliance and actively committed to wider political liberation. Aided by international pressures, economically driven shifts in employer stances, economic and demographic imperatives the trade union movement of the eighties has vigorously asserted itself in the remoulding of the collective bargaining system. New levels of bargaining (plant, company and enterprise), new labour rights through the industrial court, raised wage levels, a dramatic influence over personnel practices and a political protest presence have all been achieved in a decade. An extraordinary growth rate in numerical strength underpins the unions' power, but also gives rise to weaknesses of stretched infrastructures and services. Divisions along ideological lines have presented the union movement with crises in achieving unity, and an absence of political reform obliged a political role exacerbating divisions and bringing with it state harassment. Membership expectations, problems of leadership, control and democracy and uneasy relations at times, not only with the state and employers, but other struggle groups are further problems which have had to be faced.

The decade has been a stressful one for many employers. Economic, political and international pressures coupled with the militancy of the 'new industrial relations' have witnessed an unsteady shift from coercive or paternalistic unitarism toward more constitutional managerial styles. Still, it appears that employers have yet to develop the coherence (and the desire to create such a coherence) to act as a co-ordinated influence group in the wider society.

Collective bargaining relations have evidenced twin thrusts of disruption and institutionalisation—raised levels of industrial and political action by labour have been accompanied by a rapid growth in the use of conciliation mechanisms, the industrial court and plant, company and industry level agreements. Such apparently incompatible drives are readily explicable in the strains of an evolving democracy as parties seek to establish balances and boundaries in new power relations, especially in a context of wider conflict.

Into this delicately balanced scenario the state chose to inject the Labour Relations Amendment Act. It is trite theory that effective conflict regulation requires channels, procedures and institutions legitimised by the parties who make use of them—as such the new Act was retrogressive, creating new levels in conflict rather than contributing to its institutionalisation. Apart from steps undertaken at the level of relations with organised employer groupings, trade unions have embarked on drives to pressure employers to bargain outside the Act. Typical efforts to create a new labour dispensation beyond the Act include those of SACTWU and the principles embodied in the IG Metall Code with which German multinationals have been faced (Appendix A).

Once one has acknowledged the strains in the country's collective bargaining system, its mechanical and relationship based problems and the external pressures under which it must operate, several other points must be made. Arguably it has limitations beyond those of its internal workings.

The enormity of South Africa's political, economic and social problems is now well documented. Low growth rates, low investment confidence, poor productivity levels, inflation, the flight of capital, taxation, the population explosion, the unemployment crisis, and rapidly escalating problems in housing, education, health and welfare are national problems that will transcend the eradication of apartheid. They will demand practical solutions beyond the long-term blame which will be ascribed to apartheid, and organised labour and capital will be inescapably involved in this process. Simply, collective bargaining is unlikely to be sufficient to the task. Arguably a developing economy cannot afford ongoing high levels of industrial action and poor productivity, at some point it must address issues of unemployment and inflation and the influence of wage levels on these. Nation-building will require a capacity for labour–management parties to move beyond the adversarialism inherent in their relationship, to a more open acknowledgement of their interdependence and the creative development of co-operative endeavour as well. A glance at international trends indicates that this would not be a unique shift—it moves the relationship into a range of worker participation options, adjusts it from one confined to annual bouts of adversarial exchange to one which in addition places greater emphasis on the daily relations of the workplace in an effort to achieve optimum levels of organisational performance, and at federation levels sometimes to a focus on social policy matters.

What then, are the options beyond collective bargaining?

BEYOND COLLECTIVE BARGAINING: WORKER PARTICIPATION OPTIONS

Bilateralism and social policy options: joint endeavour beyond the enterprise

Since 1983 Douwes-Dekker has published several papers (1983, 1986, 1987, 1988) advocating that organised labour and organised employer groupings engage more meaningfully in an effort to influence social policy. His argument suggests a number of bargaining levels moving from plant level to relations through national organisations on issues of macro-significance for the country as a whole. The levels proposed are summarised in figure 1.2.

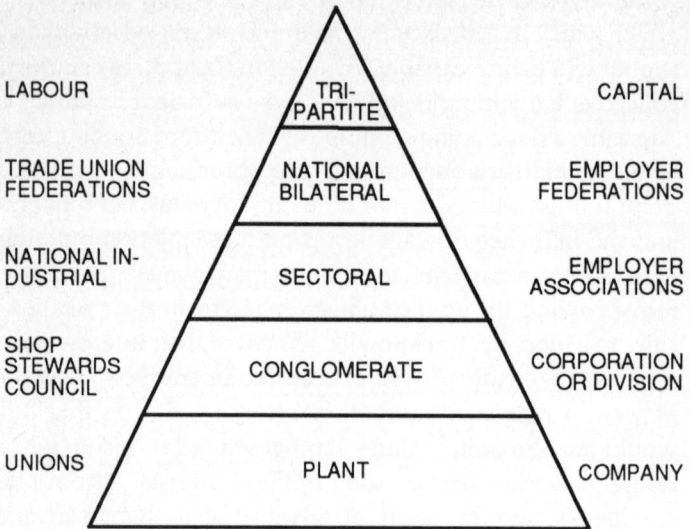

FIGURE 1.2
Levels of collective bargaining

At national level, Douwes-Dekker proposes a twofold objective for agreement between the parties:

1 the provision of a framework of basic principles to guide industrial relations practices at other levels; and

2 macroeconomic tradeoffs between employers and trade unions in response to national needs.

In short, nationally organised employer and labour groupings would act to establish collective bargaining ground rules and engage on issues of resource distribution and social policy including such matters as social security, economic development, manpower, taxation, unemployment and job creation, health and safety, education and training. A system of self-governance in industry is envisaged that would be neither proposed by the state nor require its intervention or support (1988, p 74). An effective engagement at this level could lay the base for a developing influence on government policy, allowing the evolution of tripartite relations involving the state. In this way Douwes-Dekker suggests a social corporatism might be developed to moderate state control and allow the evolution of a stable democracy. Social corporatism of this sort is evidenced in such countries as Austria, Netherlands, Sweden and Norway and in weaker form in West Germany, Belgium, Denmark, Ireland and Italy (Douwes-Dekker, 1988; Treu and Negrelli, 1987).

Since the demise of TUCSA in 1986, statutory bodies influencing government policy have lacked a labour representivity with COSATU and NACTU refusing to legitimate the system with their participation. Labour policy is seen, therefore, to emanate from state and employer interests with all the consequences of suspicion and system discreditation that this induces.

The passage of the 1988 Labour Relations Amendment Act served to entrench these negative consequences when the government decided, apparently unilaterally to promulgate the Act in full, despite a SACCOLA/COSATU/NACTU agreement that parts of it be suspended. Labour's three-day stayaway to greet the new legislation prior to its promulgation provided a dubious welcome for a piece of legislation whose primary purpose is to promote labour peace through processes of collective bargaining. 1989 witnessed a pursuance by organised labour of its objective of seeing the Act scrapped, and could give rise to extensive industrial or stayaway action in the future. Questions surround the feasibility of a social corporatism in the South African context.

• Is it appropriate in the South African context?

• Is it achievable?

• Does the necessary coherence exist in labour and management parties?

- Are the conditions right for the development of a social corporatism?

A unique opportunity would seem to exist to take a first step in the social policy area with the SACCOLA/CO-SATU/NACTU discussions on the Labour Relations Act—do the parties have the desire and/or the capacity to exploit it?The wider debate relating to employers' and trade unions' engagement on social policy issues is enlarged on by Douwes-Dekker (Chapter 6).

Worker directors and works councils: high-level co-operation within enterprises

The concept of worker directors has its origins in West Germany's system of co-determination. The idea was mooted in the 1920s by the Social Democratic Party and organised labour as they attempted to democratise the economy and later to find a passage between capitalism and socialism. The Co-determination Acts of 1951 and 1976 entrenched worker directors in organisations employing more than 2 000 persons, and the Works Constitution Acts of 1952 and 1972 a system of worker representation through elected works councils. Over the years a highly institutionalised industrial relations system has evolved based in a detailed legislation and series of court decisions which separate out the places of adversarial collective bargaining (and the right to strike) and more co-operative labour–management relations. The former is union-centred and generally takes place at industry level, the latter occurs at enterprise level where worker representatives engage with managers on a wide range of labour, personnel, administrative and welfare issues through works councils and worker directors. Enterprise co-determination is but one of the levels envisaged by organised labour as a means of democratising the entire economy—it is part of wider political process (Schregle, 1987).

Worker directors

The idea of worker directors has been pursued in other European countries such as France, Denmark and the Netherlands and, to a very limited extent, the United Kingdom. Managers in these countries tend to view the value of worker directors as a means of establishing a coalition between workers and management leading to conflict reduction, raised employee awareness of business problems, improved levels of organisational commitment, lessened resistance to managerial decisions and improved decision-making. Unions, on the other hand, are equivocal in their views, some seeing the presence of worker representatives on the board as diluting the 'challenge' role and power of the trade union, others taking the view that every opportunity should be taken to establish joint control at all levels in organisations and that board participation offers opportunities to influence key decisions affecting workers' lives (Salamon, 1987).

The co-option versus influence debate centres itself really in discussion as to whether worker participation implies involvement in the *management of* an enterprise or in *decision-making for* the enterprise (Nel, 1984). Running through this debate are questions as to whether the German two-tier system is more appropriate than a unitary single-tier structure. In the two-tier system worker directors are involved at supervisory board level in the long-term policy issues of a company rather than in the more immediate (and contentious) area of immediate strategies and decisions at Board of Director level (ie decision-making for versus management of the enterprise). Opponents of this approach propose that it negates the purpose of worker participation if elected directors are not involved in operational issues.

Whichever way a board is structured in terms of levels, weighting of representation or assigned responsibilities, worker participants face the reality that power and decision-making are likely to reside with senior management. It is this usually small group of persons who have the expertise, knowledge and current information required to run an operation, and to whom power is delegated for daily decision-making. Boards meet relatively infrequently, are reliant on information and proposals from senior management and usually occupy an endorsement rather than a direct managerial role (Salamon, 1987).

Other problems centre around the industry base of most unions. Access to strategic information at board level in one company may have direct relevance to bargaining or participation in other companies in an industry or region. In such instances clear dilemmas exist—what are the boundaries of confidentiality? To whom does the worker director owe first loyalty, the company, company employees or the wider union membership? In South Africa, of course, worker directors may find themselves unwilling partners in having to implement 'unfriendly' government laws and policies. Cooptation by the State is as real a possibility as that by capital.

Works councils
The German Works Council is

> '... not a joint body but consists of elected workers' representatives only. It is an instrument for labour–management co-operation and has both advisory and collective bargaining functions of the trade unions . . . it must not bargain on remuneration and other conditions of employment which . . . are normally fixed by collective agreement between trade unions and employer associations' (Schregle, 1987, p 320).

In West Germany, then, works councils may be equated with trade unions in other countries which bargain at enterprise level with the *important distinction* that they may not engage in 'industrial warfare' but are confined to co-operative endeavours for which they are legally empowered by the wide-ranging Works Constitution Acts. The lesson of the system is that the parties have managed to find a balance in the tension

between concurrent thrusts of adversarialism and co-operation by appropriate attention to both in an exchange of
mutual benefit.

The workings of the West German system are elucidated
by Robinson (Chapter 3), and its influences on a South African
enterprise illustrated in Smith's description of worker participation initiatives in VWSA (Chapter 9).

Worker control and ownership: gaps and dilemmas

Worker-controlled enterprises

The dilemmas associated with participation at high organisational levels, coupled with strong ideological stances, act
often to restrict trade unions to the position that worker
control is the best option and until this is attained that collective bargaining is the least compromising of the available
alternatives. The case for a socialised South African economy
has been made by several authors (Davies, 1987; Innes & Gelb,
1987).

While some believe that the full benefits of worker-controlled enterprises can only be achieved when an entire society rejects capitalism, others propose that they might be
developed in an evolutionary manner (Pillay, 1987). In addition they are perceived as having a clear place in a mixed
economy, and indeed are identified as one of the major sectors
in such a future economy for South Africa in the ANC's
constitutional guidelines (Johnson, 1988).

For many years the Yugoslav system has been used to
exemplify the values of worker self-management, but of
course off a base of social or state ownership in a single-party
system. Apart from the fact that a relocation of such a system
in South Africa is unlikely, the current crisis in the Yugoslav
system has prompted a caution as to its merits. It appears that
a revision is underway whereby not only control but ownership is being returned to private hands in a 'democratic

revolution'. The Mondragon co-operative in Spain which has been developed over a period of many years is a case where ownership and control have been successfully linked.

Worker-controlled enterprises in socially controlled or market economies face problems. In socialist societies it has been argued that they have contributed to economic stagnation and misallocation of resources as public funds are used to subsidise non-economically viable operations, and that control without ownership has witnessed a rise in wages instead of appropriate investment. In market economies they tend to be under-financed, experience problems in attracting competent managerial expertise and limit investment opportunities for worker owners who must plough back their savings into an operation which may not provide them with the best returns. Problems of ownership and control arise and may be experienced in attempting to operate in isolation in a free-enterprise context (Pillay, 1987). Nevertheless a wide variety of market, ownership, employee commitment as well as job preservation and creation questions might be addressed through the development of worker-controlled enterprises in the South African context. They may prove a useful vehicle for bridging gaps between collectively oriented groups anxious to participate in the economy and current owners of capital anxious to see the survival of a market system. They offer opportunities to extend ownership and control of the means of production and for financial institutions to extend access to capital in a business rather than a welfare spirit.

The Frame/SACTWU initiative is thus an important one for South Africa as a whole and the manner in which it is financed and structured and deals with issues of control, authority and wealth distribution will carry important lessons and indicators for future projects.

Problems and potentials of worker co-operatives are enlarged on by Jaffee (Chapter 8) and Cormack provides an early commentary on the SACTWU co-operative in Chapter 9.

Employee share ownership

A counter-thrust to the concept of socialist-type worker-controlled enterprises has arisen in the form of employee share ownership drives which have assumed a prominence in the USA and the UK over the past fifteen years. Between 1974 when Congress in the USA first passed facilitative tax laws and 1987, the number of employee owned (or partially owned) companies grew to about 8 100, and stock ownership jumped from 250 000 to between eight and eleven million (Rosen & Quarrey, 1987; Nagy, 1987). The underlying premise in this trend is that the free-enterprise system might be best preserved through an extension of ownership:

> 'Justice would be hindered by abolishing private property; instead ownership should be shared. The genius of worker capitalism ... lies in permitting the continued existence of a market economy, property rights, and political freedom while also addressing the problem of inequality by making every man a capitalist. The idea of a reformed type of capitalism more than just socialism excites liberals and conservatives alike' (p 188).
>
> Worker capitalism ought to be accepted or rejected for what it is, and it is not socialism. Socialism is the ownership of the means of production by the State, not by individuals. Some people call it capitalism when managers exercise stock options and take equity positions in the companies in which they are employed, yet they call it socialism when workers do the same thing' (p 197) (O'Toole, 1979).

The purposes of such schemes are diverse, including drives to save jobs, reform capitalism, share wealth created, increase motivation, create a sense of common identity with the company, raise capital via tax concessions, acquire other companies and settle labour disputes.

The ESOP idea has received considerable interest in South Africa, not least owing to a growing realisation that inequities in ownership require urgent redress and that a lack of widespread ownership is a very real threat to the free enterprise system employers are so anxious to promote. In a 1989 survey Maller estimated that about 120 companies had introduced some form of shareholding scheme in South Africa. The most highly publicised of these include Anglo's and Pick 'n Pay's schemes, and the Samcor trust established when Ford withdrew from the country. Internationally trade unions have voiced concerns over such schemes, pointing out that new levels of shared financial risk are seldom accompanied by new levels of organisational decision-making or information disclosure.

Doubts have been expressed over their value in improving worker commitment to the organisation. Share prices are not directly linked to worker or company performance and unions believe schemes are often introduced without proper negotiation and in many cases do not result in improved rewards for workers. Financial participation is quite unrelated to control of organisations and unions have voiced suspicion over suspected co-optive strategies on the part of employers. Heckscher (1988) in reviewing the stock ownership drive in the USA suggests that many of the boldest initiatives have been taken by companies facing serious financial crisis and that unions are uncomfortable in their new roles as partners in losing firms, feeling resentment in sharing responsibilities only at points of lowest ebb. Many schemes have not dramatically turned the fortunes of companies and extended ownership certainly does not equate with the co-determination of some Western Europe countries. In South Africa there is a view that such schemes do little to resolve fundamental inequalities and injustices in the economy (Maller, 1988; Daphne, 1988; Mastrantonis, 1987).

Cyril Ramaphosa, NUM's general secretary met the news of Anglo's scheme with a blunt 'It stinks'. Nevertheless,

Anglo's scheme has a wide participation albeit on a give-away basis at present and will receive its acid test in a few years' time when workers can choose to sell or retain their shares. When one has finished with the reservations and suspicions it is clear that ESOPs have taken off internationally and that under certain circumstances they are experienced positively. In essence it would appear that they are effective overseas to the extent that they are part of a wider approach to participation by management (a holistic thrust); involve all employees; involve disclosure of information and carry 'felt' benefits (ie meaningful levels of ownership). Beyond this ESOPs are not a substitute for an adequate wage level and unions usually insist that this area be attended to through processes of collective bargaining before showing an interest in other forms of financial participation. (Bell & Hansen, 1984; Rosen, 1987; Daphne, 1987; Maller, 1988).

International trends in financial participation are reviewed by Horwitz (Chapter 5) providing a context for Fletcher's explanation of the thinking behind Anglo American Corporation's Employee Shareholding Scheme (Chapter 11).

Shopfloor participation: co-optation or co-operation?

Direct worker participation in work process issues in which they are directly involved is perhaps the type of system most favoured by employers. It occurs at low levels in an organisation, is seen to improve productivity and organisational performance and is the least threatening of the available range of options in terms of challenges or adjustments to managerial authority.

Small group activities to raise productivity and improve labour–management relations have been in use in Japan since the 1950s. In 1986, 77% of Japanese companies employing over 10 000 employees were using such team activities. A postwar Japan firmly intent on rebuilding its economy and on establishing itself as an international competitor centred major drives on quality control, mobilising workers into participation in operational decision-making purposes. Out of these drives arose the *quality circle* concept which developed into a national movement contributing to the transformation of the Japanese economy. In many senses it has been successful in Japan owing to its 'natural fit' into cultural values of a unitary nature with an emphasis on collectivism and paternalism, its acceptance by managers and unions alike in a common spirit of nation-building, the company versus industry focus of unions, participative management philosophies, nationwide promotion of the method coupled with training and the lifetime employment practices of many Japanese companies (Crocker et al, 1986).

In the early 1970s companies in the USA made some tentative moves to introduce quality circles as they recognised the necessity of identifying more efficient production methods in the face of stiffening international competition, especially from Japan and other Asian countries. Heckscher (1988) writes:

'The entry of nations with lower standards of living into markets traditionally dominated by US firms has produced major dislocation including absolute declines in employment in the formerly core manufacturing sector' (p 56).

The consequence was a major shift in the profile of jobs in an urgent economic and organisational restructuring of American industry reflecting a major shift to a post industrial society—a service rather than a manufacturing-based economy. Traditional patterns of adversarialism and legalism and the power of the strike weapon were rendered increasingly inappropriate in the face of automation, declining union strength in a diminishing manufacturing sector and as a consequence of wider social changes (Heckscher, 1988). One method by which employers sought to improve organisational performance levels was worker participation at operational levels and adapting the Japanese quality circle to American culture. Two major themes have emerged in US labour relations as efforts are made to move beyond traditional collective bargaining into a new participatory engagement with returns for all—'managerialism' (managing without unions) and programmes of labour–management co-operation (Quality of Work Life or QWL) (Anstey, 1989).

In the first—*managerialism*—trade unions are seen as an obstacle or at least unnecessary to participation. The 'new managerialism' suggests that effective management leading to economic growth should be based on the co-ordinated independence of small groups operating in an innovative autonomous manner rather than through a bureaucratic work rule approach underpinned by an inflexible base of legalism built up over the years by trade unions anxious to secure their members' rights in an age of different problems and challenges. Wide-ranging communication channels, protections against arbitrary power, job security, personal planning and organisation development thrusts are offered in place of unions. (Foulkes 1981; Heckscher 1988). Procter & Gamble, Honeywell, Hewlett-Packard, Westinghouse and IBM are some of the names associated with this kind of thinking.

The other drive—*QWL*—is based in a recognition that while old-style unionism and collective bargaining may be inappropriate to new challenges, this does not render their usefulness suddenly redundant. Abuses of power and the ongoing existence of grievances and conflicts in places of work mean that independent representation of worker interests is still important. A realisation was reached that managerialism could not substitute the values of traditional unionism effectively, but neither could traditional unionism remain immutable in a changing environment. Trade unions under pressure have been required to move beyond collective bar-

gaining and the strike weapon to other forms of representation and participation to continue to effectively articulate concerns, set standards and represent members' interests.
They face a real dilemma—a continuation of traditional adversarialism could well see a continuation of an already long-
term decline, a step into participation demands fundamental
changes in structures, policies and practices.

Quality of Work Life programmes tend to be programmes
of co-operation between organised labour and management
based in a common endeavour to see their enterprises survive
and grow in an increasingly competitive environment. Large
unions such as the UAW and CWA have committed themselves to such initiatives as have many unionised employers.
Dramatic changes are required: management styles have had
to be shifted at all levels, new levels of information sharing
embarked on, authority relations adjusted and 'union bash-
ing' dropped as a tactic; unions have had to risk moving
beyond the challenge role into organisation building and
training roles, to adjust their philosophies and risk members'
perceptions of co-option by management. Importantly, QWL
has not attempted to replace collective bargaining—it has
recognised that labour-management relations have an inevitable adversarial component, but that more is required. As a
consequence some novel tradeoffs as regards peace obligations, job security, wage improvements and organisational
growth have been evidenced. (Heckscher, 1988; Kochan &
Katz, 1988; Anstey, 1989).

Power (Chapter 4) explores the major shifts in US labour–
management relations underpinning the move to employee
involvement programmes, and in more practical vein outlines
the key elements of what makes such initiatives successful.
Dewar (Chapter 10) outlines the philosophy and practices of
Toyota's Total Worker Involvement Programme as an

example of a South African approach which has its roots in the drives evidenced in Japan and the USA.

SOME REQUIREMENTS FOR A MOVE BEYOND ADVERSARIALISM

Worker participation has been proposed to hold the key to the achievement of a wide range of organisational, individual and nation-building objectives. Increased job satisfaction is proposed as the vehicle for improved motivation and enhanced productivity; a sense of belonging and relevance is proposed to increase organisational loyalty; adjustments of traditional autocratic decision-making structures and improved communication channels are mooted as the means to a more meaningful industrial democracy allowing the proper expression of worker rights as organisational stakeholders and as having the consequence of improved problem-solving and lowered resistance to decisions. Improved supervisory relations, new efficiencies, raised levels of competitiveness, a new regard for worker rights, and co-operative endeavour in nation-building are themes which run through the literature.

However, also clearly reflected are the obstacles: autocratic management styles, union suspicion and resistance, racial attitudes, educational levels, inadequate basic wages and conditions of employment, ideological differences, the absence of shared values, the volatile socio-political context, role dilemmas for the parties, the sharing of strategic information are all cited as problems.

Several questions must be addressed in the South African context:

- Is worker participation a desirable process?
- What forms should it take?
- Is it an achievable objective and which forms are most attainable/acceptable in the first instance?

It is suggested here that whatever forms are pursued several prerequisites exist.

New vision

Strong ideological stances have an important mobilising value but can create a rigidity in positions prohibiting the development of strategic alliances, movement off positions or engagement with opponents to search for settlements in no-win scenarios. Thompson (1988) has observed that since the 1970s unions have been indiscriminate in their responses to employers, failing to separate progressive elements from others and thus limiting scope 'for a creative dialectic'. He argues that there is a compelling and urgent need for such unions to re-evaluate their strategies towards employers if they are to strengthen themselves into the future.

Blind confrontationalism is a crude form of engagement inadequate for nation-building purposes. It may have been necessary for some unions to oblige recalcitrant employers to the bargaining table or recognise fair employment practices, and for some employers desirous of establishing reality-based boundaries on employee behaviour. However, all too often coercion and disruption are really the product of clumsy mismanagement of industrial relations, of loss of control, of misjudged power realities or ignorance or malice. A blunt reliance on stayaways, strikes, dismissals and interdicts reduces the relationship to one of coercion only; efforts to render conflictual relations manageable solely through procedural and legal measures move to a rigidity in exchange.

Entrapment in the conflict process limits possibilities of a more creative engagement between parties. Determinists will argue that the process is so irrevocably advanced in the wider society as to render the relationship-building and organisational restructuring required for effective worker participation progress a hopeless dream. Indeed there are popular beliefs that such programmes merely blunt the thrust necessary for full liberation, or represent appeasement of militant elements who should rather be 'tamed'. The question really centres around whether in an escalating conflict situation parties will retain the desire or capacity to create or exploit co-operative opportunities.

A softening, at least on a selective basis, will be required if labour–management relations are to move beyond adversarialism. Trade unions are not attracted to the idea of co-operative endeavour with employers whom they perceive to be architects in oppressive laws, or allies in their use. In this regard clearer, more coherent stances on apartheid and labour laws are required from employers. Likewise employers are not excited by calls to move outside the framework of the law or share decision-making with trade unions unable or unwilling to abide by agreed procedures, whose members are involved in acts of intimidation and violence, who advocate measures likely to damage company viability and who promise a future of blanket worker control.

It has also been argued that the required flexibility can emerge only when all parties to a problem share a perception of common crisis—as long as a party believes it can prevail, a lifting of pressure on the other is unlikely, and is even seen as dangerous to the achievement of an end goal. The problem is that parties bent on creating crises for others may fail to recognise their own and the consequent need to move out of confrontationalism. As long as parties deny the legitimacy of others seeing them as part of the problem rather than solutions then we will be locked into direct conflict.

Ideological softening requires the development of a new vision on the part of organised labour and employers. International shifts away from the 'isms'—capitalism and socialism—to political economies structured around pragmatic questions of economic growth, employment creation, foreign trade and investment, and competitiveness in world markets have supplanted the dogma of previous years. A South African shift would not represent something unique in the world picture; the question really centres on whether labour and management in this country can or want to move beyond the wider civil conflict in a joint nationbuilding endeavour.

Organisation

If new vision is to be carried through in action it will require organisation and the commitment of constituencies. Sectional interests of a racial, cultural or ideological nature will have to give way to a national concern. Internal coherence is required within interest groups for either struggle or co-operative endeavour. Current levels of fragmentation and division in both union and employer camps are a contribution to the status quo. A courageous and responsible leadership is required to lead shifts in strategy and position. Koopman's Cashbuild initiative has stimulated discussion on new forms of labour–management engagement with its clear bottom-line impact. Its success was no doubt due to a wide variety of factors including not only a new management–worker ethos but the context in which this was developed—a small and scattered organisation and its wholesale character were no doubt of assistance. The 'model' may have limited applicability to other more centralised, industrial companies with large unionised workforces, but to limit the critique to these observations would be to miss the point. The fact is that Cashbuild was a success. A leader with some vision was able to regenerate an organisation, restructure its operations and improve its performance through a more creative engagement with workers, and the qualities of leadership to see his vision through. The process is the message rather than the model.

Risk

If parties are unable to build a mutual respect or trust through the manner in which they conduct their adversarial relations then their capacity to move to endeavours of joint co-operation will be sharply constrained. Industrial relations becomes limited to annual substantive negotiations of a distributive nature and further contact to disputes which arise on an ad hoc basis.

A move beyond adversarialism demands new managerial styles, new union roles, new areas of joint responsibility and shared decision-making styles, new union roles, organisational restructuring and information sharing, new communication systems, joint training and commitment from top management and trade union representatives. It involves a step into the unknown for both. Recent initiatives with Relationship by Objectives (RbO) programmes in South Africa have been positive in helping parties engage in long-term relationship building, but indicate how difficult such steps can be after periods of prolonged confrontation (Anstey, 1989). When parties enter the process, however, they convey a signal of willingness to each other that they are desirous of building a new accord. The risk, of course, is not only embarking on new courses of action with uncertain outcomes, but letting go of old entrenched modes of exchange—adversarial roles may be what holds some unions and employer groupings tenuously together; moves beyond this may rupture already weak alliances and expose internal disorganisation.

CONCLUSIONS

This paper has proposed, *inter alia*, that the diversity of forms of worker participation internationally has served to both invigorate and confuse debate in South Africa on the issue. A broad framework has been outlined based on Salamon's (1987) proposals to assist in clarifying concepts and forms of workers participation. A brief introduction to these various forms has been provided in an effort to highlight some of the major issues of debate in their introduction and implementation. The following major proposals were made:

1   While the major developments internationally and in South Africa to date have been in collective bargaining this is a stressed process currently and will, in isolation, be inadequate for nationbuilding purposes in the future.

2   Opportunities exist for an accord on social policy issues with possible far-reaching implications for the development of a stable economy. Obstacles to seizing these exist in the form of ideological caution, division within employer and employee camps and environmental factors.

3   Obstacles to progress in the direction of worker directors lie in role dilemmas, levels of influence and ideological stances.

4   Worker-controlled enterprises, while having a largely uninspiring international track-record, could hold potentials for South Africa in bridging ideological gaps, job creation and the development of a broader based market economy. Problems lie in the area of financing, managerial expertise and dilemmas of authority/control.

5   Employee share ownership schemes have made progress internationally and are being introduced in South Africa, but are not really forms of participation generally in senses beyond the financial.

6   Forms of shopfloor participation have been successfully introduced in countries where a greater ideological consensus exists and in the face of threats to the national economy. Problems arise where they are seen as a means to subvert trade unions, and in their limited scope by unions intent on a wider reorganisation of control in places of work.

South African employers and unions will have to move beyond adversarialism for nation building purposes in the future. In this regard it is proposed that:

1 New vision is required involving a softening of ideological stances and adversarial action to move to more creative joint endeavours.

2 New levels of internal coherence and courageous and responsible leadership will be required to lead shifts in strategy and position.

3 Relationships must become focused on matters other than adversarial exchange involving a risk on the part of both to engage in new structures and systems of joint decision-making.

This book considers some relevant overseas trends and gives more detailed consideration to some of the options available to South African labour–management parties and to some of the initiatives already undertaken.

REFERENCES

Anstey, M 'Bilateralism: Some Perspectives for South African Industrial Relations' Unpublished paper delivered at Natal Chamber of Industries. June, 1989

Anstey, M 'The Labour Movement in the USA: History and Prospect' *I R Research and Topics Series No 2* IR Unit University of Port Elizabeth, June, 1989. ISBN 0869 883844.

Anstey, M 'Relationships by Objectives: Some Early Observations of Theory & Practice in South Africa' *Industrial Relations Journal of South Africa* Vol 9 No 3 1989, pp 47–60.

Bell, D W & Hansen, C G *Profit Sharing and Employee Shareholding Attitude Survey* Industrial Participation Association. 1984.

Cordova, E 'Workers' Participation in Decisions within Enterprises' *International Labour Review* Vol 121, No 2, March–April, 1982, pp 125–139.

Crocker, O L, Charney, S & Sik Leung Chiv, J *Quality Circles: A Guide to Participation and Productivity* New York; Mentor Books. 1984.

Daphne, J 'Worker Ownership of Shares at Pick 'n Pay—Union Comment' *SA Labour Bulletin*. October, 1987. pp 2–5.

Davies, R 'Nationalisation, Socialisation and the Freedom Charter' *SA Labour Bulletin* Vol 12, No 2. 1987.

Douwes-Dekker, L C G 'Social Policy and the Role of Employers' Associations' *SA Journal of Labour Relations* Vol 7, No 4, December 1983. pp 40–57.

Douwes-Dekker, L C G 'Research Note on the Concept of Corporatism from an Industrial Relations Perspective' Unpublished paper, Wits Business School, July, 1986.

Douwes-Dekker, L C G 'Workers' Participation in South Africa: Some suggestions' *Industrial Relations Journal of South Africa* Vol 7, No 4. 1987.

Douwes-Dekker, L C G 'Tripartism *SA Journal of Labour Relations* Vol 11, No 4. December 1987. pp 18–29.

Douwes-Dekker, L C G 'The Role of Federations of Unions and Employers' Associations in Negotiating the Parameters of Social Policy' *Research Paper No 9* Wits Business School. December, 1988. ISBN 1 868140806.

Douwes-Dekker, L C G 'Towards Bilaterial Self Governance' *Indicator SA* Vol 5 No 4. Spring 1988. pp 72–75.

Fowkes, F K 'How Top Non-Union Companies Manage Employees' *Harvard Business Review* Vol 59, No 5. September–October 1981. pp 90–96.

Heckscher, C C *The New Unionism* New York; Basic Books. 1988.

Innes, D & Gelb, S 'Towards a Democratic South Africa' *Third World Quarterly* April, 1987.

Johnson, S 'Charting a new Course for the Charter' *Weekly Mail* August, 12–18 1988.

Kochan, T & Katz H C *Collective Bargaining and Industrial Relations* (2 ed) Homewood; Illinois; Irwin Books. 1988.

Maller, J *ESOP's Fables* Johannesburg; Labour & Economic Research Centre. 1988.

Mastrantonis, H 'ESOPs—Towards Worker Commitment or Worker Control?' *Information Sheet* Institute for Industrial Relations. October, 1987. pp 1–4.

Nagy, J 'Share Schemes: The Need for a Radical Reassessment' *IPM Journal* April, 1987. pp 4–7.

Nel, P S 'A Critical Overview of the Concepts Democracy, Industrial Democracy, Participation and Representation' *SA Journal of Labour Relations*.

Nupen, C 'Making Amends for the LRA' *Indicator SA* Vol 5, No 4. Spring 1988. pp 76–79.

O'Toole, J 'The Uneven Record of Employee Ownership' *Harvard Business Review* November/December 1979. pp 185–197.

Pillay, P 'Worker Control of Enterprises' *Industrial Relations Journal of South Africa* Vol 7, No 1. 1987.

Rosen, C & Quarrey, M 'How Well is Employee Ownership Working?' *Harvard Business Review* September/October 1979. pp 185–197.

Rosen, C 'Starting an Employee Owned Business' in Eds. *Employee Ownership: A Reader* Virginia, National Centre for Employee Ownership, 1986.

Reum, W R & Reum, S M 'Employee Stock Ownership Plans: Pluses and Minuses' *Harvard Business Review* July/August 1976. pp 133–143.

Salamon, M *Industrial Relations: Theory & Practice* Englewood Cliffs, New Jersey; Prentice Hall. 1987.

Schregle, J 'Workers' Participation in the Federal Republic of Germany in an International Perspective' *International Labour Review* Vol 126, No 3. May/June 1987. pp 317–327.

Singleton, W T 'Occupational Health and Safety Systems: A Three-Country Comparison' *International Labour Review* Vol 122, No 2. March/April 1983. pp 155–168.

Sisson, K *The Management of Collective Bargaining: An International Comparison* Oxford; Basil Blackwell. 1987.

Thompson, C 'Beyond Recognition: A New Social Contract' *Indicator SA* Vol 5, No 4. Spring 1988. pp 67–71.

Treu, T & Negrelli, S 'Workers' Participation and Personnel Management Policies in Italy' *International Labour Review* Vol 126, No 1. January/February 1987. pp 81–94.

Viljoen, J 'Worker Participation in a South African Context' *SA Journal of Labour Relations* Vol 10, No 1. March, 1986. pp 53–58.

APPENDIX A
THE I G METALL CODE

- Renounce use of apartheid, security and emergency laws, and exploitation arising from their use.
- Negotiate at company level with a representative trade union on all internal company affairs.
- Rights of access to company premises.
- Provision of meeting and voting facilities without management interference.
- Shop steward rights.
- Rights of representation in disciplinary and grievance proceedings.
- No dismissal in 'competent' strikes.
- A right to picket peacefully on company premises.
- No use of undemocratic industrial council means of 'illegalising' strikes.
- Any disputes adjudicable before a court to be referred to a mutually agreed arbitrator.
- No threat to rights of residence in company accommodation except in cases of fair termination of the employment relationship.
- Maintenance of such standards amongst franchisees and South African affiliates.
- Annual report to South African trade unions and Germany parent company's works council.

SACTWU DEMANDS

- Fair disciplinary procedures regardless of length of service.
- Fair retrenchment practices with relevant information disclosure and proper use of consultation.
- Rights disputes to private arbitration rather than the industrial court.
- In interests disputes protection against dismissals via:

- —Reasonable notice of intention to dismiss
- —Collective vs selective dismissal
- —Collective vs selective re-employment
- Renunciation of right to litigate vs SACTWU re: industrial action where this is based solely on the LRA.
- Employer to bargain with majority union on collective conditions and not introduce unilateral changes.
- Employers in homelands not to rely on homeland laws to refuse to recognise a majority union.
- Support labour's efforts to secure labour rights for workers excluded from the LRA: (Agricultural, domestic, post office, education, health and transport (SATS) workers).

2

Charles Nupen

COLLECTIVE BARGAINING REALITIES IN SOUTH AFRICA: PROBLEMS AND POTENTIALS

INTRODUCTION

This paper addresses the problems and potentials associated with collective bargaining in South Africa. I could spend a considerable time reflecting on the remarkable progress that has been made in the ten years since Wiehahn—the culture of negotiation that has emerged from the recognition battles of the early 1980s, the detailed procedures which set the parameters within which collective bargaining takes place and which are expressed through many thousands of recognition agreements which have been concluded in the past decade. I could dwell on how many employers have incorporated notions of equity and fairness into their employment practices—notions which were foreign to many and certainly not supported by the common law of the land. I could refer in detail to an increasing sophistication and maturity that has developed in dealing with conflict on the shop floor.

These are developments which are worthy of praise in a context where recognition for achievements is perhaps conferred too infrequently.

My experience of collective bargaining comes through the practice of law and in recent years, through mediation. I engage employers and trade unions when they are in conflict, and most often precisely at the moment when they face a crucial choice between agreement or a resort to force. It is an experience of collective bargaining at its most critical stage.

If I use this space not to dwell on past achievements but on some of the more sober realities of collective bargaining and the immediate challenges that they present, it is because my particular experience of collective bargaining compels me to do so.

THE CHARACTER OF COLLECTIVE BARGAINING IN SOUTH AFRICA

Why has collective bargaining asserted itself as the dominant form of worker participation? Trade unions will argue that collective bargaining allows parties with conflicting world views and conflicting interests to engage on issues of substance within the parameters of agreed procedures, in a manner which does not undermine those respective world views or interests.

South African management has been more ambivalent about collective bargaining. Most managers would have at some time or another, usually during the heat of conflict, postulated a unitarist vision of the enterprise, sans conflict, sans trade union, where relationships and the quality of working life have reached a level which would render these things superfluous—the new managerialism to which Mark Anstey has referred. Inherent within the command or even consensus structure within management lies a view that an entity which asserts the independence of labour, that collective disputes, that stresses the conflict rather than the harmony of interests, must be counter productive. *Nowhere does management institute collective bargaining, it concedes it*, and in doing so it narrows the range of issues historically falling within the realm of its prerogative.

It is a fact that trade unions proliferate in South Africa in a manner unequalled anywhere else in the world. The question, therefore, is not *whether* to have collective bargaining, but *how* to develop it in a manner which has more consistently beneficial consequences for both management and labour.

In addressing this question it is important to make some observations about the political context in which collective bargaining takes place, because political factors impact on the work place more profoundly in South African than in most other societies.

Political unionism is not unique to South Africa, but unlike that in South Africa, organised labour in democratic societies influences political policies primarily through the constitutional process. Where the franchise is denied, that option is unavailable and organised labour must needs find other avenues of political expression. The protests against the Labour Relations Amendment Act are the most recent dramatic example of political expression by other means. The political role becomes more pronounced when popular organisations are severely restricted.

Compounding the issue is the view held by wide sections of organised labour, that in creating a dispensation which places its constituency at such political and material disadvantage, the role of the state and business is largely indivisible. It is a fact that the ideas of radical historians such as Wolpe, Legassik, Davies and others have much greater currency among large sections of organised labour than the views of liberal commentators like O'Dowd. The radical historians argue an alliance between capital and the state in the construction and perpetuation of apartheid. The liberals dispute such an alliance and argue that business and economic growth is a progressive force for change in our society.

It is from the radical perspective that strategies for change such as comprehensive and mandatory sanctions, which do not distinguish between business and the state as targets, are justified.

The legacy of the apartheid system, and the strategies adopted to change it, is a collective bargaining environment where the major players on both sides are demonised, where the explanation for disputes is often sought not on the ground or on the merits but in terms of hidden agendas and strategies devised by players removed from the immediate point of conflict. My exposure as a mediator to that kind of analysis in many disputes is that it is for the most part misplaced.

What is urgently needed if the demonising is to stop, and a more fruitful collective bargaining environment is to be established, is the creation of a forum or process within which employers and trade unions can debate issues of broader political significance beyond the immediacy of the shop floor. Where political perceptions can be clarified and better understood, and where the possibility of strategic alliances on political initiatives, unthinkable at the moment can at least be explored. That is not all. What lies open to management, if it seeks to separate itself in the minds of workers from the political policies of the state, is to play a more assertive role in the political arena in opposition to apartheid and in defence of human rights.

Let me give an example. When I was called in with Gavin Brown to mediate five weeks into the 1987 OK Bazaars strike, tension between the parties was very high. There had been incidents of industrial sabotage, a bomb had exploded at the main Johannesburg branch of the OK, many workers had been detained without trial under the emergency regulations and many more had been dismissed. It was clear at the outset that the atmosphere prevailing between the parties was one which did not allow for a sober concentration on the issues that were dividing them. The mediators determined in the first instance to work towards forging an agreement between the parties which would compel restraint, cool tempers and create a climate conducive to the rational resolution of the dispute. Foremost in the minds of the union team was a perception that the company was co-operating closely with the police in the arrest and detention of its members. Under the restraint agreement, the company agreed to seek an audience with the Minister of Law and Order to attempt to secure the release of union members from detention and the Managing Director delivered on that agreement. There is no doubt in my mind that that single gesture, more than any other, fundamentally altered the perception of the company in the union caucus and created a climate for constructive bargaining.

That sort of experience compels one to ask the question: What positive impact would be made on the collective bargaining environment by more wide ranging and assertive political initiatives undertaken by management?

One initiative already embarked upon by employers to transform the ideological mind-set which places them in the same camp as the state, is to offer workers more tangible benefits of the free enterprise system through equity share option schemes. A report by the Labour and Economic Research Centre on these schemes referred to a recent survey of urban-based black South Africans, showing that 77% favoured a socialist vision of the economic future of the country. The report goes on to quote Zach de Beer as saying:

'During many long decades, while they have suffered adverse discrimination and a capitalistic society, many black people have come to associate capitalism with apartheid. It behoves every committed supporter of free enterprise to start now, working to bring the benefits of the system more and more within the reach of our black citizens, so that they too can become believers in it. Certainly this means active black advancement programmes—and it means the extension of share ownership to employees to the maximum extent that this is feasible.'

Consider the view, by no means uncharacteristic, of David Thathe, a senior FAWU shop steward (quoted in the *South African Labour Bulletin,* September 1988 edition):

'We are not looking forward to becoming economic citizens. We need total control over the country. They must un-ban all our political organisations and return our voting rights.'

If political rights are an issue of great importance to workers management of its own volition cannot extend them. But to those employers who look to more modest initiatives in the form of worker participation schemes, to alter the ideological mind-set, let me suggest that to enjoy support, they need to be negotiated, and need to address not only questions of economic benefit but also questions of meaningful participation and control. It is no surprise to me, for example, that provident fund schemes and co-operatives which address these considerations are far more attractive to unions than share schemes which don't. A common response is 'don't give us shares, raise our wages'.

The political context adversely affects the collective bargaining environment, and there is indeed a greater onus on the parties to ensure that the process itself works and works effectively. Let me illustrate the point by reference to some of the key issues in the substantive and procedural areas of collective bargaining.

Wage bargaining has developed dramatically in the post-Wiehahn era. In many industries the material position of workers has been significantly improved as a result, and yet it is my abiding impression that for many participants the experience of wage bargaining is a negative one, viewed as an ordeal, rather than a challenge which offers the prospect of building trust and strengthening relationships. My experience and that of my colleagues in mediating wage disputes confirm that view. In many instances, after several years experience of collective bargaining, parties have deadlocked in 1989 at points as far if not further apart than they have done before. Current economic imperatives and rising expectations are a factor, but there is more to it. It is clear that parties are deadlocking at points where there is still flexibility in their mandates and in circumstances where they have not bargained the issues through in a serious manner.

Investigations show that dispute meetings are often followed as a matter of procedural necessity rather than in a serious endeavour to promote resolution. It is not uncommon for a mediator to confront 10 to 15 items which form the subject or dispute and discover that *the* only item which has been bargained is wages.

Why is this so?

The primary objective of any negotiating team must be to get members of the opposing team to adopt the positions and the supporting arguments that it advances, and if not to adopt them then at least to attach validity to the propositions advanced such that they form the subject of meaningful debate within the other team, and between it and its constituency. Such an approach demands thorough preparation not only of ones own position but in anticipation of the proposals that will be advanced by the other side. It also demands thorough motivation at the table accompanied by appropriate disclosure. Destabilising tactics and the use of threats undermine the process and are self defeating because they create uncertainty and make responses difficult to predict.

These observations are, I believe, acutely pertinent to the South African collective bargaining experience. With rare exceptions, we have fallen victim to a syndrome which I can best characterise as the poverty of positional bargaining. Proposals are made at the bargaining table, positions adjusted and concessions made, without motivation, or when it is offered, it is little more than cursory. Reasonableness in approach is based only on the extent of the moves made. To the extent that preparation is done it focuses on justifying one's own position and takes little account of the interests of the other party. Items are bargained on a piecemeal basis with little creative thought given to linkages and trade-offs. Quid quo pro bargaining is virtually non-existent. Little wonder that we witness in 1989 the emergence of a new bargaining phenomenon where one party makes the moves and the other hangs back, way out of range, hoping that an acceptable proposal will eventually come on to the table. Power realities, an important backdrop to any collective bargaining experience, are thrust prematurely centre stage. Unreasonableness and bad faith become the clarion calls of each negotiating team but make little impression on the other.

As one leader of a negotiating team remarked to me this week:

> 'There is too much emotive bargaining. Our bargaining culture is one dominated by threats and power. We talk past each other and seldom engage on the merits.'

What hope is there of developing a coherent and fulfilling bargaining culture. My assessment is that the situation is serious. We have to explore new ways.

SOME SUGGESTIONS

I offer two suggestions to break the malaise. The first phase of wage negotiations should not focus on the specifics of the items tabled but should be spent trying to *establish an understanding of the issues which inform and establish the positions of the parties.* Wage policy, the concept of a living wage, the relevance of the consumer price index, minimum effective levels, household effective levels, the impact of inflation, profitability and comparative wage rates, a discussion of interests and expectations, the disclosure of information to support arguments. I don't suggest necessarily that there will be consensus on these issues, but a better understanding will set the parameters for the negotiation to follow and will encourage a more informed and constructive negotiating experience.

We need to *draw the concept of good faith out of the realms of rhetoric and give it practical expression.* Serious and not superficial bargaining on the merits, considered responses to proposals, no matter how untenable they may appear, adherence to procedures, accurate flows of information between representative and constituency. There are parties who follow this approach and their experience of collective bargaining is invariably positive. They negotiate professionally and maturely and their relationship is sound.

Another observation: *negotiating teams are not sufficiently empowered by their constituencies with the necessary degree of flexibility to strike deals where settlement is close at hand.* I am not suggesting an open hand but what I argue against is the determination of absolute and inflexible parameters by constituents who have little experience of the negotiation process and who are not exposed to the debates and often remain impervious to them.

It is easy for an unempowered negotiating team to evade the responsibilities of leadership and guidance which are intrinsic to their function in collective bargaining. I believe that much more attention has to be paid in negotiation skills training to the crucially important interaction between bargaining representatives and their respective constituencies.

Questions of procedure in collective bargaining are probably more problematic at present than those raised on matters of substance. The most fundamental challenge the industrial relations community faces is to enhance a genuine respect for procedure, and there is much work to be done. Parfitt's (1989) survey on strikes in the Eastern Cape shows that in 80 incidents of strikes surveyed, 76 were unprocedural in the sense that the procedural requirements of the Labour Relations Act were not followed. What use are procedures when they are honoured more in the breach than in the observance? If it is only to provide a superficial gloss to the strategy of results by power, or to provide a basis for workers to be fired or processed through the criminal courts, then we have reached new levels of sophistry in our industrial relations.

I do not wish to debate the Labour Relations Amendment Act at length here. My views on the subject are well known. The new law has exacerbated an already problematic situation. Section 79 has introduced a new reality into collective bargaining. Trade unionism remains influential on the shop floor, but in times of unprocedural strikes trade unionists are rarely to be found, and with good reason.

The introduction of elaborate adjudication procedures offers justice to those who can afford it and denies it to those who can't. Trade unions who made prolific use of adjudication under the statute now choose to ignore it. Employers may gain some succour from less frequent appearances in the Industrial Court, but the underlying discontent on issues which were channelled procedurally to adjudication in that forum, will now be expressed in other ways. Although I promote private processes of dispute resolution I recognise that the consensus which is needed to give effect to these processes, while growing, can never match the universal application of law. I remain firmly convinced that we need a statute which enjoys legitimacy, is fair and workable. In its absence, however, we are driven to examine alternatives.

Some parties have chosen the route of contracting out—of negotiating an entirely private procedural regime which in the event of conflict, eschews resort to the statutory procedures. I am aware that there are two aspects to this initiative which cause difficulty for employers. The extent of the right to strike which is granted and the nature of disputes which are referred to private arbitration.

There are a number of creative possibilities in these two areas. The right to strike can be limited to certain defined issues. The right can be extended only insofar as procedures are observed and certain standards of conduct are adhered to;

adjudication on the validity of continuing the strike can be invoked at that point where the employer alleges permanent harm to the enterprise; time limits can be agreed, the right to strike can be balanced by a corresponding right to lock out.

There must be salutary consequences for the parties to collective bargaining, if a negotiated right to strike lends predictability to the way in which conflict expresses itself in the work place.

The major advantage of adjudication through private arbitration is that it establishes certainty in processing rights disputes; disputes which are characterised by a high degree of unprocedural conflict. Parfitt's (1989) survey shows that fully 70 % of man days lost in unprocedural strikes in the Eastern Cape concerned perceived unfairness in the handling of disciplinary matters. Referral to private arbitration does not have to be comprehensive but can be limited to individual dismissal disputes. On those rights issues where referral to arbitration is agreed, the union usually concedes the right to strike.

If the effect of these private arrangements is that they evidence over time a joint commitment to procedure, then there is much to be gained by exploring them. There seems to me to be a qualitative difference in the legitimacy and commitment to procedures which have been negotiated rather than imposed, and indeed in the acceptance of the sanction in the event of breach.

Another issue of growing importance is the debate over appropriate levels and forums for collective bargaining. Recent events in the printing industry and the motor industry bear testimony to this. In the former, the Industrial Council has effectively collapsed and in the latter the union is trying to engineer a commitment from employers to bargain at industry level.

What is clear is that there is a new perspective on the part of unions to industry level bargaining through Industrial Councils. No longer is there a uniform adherence to the notion of Industrial Councils as institutions for bargaining minimum standards, to be complemented by more realistic plant level bargaining on substantive issues. Industrial Councils are beginning to be viewed as forums for single-tier bargaining where realistic agreements can be struck.

It seems to me a recipe for conflict if positions are taken on this issue as a matter of firm principle. Let parties find appropriate forums for bargaining through the negotiation process itself. What is needed is a pragmatic approach which takes into consideration questions of power and convenience.

South Africa is rapidly entering a new political era that must profoundly affect relationships and the order of things in the workplace. Those who bargain matters of substance and procedure with this in mind will secure the greatest advantage from collective bargaining. Those who continue to defend and assert the old order will know only problems in a process that will remain an ordeal.

REFERENCES

Parfitt J 'Industrial Relations Trends in the Eastern Cape: Strikes and Stayaways' *IR Research and Topics Series* No 3, IR Unit, UPE, June 1989, ISBN 0 8698 8387 9.

Thathe D 'Samcor—Workers Strike Against Share Ownership' *SA Labour Bulletin* Vol 13 No 6 1988, pp 24–43.

3

Brian Robinson

WORKER PARTICIPATION: TRENDS IN WEST GERMANY

This chapter seeks to provide:

- a brief description of the key legislation on worker participation in West Germany;
- an outline of employee participation at VOLKSWAGEN AG (VW AG) and trends within VW AG;
- trends within West Germany generally; and
- current trends in Europe.

WORKER CO-DETERMINATION IN WEST GERMANY: A BACKGROUND

Since World War II, West Germany has been experiencing a peaceful revolution in industrial relations. To an extent unmatched in the rest of the Western world, many German workers have been participating directly in corporate decision-making. This worker participation, or industrial democracy as it is frequently called, grew out of the ashes of World War II. While the first possibilities for elected worker representations in German companies were contained in a 1920 Works Council Act, the main impetus came (ironically!) from British occupation authorities and German trade unionists who were committed to ensuring that the nation would never again fall into the dictatorial pattern of the Third Reich.

In 1951, in the two-year-old Federal Republic, the first major labour legislation was introduced (Montan-Mitbestimmungsgesetz) which gave workers in the mining and steel

industry important co-determination rights as well as representation at board level. A Works Constitution Act (Betriebs-
verfassungsgesetz) promulgated the following year brought
workers in almost all companies co-determination rights in
social welfare and personnel matters and the right to be heard
in business policy decisions.

It was another 20 years before further changes were made,
in a new Works Constitution Act, introduced in 1972. Another
significant milestone for worker representation was the revised general Co-determination Act of 1976. West Germany
is sometimes aptly described as a 'constitutional factory' by
virtue of its highly legalised labour relations system. The two
key acts influencing management labour relations — and
indeed that determine the degree of employee participation
— are those just mentioned:

- The Works Constitution Act of 1972 — which deals with
  shop-floor level participation; and
- The Co-determination Act of 1976 — which deals with
  enterprise level participation.

Shop-floor-level participation

The Works Council (Betriebsrat), sometimes called Workers'
Council, is the main instrument of employee representation,
at factory-floor level. All workers, from the age of 18, including foreigners, may vote and be elected, as long as they have
worked for at least 6 months in that company. It is also
(theoretically) not necessary to be a member of a Trade Union,
but particularly in large companies — such as VW AG — the
Trade Unions have a powerful say on the composition of
candidates lists.

The number of Works Councillors depends on the size of
the company (headcount) and this also has a bearing on
whether they operate on a full-time or part-time basis.

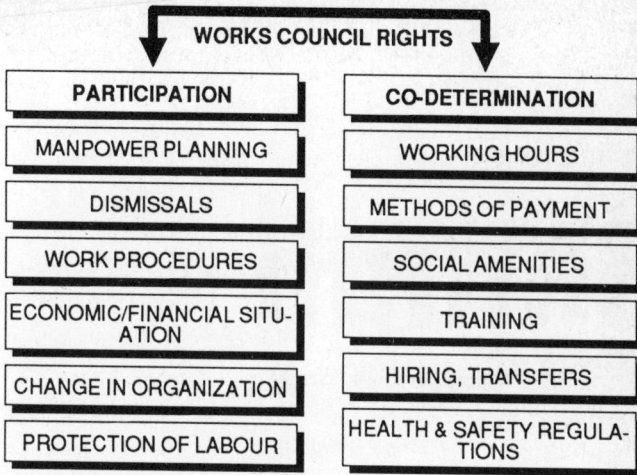

WORKS COUNCIL RIGHTS

PARTICIPATION	CO-DETERMINATION
MANPOWER PLANNING	WORKING HOURS
DISMISSALS	METHODS OF PAYMENT
WORK PROCEDURES	SOCIAL AMENITIES
ECONOMIC/FINANCIAL SITUATION	TRAINING
CHANGE IN ORGANIZATION	HIRING, TRANSFERS
PROTECTION OF LABOUR	HEALTH & SAFETY REGULATIONS

FIGURE 3.1
Works Council Rights (Source: *Facts About Germany*)

The election process and the composition of the Works Councils in the VW AG factories is explained in a later section. At this stage the most important aspect is that of the *Works Council rights* (see figure 3.1). The Works Council has wide-ranging powers, particularly, of course, in social welfare and personnel affairs, and these range from the right to be consulted through participation in decision-making to genuine co-determination where management cannot decide without the approval of the Works Council. If deadlock is reached the matter can be referred to a Labour Court or an Arbitration Panel, on which management and labour are equally represented, together with a neutral chairman.

In practice, the Works Council and the employer seldom seem to get into irreconcilable confrontation and do in fact seek out — in the spirit of the labour relations system — suitable compromises. The 'balance of power' between the two parties obviously influences decision-making and it should be pointed out that even in matters where the Works Council has only a consultative right, skilful negotiating can,

COMPOSITION OF THE SUPERVISORY BOARD

CAPITAL OWNERS   WORKERS

. . . according to the Works Constitution Act

CAPITAL OWNERS   Neutral   WORKERS
                            Member

. . . in Mining, Iron and Steel

CAPITAL OWNERS   Chairman   Managerial   WORKERS
                  with casting staff
                  vote   member

. . . according to the 1976 Codetermination Act

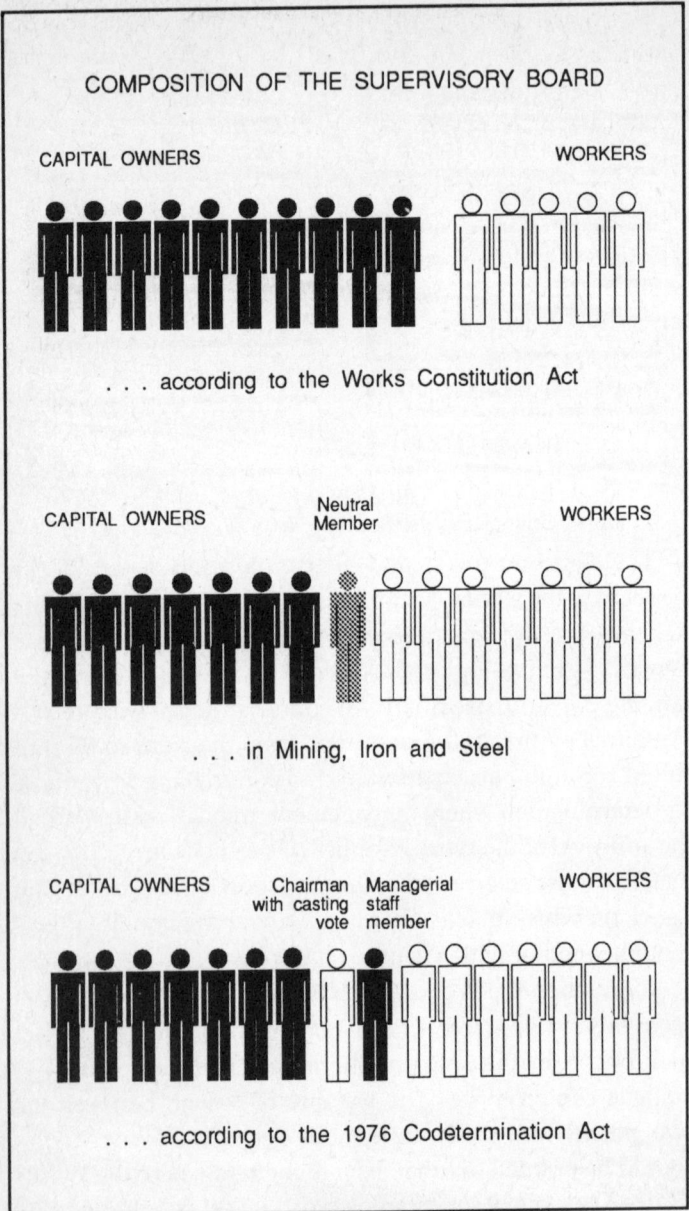

FIGURE 3.2
Composition of the Supervisory Board
Source: *Facts About Germany*

in fact, result in employee representatives having a significant influence on decisions taken.

Enterprise level employee participation

Co-determination in large enterprises

The Works Council has no co-determination right in terms of the actual management of the business; in this respect it has only information and consultation rights in firms with more than 100 employees. But in most larger enterprises there are various other forms of co-determination. In West Germany many large enterprises are joint-stock companies. The German joint-stock company (Aktiengesellschaft) has two levels of control:

The Aufsichtsrat (Supervisory Board) as the control organ, and the Vorstand (Board of Management) responsible for day-to-day management. (See figure 3.2 for the composition of the Supervisory Board.)

As early as 1952 one-third of the Supervisory Board members of every stock company had to be elected employee representatives. This provision still applies to small and medium-size joint-stock companies (up to 2 000 employees) and for other enterprises with 500 to 2 000 employees.

For larger enterprises there are two special co-determination systems. In mining and steel companies with more than 1 000 employees the 'Montan-Mitbestimmungsgesetz' has applied since 1951. According to this law, the owners and labour each have half the seats on the Aufsichtsrat and have to agree on a further, neutral member. On the Board of Management there has to be a 'Labour Director' with fully equal rights who cannot be appointed against the will of the labour representatives in the Aufsichtsrat.

For other large enterprises employing more than 2 000, a general Co-determination Act, adopted in 1976, is applied. In this law, which covers just under 500 enterprises of all branches except mining and steelmaking and the press, the provisions are somewhat more complicated. On a numerical basis there is full labour/capital parity in the Aufsichtsrat. But in tied votes, the deciding vote is that of the Chairman, who in practice, because of the electoral system, must always be a representative of the capital owners. Moreover, the labour side must include at least one representative of the 'leading personnel' ie a staff member with managerial functions. The unions are not satisfied about this and have, in fact, made several attempts to get the law changed to adjust the 'balance of power' but to date to no avail.

In the following section, this overview of legislated worker participation in West Germany is elucidated through a description of practices in VW AG.

EMPLOYEE PARTICIPATION AT VW AG

At enterprise level

Co-determination in VW AG

The composition of the Supervisory Board at VW AG is illustrated in Figure 3.3. It comprises 20 members, 10 of whom are employee representatives (including a member of management). Of these 10, seven must be company employees. The other 10 represent the shareholders, who also provide the Chairman with a casting vote. The Vice-Chairman is always from Labour (in the case of VW, it is traditionally the President of the German Metalworkers' Union, IG Metall). Shareholder representatives are elected at the Annual General Meeting (i e they are not company employees). The Supervisory Board is elected for 5 years. It is customary at VW AG that decisions are made by consensus.

There are, however, some special peculiarities of the VW AG Supervisory Board that tend to redress the 'balance of power'. Through the VW Act of 1960 and the Articles of Association of VW AG some provisions apply that deviate

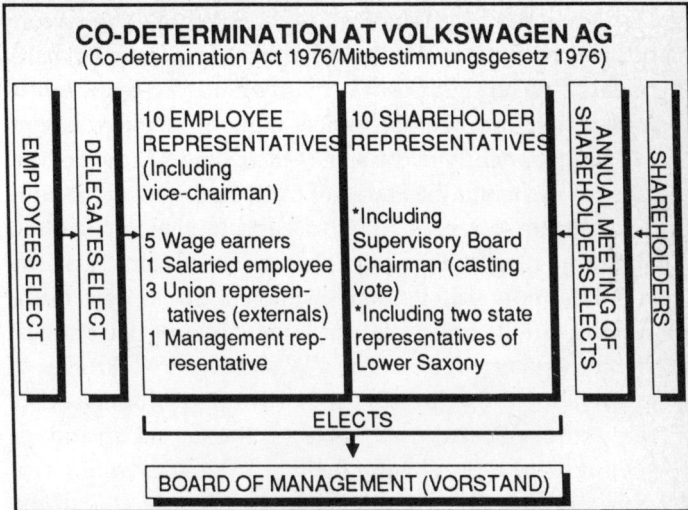

CO-DETERMINATION AT VOLKSWAGEN AG
(Co-determination Act 1976/Mitbestimmungsgesetz 1976)

EMPLOYEES ELECT	DELEGATES ELECT	10 EMPLOYEE REPRESENTATIVES (Including vice-chairman) 5 Wage earners 1 Salaried employee 3 Union representatives (externals) 1 Management representative	10 SHAREHOLDER REPRESENTATIVES *Including Supervisory Board Chairman (casting vote) *Including two state representatives of Lower Saxony	ANNUAL MEETING OF SHAREHOLDERS ELECTS	SHAREHOLDERS

ELECTS

BOARD OF MANAGEMENT (VORSTAND)

FIGURE 3.3
Composition of the Supervisory Board at VW AG
Source: *Co-determination at VW AG*

both from the Co-determination Act of 1976 and from the Limited Companies Act.

The following important deviations exist:

1 In line with the VW Act and the Articles of Association of VW AG, voting rights from the possession of shares are restricted to 20 % of the votes cast. A shareholding of more than 20 % does not give increased voting rights.

2 The VW Act and Articles of Association require a majority of over 80 % for all resolutions of the Annual Meeting of Shareholders for which the Limited Companies Act requires a majority of 75 %. This increased requirement affects, for example, votes on capital increases, relocation of group headquarters and all alterations to the VW Articles of Association.

3 On the other hand, a recent event has swung the pendulum back in favour of capital, to the concern of the unions.

The Federal Government and the State of Lower Saxony each held 20 % of the capital stock. Until recently, this meant that no significant decisions could be made by the annual meeting of stockholders without their agreement.

Independently of the size of their holding, the Federal Government and the State of Lower Saxony had the right to delegate 2 representatives each to the Supervisory Board as long as they held shares. The Federal Government has now sold its shares, much to the concern of the unions, but the provincial parliament retains two seats on the Supervisory Board. The VW Act and VW Articles of Association prescribe a 2/3 majority for resolutions of the Supervisory Board, whose object is the setting up and/or relocation of a production facility. In such cases the employees cannot be overridden by the double vote of the Chairman of the Supervisory Board.

Functions of the Supervisory Board

The tasks of the Supervisory Board are laid down in the Limited Companies Act. They include:

1 overall powers to set general company policy and to supervise the management of the company;

2 approval of the annual financial statements;

3 the Board of Management is required to inform the Supervisory Board comprehensively regarding the company situation including:

(a) intended business policy and conduct

(b) profitability/financial situation

(c) resales situation

In the framework of its control functions the Supervisory Board must agree to various types of decisions of the Board of Management before they can be implemented. For example:

1   establishment and discontinuation of subsidiary companies;
2   setting-up and re-location of production facilities;
3   acquisition and selling-off of holdings in other companies;
4   capital investments;
5   loans or credits;
6   acquisition and sale of property;
7   appointment of senior executives;
8   matters concerning subsidiaries; and
9   introduction of permanent social measures outside of agreements reached with the Works Council.

Employee participation at VW AG at shop-floor level

As mentioned earlier, the main vehicle of employee participation is through the Works Council. Employee parties' powers are underpinned by a legal empowerment within the West German Labour Relations System. The degree to which Works Council 'rights' are exercised depends very much on the relationship — the power balance — that has been developed between the employer and employee parties over the years. The extent to which, and the nature in which these rights are exercised varies greatly:

1   within industries;
2   within enterprises;
3   even between plants within the same organisation.

Historically, at VW AG, the Works Council has played a prominent role in company affairs and as 90 % of the Works Councillors belong to the IG Metall, the union influence at shop-floor level is also strong.

The *Works Council election process*, briefly referred to earlier, is illustrated in Figure 3.4.

The dominance of the IG Metall within the VW AG factories can be seen in Table 3.1, Composition of the Works Councils at the VW AG Factories. There are six Works Councils within VW AG (one for each separate plant) and to ensure

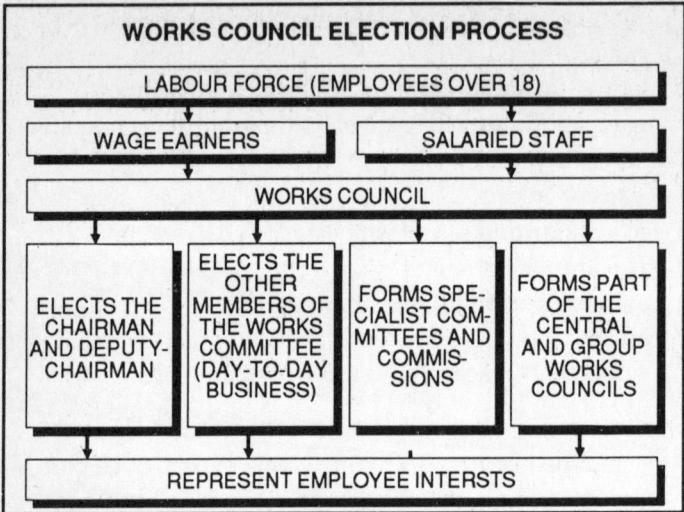

WORKS COUNCIL ELECTION PROCESS

LABOUR FORCE (EMPLOYEES OVER 18)

WAGE EARNERS

SALARIED STAFF

WORKS COUNCIL

ELECTS THE CHAIRMAN AND DEPUTY-CHAIRMAN

ELECTS THE OTHER MEMBERS OF THE WORKS COMMITTEE (DAY-TO-DAY BUSINESS)

FORMS SPECIALIST COMMITTEES AND COMMISSIONS

FORMS PART OF THE CENTRAL AND GROUP WORKS COUNCILS

REPRESENT EMPLOYEE INTERSTS

FIGURE 3.4
The Works Council election process
Source: *Co-determination at VW AG*

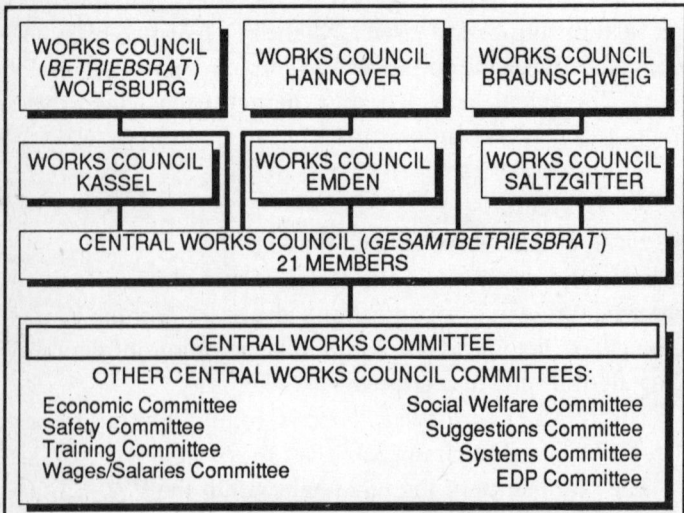

WORKS COUNCIL (*BETRIEBSRAT*) WOLFSBURG

WORKS COUNCIL HANNOVER

WORKS COUNCIL BRAUNSCHWEIG

WORKS COUNCIL KASSEL

WORKS COUNCIL EMDEN

WORKS COUNCIL SALTZGITTER

CENTRAL WORKS COUNCIL (*GESAMTBETRIESBRAT*) 21 MEMBERS

CENTRAL WORKS COMMITTEE

OTHER CENTRAL WORKS COUNCIL COMMITTEES:

Economic Committee
Safety Committee
Training Committee
Wages/Salaries Committee

Social Welfare Committee
Suggestions Committee
Systems Committee
EDP Committee

FIGURE 3.5
The central works council at VW AG
(Works Constitution Act 1972)

effective coordination between the various plants there is also a *Central Works Council*, consisting of 21 members elected by the Works Councils of the various factories (figure 3.5).

TABLE 3.1
Composition of the Works Councils at the VWAG factories
(1987–1990)

Factory	Total	Wage Earners	Salaried Staff
Wolfsburg	69	IGM: 49 CMV: 3 CCSA: 1	IGM: 13 DAG: 3
Hannover	39	IGM: 32 CMV: 2	IGM: 5
Braunschweig	31	IGM: 26	IGM: 5
Kassel	39	IGM: 32 CMV: 2	IGM: 4 DAG: 1
Emden	33	IGM: 28	IGM: 5
Salzgitter	33	IGM: 25 CMV: 3	IGM: 4 DAG: 1
VW AG	244	IGM: 192 CMV: 10 CCSA: 1	IGM: 36 DAG: 5

IGM = IG METALL
CMV = CHRISTLICHE METALLVERBAND
CSSA = CHRISTDEMOKRATISCHE UND CHRISTLICH-SOZIALE
ARBEITSNEHMERSCHAFT
DAG = DEUTSCHE ANGESTELLTEN-GEWERKSCHAFT

The Chairman and Vice-Chairman of each plant council are members of this central committee, that meets at least 4 times a year and is responsible for matters concerning the Company as a whole or several factories or matters that have been referred to it by a particular plant Works Council.

(It should be pointed out that the Chairman and Vice-Chairman of each Works Council are traditionally a blue-collar and white-collar representative respectively.)

A *Central Works Committee* conducts the day-to-day business of the Central Works Council and a number of other specialist committees exist, in which all the factories are represented. It should also be noted that the individual plant Works Councils are not subordinate to the central one.

The central Works Council is the highest level employee body and members regularly deal with members of the Board of Management.

Factory meetings

Factory meetings are held quarterly, in all factories, during working hours. In these the Works Council reports on its activities and the Board of Management reports on the company situation. Every employee has the right to participate in these meetings (such meetings are required in terms of the Works Constitution Act).

Works Council/Trade Union relationships

The Works Constitution Act provides for a close co-operation between Works Councils and the unions represented in the company. This is essential since the Works Council would not be able to function effectively without the active support of the unions. Within VW AG, there are 244 Works Council members and over 5 000 IGM shop stewards. Over 90 % of the Works Council members belong to IGM, and all employee representatives on the Supervisory Board are IGM members. Shop stewards are elected for 3 years and keep in close contact with IGM officials and the Works Council.

Industrial agreements contain provisions on such matters as:

1   wages and salaries;
2   principles of remuneration;
3   wage differentials;

4   hours of work; and
5   general industrial agreement.

Senior Works Council members in VW AG are in a unique situation when it is considered that they are members of the top policy-making body of the company (the Supervisory Board) and at the same time take part in wage negotiations as part of the union team.

Company agreements are legally binding between the Works Council and the company and apply to *all* employees. Remuneration and other conditions of employment cannot be the subject of a company agreement except when an industrial agreement expressly permits complementary company agreements.

The most important company agreements contain provisions on:

1   company pension scheme;
2   factory regulations;
3   suggestion scheme;
4   information/consultation on systems projects etc;
5   personal data protection;
6   organisation of work at VDUs;
7   free shifts as per industrial agreement on working time;
8   regulation of employee early retirement; and
9   introduction and objectives of quality circles.

Another important body existing within VW's operations in Germany is the *Group Works Council* (Konzernbetriebsrat) made up of representatives of the Works Councils of all German subsidiaries (see figure 3.6).

It should be noted that it is a long-established aspect of VW labour relations philosophy that contact and dialogue between employee and management representatives, throughout the VW world, is actively encouraged. For example, as far back as 1978 Volkswagen of South Africa

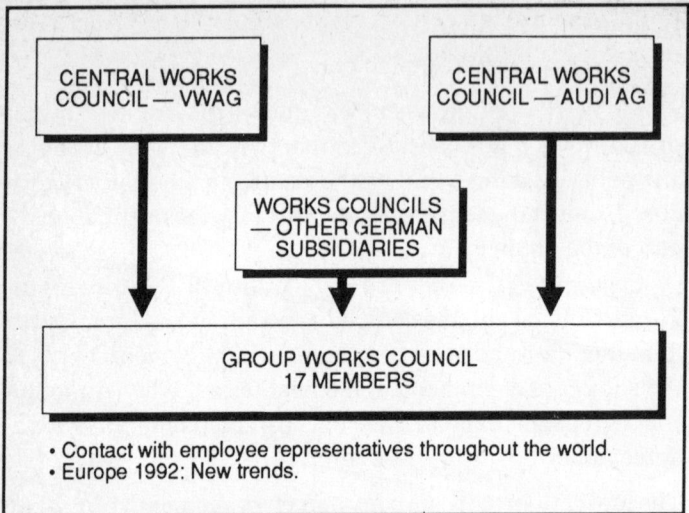

FIGURE 3.6
The VW AG Group works council (*Konzernbetriebsrat*)
Source: *Personalwesen Konzern*, July 1989

pioneered a joint management/shop steward study tour to
Europe to examine various labour relations systems first-
hand. In 1979 and 1986 the VW AG Group Works Council
hosted conferences in Germany for worker representatives
from the VW operations throughout the world. VW is neatly
poised, therefore, to meet the newly emerging trends for
cross-national forms of worker participation being precipi-
tated by 'Europa 1992'.

TRENDS IN WORKER PARTICIPATION

A considerable space has been allocated to a detailed description of the current situation in Germany. The reason for this
is to emphasise the dominance of legalism in the labour-management relationship. My impression is that this results,
generally speaking, in a more formal relationship between
management and labour than has been my experience in the

South African situation. The legal nature of the relationship has also been stressed because it means that changes in the system take a long time to come about. For example, a new law, that will operate in conjunction with the Works Constitution Act — has been years in the making.

Management representation

With effect from 1 January 1989 there is now a 'business class' supplement to the Works Constitution Act. Senior executives can elect a special in-company body to represent their special interests (Sprecher-Ausschuss). There seems to be a German tendency to be always looking for groups to protect or represent! Under 18s, Over 18s, Handicapped, Women, Foreigners, etc, and now the 'Fat Cats'!!! The new law is known as the Spokemen's Committee Law (Sprecher Ausschussgesetz) and consists of 39 articles. What it doesn't make clear is who will organise management — unions or others? Nor does it define too clearly who is and who is not a manager — although the intention is that only a relatively small group of people will fall within it. Anyway, as long as there are at least 10 managers in a company, and the majority vote in favour, a Spokesmen's Committee Group must be formed. These bodies are primarily consultative, but they are empowered to sign agreements on the content of individual employment contracts for executives, and they can have an extensive say in dismissals of their constituents. There does not appear to be much enthusiasm for the Act, either on the part of employers — the BDA (Employer's Association) sees it as unnecessary institutionalisation — or on the part of the Unions who don't really want a further split in employee representation. The first elections of Executives' Committees are scheduled between 1 March and 31 May in 1990. The new legislation primarily affects large national and international companies, and follows very similar patterns to the Works Constitution Act in terms of

1   individual committees for each geographical unit;
2   a Group Committee (gesamtsprecherausschuss) for organisations that have several Company or Enterprise Committees; and
3   a special form of Group Committee (Konzernsprecherausschuss) which may be set up to represent eligible executives throughout the organisation.

Contents of the new legislation specify:

1   men and women must be represented proportionally;
2   costs of elections, paid time, facilities (office, materials, clerical support) to be provided by the company; and
3   the Committee is required to hold a meeting of all senior executives annually.

It is too early to tell how effective these committees are going to be, and how the functions of these committees are going to clash with those of the Works Councils. There is provision for Works Council members to attend meetings of Executives' Committees, at their invitation. Some employers' duties to the Committees are defined in terms of the Works Constitution Act. e g To inform on the economic situation and plans for major changes in the company 'in the sense of the Works Constitution Act and to the same extent as Works Councils are informed'.

Other reforms

In addition to new representative arrangement for executives, reforms to the 1972 Works Constitution Act earlier this year affect the organisation of Works Councils and Youth Delegations. For example, previously candidates wishing to stand for election to a Council needed to have their nomination supported by the signatures of 10 % of the workforce or 100 people, whichever was the lower. It is now 5 % or 50 people. In addition, trade unions receive an automatic right to nominate candidates, *without* being required to document their workforce support. This makes it easier for the smaller labour groups, notably the Christian trade unions, to secure representation. Minority groups are now guaranteed Works council places according to their scale of support:

up to 50: 1
51 to 200: 2
201 to 600: 3
. . .
more than 15 000: 9

Also included are new rules of full-time release and further privileges for those who sit on Council Committees. Proportional voting has supplanted simple majoritarianism. This means even if small groups succeed in placing candidates on the Councils, they will not necessarily occupy key positions unless they have significant workforce support. Traditional unions resent the changes — and are unlikely to hand over the most influential posts unless weight of numbers forces them to. As already indicated, periods of office of Works Council members have been extended from 3 to 4 years. Youth delegations now cover apprentices and trainees under 25 as well.

New technology

The rights of Works Councils to be informed and consulted on new technology have been redefined and extended. When informing, the employer must now provide all relevant documents, and allow time for them to be studied. The employer must also consult the Council about all the implications and repercussions of the change, again allowing time for the Council to formulate its response. Finally, the employer must inform each worker affected by the innovations of what those mean to the individual's job, and discuss any vocational retraining necessary.

Stock-option/share participation/profit sharing schemes

I am unable to comment as to whether there is a *trend* in this regard. Certainly a wide variety of schemes appear to exist, mainly in smaller companies. The possibility of a share-participation scheme at VW AG is currently being investigated The fairly unusual step was taken last year of giving every single employee of our German company (134 525) one share to mark VW's fiftieth anniversary. Which goes a long way to explain why VW is the largest public company in West Germany, with around 728 000 stockholders! Another reason is the wide distribution of the shares sold by the West German government in March, 1988.

Group work (Gruppenarbeit)

Another trend within West Germany, and certainly within VW AG, is towards different work organisation and work structures, and experiments and investigations are being undertaken at all levels within the organisation from the factory floor to the boardroom to reduce hierarchies, to increase individual accountability and involvement and to allow greater opportunity for team work.

Tendencies/trends in co-determination

It is reasonable to assume that there will be further changes in Mitbestimmung. It may be slowed up by the thorough and legalistic approach — but it is clearly a dynamic process. As jobs change, as structures change, the Works Council is always going to be on the alert to protect their members, to gain more rights, to have more involvement in matters that affect the employees, and one senses that individuals themselves are questioning more and demanding more say over their jobs, their work environment, and their futures. These demands are going to require different managers and different employee representatives in the future.

Europa 1992

The world is becoming smaller and smaller, borders are disappearing — Europa 1992 is the 'flavour of the month' and this will create very interesting challenges and opportunities. What are the chances for a European Co-determination Act? The German system is, of course, very firmly rooted in German society. It many not be transferable without considerable modifications. For one thing the German unions are by and large prosperous and sympathetic to the profit motive. They own banks and businesses, have powerful political influence, are well organised, engage in steady dialogue with government and industry on economic policy. Obviously, not every country within Europe is in the same position. Widely differing labour relations systems, social systems, legal systems and ideologies exist across Europe. As far back as 1980 the EEC Commission undertook a study and produced guidelines to improve the rights of employees in trans-European companies to information and participation. To date no results have been evidenced.

Apart from these 'Vredeling Guidelines', the EEC Commission completed another study in July last year, ie to create a framework of uniform rules for European-wide concerns ('Europa Limited Company'). In the draft it appears that one can choose from 3 different models of co-determination:

1 the German model;
2 the French system of employee-only Works Councils, to be consulted on most decisions; or
3 other arrangements agreed through Collective Bargaining.

And if that choice was not confusing enough, the commission declared that the rules were not intended to be obligatory! At

---

EEC SOCIAL CHARTER

INCLUDES PROVISIONS FOR:
- A ceiling to working hours
- Free movement of labour
- Fair and reasonable pay
- Minimum rates of social security
- Freedom of Association
- Free collective bargaining
- Access to training
- Sexual equality
- Development of worker participation
- Health and safety
- Child/Youth protection
- Supporting the old
- Promoting employment to handicapped

In no case should a country use the charter as an argument for reducing, rather than increasing, worker protection.

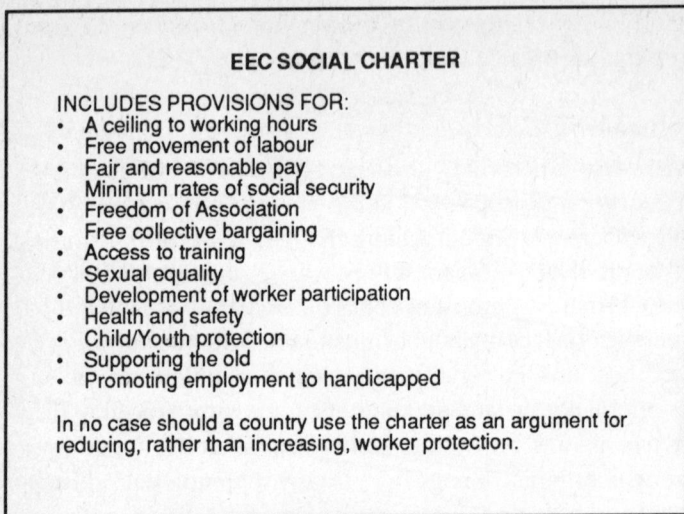

FIGURE 3.7
European Economic Community Social Charter
Source: *Personalwesen Konzern*, August 1989

this stage it seems merely a possibility to operate under a set of European rules. The latest offering of the Eurocrats is a Social Charter (figure 3.7).

What is clear is that nothing is likely to happen at parliamentary level, be it the Vredeling Guidelines or the Europa-AG or the Social Charter, before the inauguration of the single European market on January 1, 1993.

What, then, is happening at the non-parliamentary levels? What is business, what are the unions thinking or doing about trans-national worker participation?

Employers

Employers appear to be resisting any consideration of the Vredeling Guidelines, seeing them as containing unjustifiable administrative costs/expenses. German employers are happy with existing national structures and do not support the concept of the 'Europa Limited' company as presently envisaged.

The concept is too confusing, and the draft goes beyond German co-determination. Nevertheless, there are two known examples of European Agreements. A well-known French company, Thomson, made two agreements in 1985, for two years, that in 1987 were renewed indefinitely and operate at two levels:

1   A Verbindungsausschuss or Liaison Committee that meets twice per annum with delegates of the European Metalworkers' Federation; and

2   a European 'Branchenkomission' of 26 employee representatives from all the European countries in which Thomson is represented. This meets once per annum, and its costs are borne by the company, but it has no co-determination rights.

The second example is also a French company — Bull (computer manufacturers).

Trade unions

The German (and European) unions are supporting the establishment of an EEC-regulated form of trans-national employee representation. Understandably, the German trade union movement is in favour of a participation model based on co-determination. On the other hand, they do not reckon that in the foreseeable future, the legal foundations will be established. Therefore, as an interim measure, they are striving for information-sharing bodies at the European level. The union federations and individual unions need time to get consensus amongst themselves. Differences of opinion abound across industry, regional and national boundaries.

Concrete steps have already been taken by the VW AG Group Works Council and the IG Metall is preparing the ground for a form of worker representation incorporating the

European manufacturing operations and this will be taken a step further at a meeting of worker representatives from all VW plants in Europe, in November 1989.

From my point of view, these developments across national borders are inevitable and logical — and, as mentioned previously, fit in with our company's overall labour relations philosophies. From the management side, while respecting the individuality of each of our subsidiaries, there is a clear interdependence and increasing interlinking between the various European (and, for that matter world-wide) plants.

This 'Networking' clearly has labour implications and consequences and employee representatives have a justifiable interest and right to be informed and involved on matters that affect them, directly and indirectly.

CONCLUSION

The purpose of my paper was to present an overview of what is happening on the German and European labour scenes. Clearly, it is a dynamic situation, enriched and complicated by the values, traditions and social and legal systems of the various countries.

It will be interesting to see whether a new, non-national or cross-national European form of worker participation evolves. It is unlikely that a completely new form will emerge across national European boundaries in the foreseeable future. It may be true that the borders between the many countries of Europe will disappear from January 1993, and it may be true that labour will move even more freely that it does right now — and over time there will be adaptations to individual country labour systems, influenced by the wider dissemination of knowledge of other systems.

Of course it will be interesting to see, on the European scene, to what extent the labour relations system of one of the strongest members of the EEC with one of the most powerful and well-organised trade union movements in the world will influence the European worker participation model but no system is exportable in its entirety, and certainly, there are no takers for the German model amongst the European heads of state right now — least of all from the other dominant member of the EEC, Maggie Thatcher!

It is more likely that initial cross-national forms of worker participation will be initiated, within multinational companies, by the trade unions and worker representatives (and perhaps by some far-sighted employers?!) and that these individually negotiated structures will be watched with interest by the Eurocrats and could well be models for a future, legislated European-wide worker participation system.

Abbreviations

VW AG = Volkswagen Aktiengesellschaft, referring to the VW company
and plants Germany.

IGM = Industrie Gewerkschaft Metall, the German Metalworkers' Union.

EEC = European Economic Community.

BDA = Bundesvereinigung der deutschen ArbeitgeberverbaÄnde, the
Confederation of German Employers' Associations.

REFERENCES

In compiling this paper the presenter wishes to acknowledge
that he made substantial use of two booklets:

Facts About Germany, published by Lexikon-Institut Bertelsmann. Chapter
    on Industrial Relations pp 251–6 Worker Co-determination pp 257–62.
Co-determination at Volkswagen AG, issued by the General Works Council of
    VW AG.

4

Don Power

EMPLOYEE INVOLVEMENT IN THE USA

A PROCESS FOR DEVELOPING AND MAINTAINING VIABLE LABOUR–MANAGEMENT RELATIONS INTO THE NINETIES

It is becoming evident as the 1980s come to a close, that the collective bargaining process that has served the parties and the U.S nation so well over the last 40 years, is in serious need of repair and redirection. With this thought in mind, three major areas of concern must be addressed.

1. Observations/perceptions as to the problems the parties face as they consider efforts in restructuring.
2. Recommendations for achieving meaningful change.
3. Three levels of courage necessary to accomplish the needed changes.

The following *observations and perceptions* should be taken into consideration when developing and maintaining a viable labour–management relationship under the current environment.

1. Most union management failures today and in the past were not structural in nature, but involved people failures. This has in part been due to the parties' inability to understand, accept and work with differences.
2. Trust in institutions, leaders and processes in the USA are at an all-time low. It is generally felt that the institution of labour and management have lost some of their direction and focus and that there is a developing gap between

those that lead and those that are directed and served by leaders.

3. Individual gain at the expense of the whole is becoming more prevalent and destructive. This is due in part to a lack of understanding of the terms 'union' and 'collective'. The parties have forgotten that underlying the concept of union is uniformity of application to all those involved. This is the very heart of a concept of routing discrimination out of the work setting. The term collective refers to the collective good of the whole and does not contemplate the destruction of the whole body by the excesses of a small group.

4. Individual and organisational excellence is decreasing in all segments of the process. Unions and employers are suffering a loss of excellence due to an inability to adjust to and cope with the dramatic need for both of them to develop new purposes and to reaffirm old valid purposes. The parties are, at best, suffering from the rigidity of their past successes.

5. The bargaining process, as currently structured, is no longer mutually productive for the parties in a majority of cases. The process is not being focused by the parties to solve the complex problems that both unions and management face today. We are still involved in the theatrics of the past and not in developing a new responsive collective bargaining system.

6. Management and labour have only one option in a world market, and that is to restructure the bargaining process to be mutually productive again, and to develop the day-to-day relationship necessary to support this bargaining process change.

The following factors should be considered in any attempt to *develop and maintain a viable labour/management relationship*. All parties and individuals that make up the institution of collective bargaining must come to the point of accepting each other's continued existence. The parties must accept and understand the strengths, weaknesses and differences that both labour and management bring to the process. Labour and management must develop a structure to allow for meaningful change to take place. This structure must allow for real union/management input and in addition, must allow for meaningful results to be developed. The parties must redevelop the lost concept of trust. This must be accomplished by deeds and not through words. This trust will only be developed when the parties readopt the concept that 'my word is my bond'. Lastly, the bargaining process must be restructured such that the problems of today can be solved. This will be accomplished only by a bargaining process that contains the following component parts:

- is mutually productive;
- is target specific;
- reduces proposal inflation;
- increases the information flow to workers which is necessary to address complex problems; and
- is accepting of an expanded employee role in the daily decision-making process of that organisation.

It is important to point out that there are *three levels of courage* necessary to accomplish this change in direction for the collective bargaining process. Level I requires that both labour and management recognise a need for change and make plans to come together to discuss the possibilities. This level, in some measure, is being addressed by the parties today. Unfortunately, this effort is at best marginal. Level II requires that labour and management establish a structure to accomplish a new direction. This in part is being accomplished successfully but the effort is being hampered by individuals and organisations that have created structures that are at best a sham and do not allow for real input and change. Level III is the accomplishment of a new direction. This can be achieved only through a recognition of a mutual goal of survival for both unions and management. *It is of grave importance that we note* that the American Labor Movement, over 50 years ago, accepted the continued existence of the American business system by forgoing the attempt to control the means of production, and accepting collective bargaining as a process of sharing in the wealth of the system. But American business as an institution has never accepted the continued existence of the American Labor Movement as demonstrated by continuous efforts to destroy trade unions. Co-operation requires understanding, truth and acceptance of each other's right to exist. One approach to improving labour management relations is that of employee involvement.

THE PROCESS OF EMPLOYEE INVOLVEMENT

A step-by-step approach to establishing and structuring an in-plant worksite labour–management committee and its logical extension, the employee involvement process, to assist in achieving required structural changes is outlined. The model that is presented here is not necessarily a perfect one. It is a model that was developed for a variety of different organisations in both the public and private sectors. Before adopting an employee involvement process the parties must give serious consideration to various tests to determine whether the joint venture will have any chance for success. These set the stage for employee involvement:

1. Will on the Part of the Parties
2. Not a Process for Everyone
3. Timing & Expectancy Factor
4. Not a Replacement for Collective Bargaining
5. Traditional Roles & Politics
6. Training Needs.

The first test is that there must be *a will on the part of the parties* to change for the process to work. It has been noted that the most successful programmes involving joint ventures between labour and management have arisen from the worst of relationships. The reverse is also true—the failure rate for these programmes rises with the improved relationship level. This phenomenon arises from the fact that the parties with acceptable relationships find it very difficult to recognise a need for change and to sustain it. In essence, the pain of the status quo is less than the pain required to move forward in a new process.

The second test involves the realisation that employee involvement is *not a process for everyone*. This stems from several factors. A number of programmes that exist today can trace their origins to faddism. In essence they were created by an individual or group of individuals who thought that they were the 'in thing to do today' in human resource management circles. These employee involvement programmes meet the same fate that all other fads meet: here today, gone tomorrow. Some programmes are due today to a misguided theory that they are good tools to get rid of or keep a union out of one's business. The creators of these programmes have ignored the underlying concept of employee involvement, which is to harness and utilise properly the human brain power of the organisation for the good of the whole. Financial difficulties are sometimes a propellant that drives organisations to consider employee involvement. A quick fix flies in the face of the fact that an employee involvement programme will require between five and seven years to establish firmly as a fully viable structure. There must also come a realisation that some companies and unions are not now able, nor will they ever be able, to change enough to accommodate an employee involvement programme.

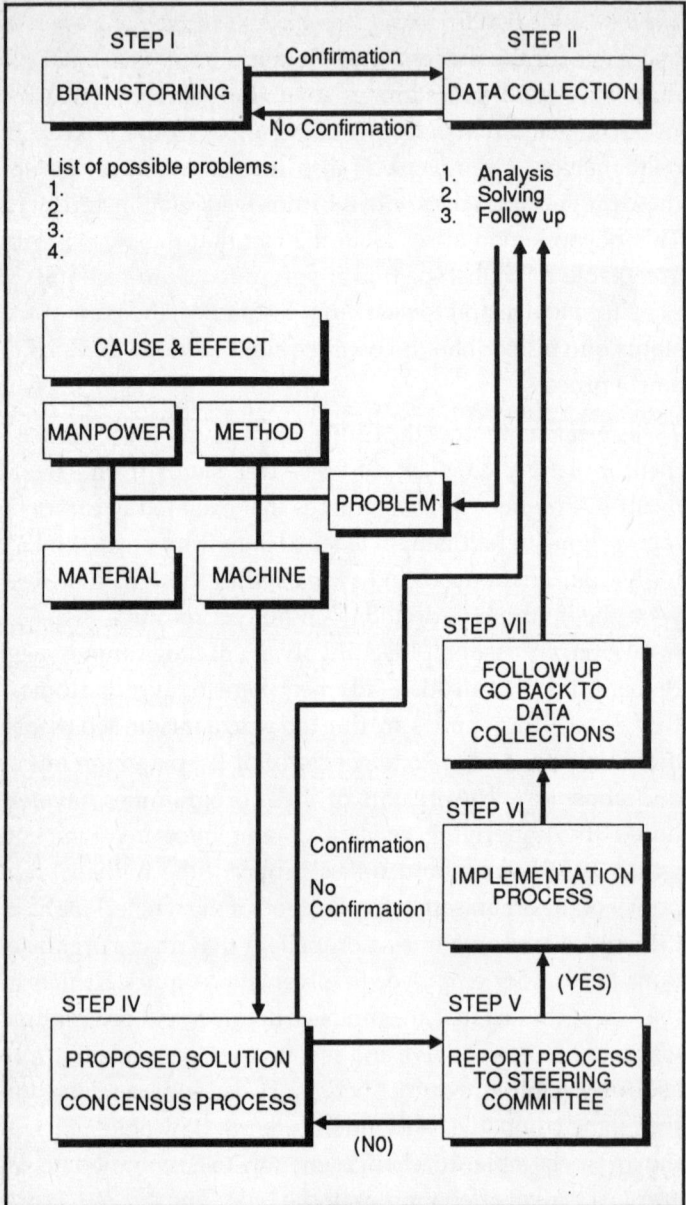

FIGURE 4.1
Steps in the problem-solving process

The third test of importance is the *timing and expectancy factor*. A worthwhile and workable in-plant labour management committee will require at least a year to build; to extend the labour management committee into a full-blown employee involvement programme, roughly five to seven years will be required to bring it to a point of being fully functional.

The question must be asked: Why is so much time required?

There are three factors that contribute to the timing issue. We must construct an employee involvement system, such that it will withstand any serious problems that may occur with the relationship between the employer and the union. This requires that the process be assembled one part at a time, and not moved along until the last problem-solving group constructed is fully and satisfactorily operating. It is very important to note that a great deal of time will be required to take two distinctly different organisational structures (union and management) from an adversarial system which selects leaders differently and defines leadership differently; where priority selection and decision-making processes are not remotely related; and where decisions in the past have been achieved through muscle and lack of information, and create a structure and process of total jointness. To accomplish this transformation, many hours must be spent training present and future participants in a joint, fair and neutral problem-solving process (Figure 4.1).

This process, as set forth in Figure 4.1, requires that the parties abandon old problem-solving methods used in an adversarial system and adopt new, neutral methods. It requires that we substitute the brainstorming process for the unilateral process for the generation of ideas. Once ideas or problems are identified, they must be validated by data, not by assumptions. Once validated, those problems will be moved to the cause and effect phase of the process where

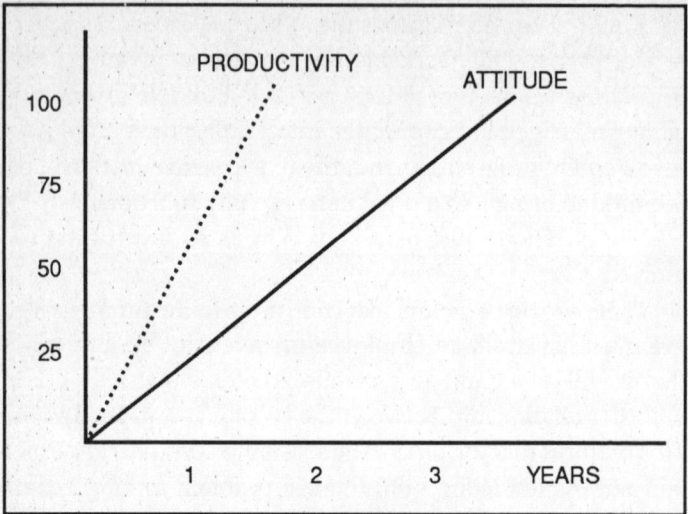

FIGURE 4.2
The expectancy factor in employee involvement programmes

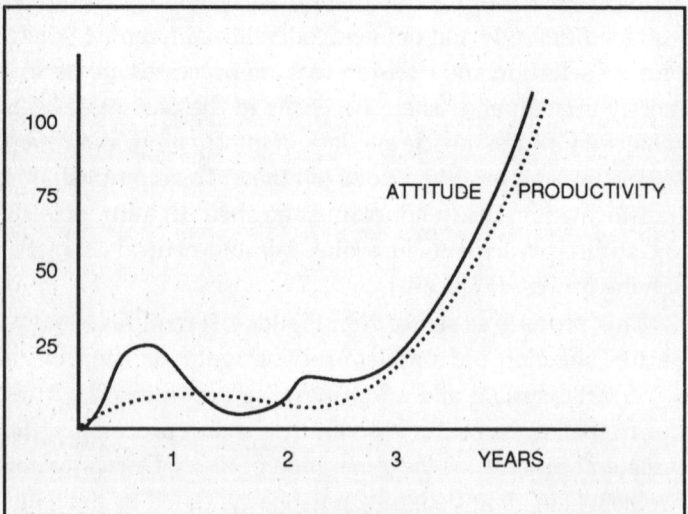

FIGURE 4.3
Actual occurrence factor in employee involvement programmes

labour and management will be asked to identify the possible causes of these valid problems. This step requires that the parties build a graphic model which will group the various causes around four standard cause areas: manpower, methods, materials and machines. Once this step is completed, the proposed solution phase of the process can be moved to. Here again the parties are required to validate or reject their suggested causes. Once validated, the parties formulate proposed solutions for each cause, making certain to analyse and report to a steering committee of top union and management leaders not only the proposed solution, but the projected outcome, cost of proposal, time required and follow-up procedure. The problem-solving process does not stop here. The parties must institute a follow-up procedure which requires that the implemented solution is checked for performance once a month for several months following implementation. In addition, the joint effort requires the pursuit of further improvements on the implemented solution.

It is important to address the expectancy factor. There is often a large gap between what both managements and unions expect to receive from the process, in productivity and changed attitudes, and what they actually receive (the occurrence factor).

When charting the management and union expectancy factor, we find that both management and labour expect that their attitudes about one another will be automatically improved. In addition management also believes that productivity will increase sharply simply because an employee involvement programme has been established.

When compared with the actual occurrence factor, however, substantial differences appear in both attitude and productivity plots. (Figure 4.3)

On the productivity side the plot of the curve is very flat for the first two years or so because the management structure has primary control over the factors that would help improve productivity and have failed to get their own house in order so that employee input might be utilised properly. Management controls the following productivity factors:

1. Product Design
2. Training and Retraining of Workers
3. Materials
4. Process
5. Machinery and Tooling Selection
6. Preventative Maintenance Programmes.

Workers cannot work at top efficiency when: the product design is defective; they are not properly trained; the raw materials are substandard; the process is not in sequence and the machinery and tooling does not adequately meet the needs of the job. It has, over the years, been very convenient to blame workers for poor productivity when in fact, management has substantial control over the causes and failed to recognise it. Management must, in addition, before starting an employee involvement programme, give serious consideration to how they are going to utilise effectively, and give feedback to, worker suggestions. In the initial stages of employee involvement, most worker suggestions will centre on repair and design. With this thought in mind, management must make certain, in advance of the idea onslaught, that the engineering and maintenance departments are staffed and fully capable of responding quickly. If this is not accomplished, we have observed a high rate of worker frustration due to managements' slow response rate to suggestions. This inevitably leads to worker claims that management does not care. The management team must also identify, develop and make available a clear, reliable source of information for worker team usage. Without data to solve problems, the parties will revert to their previous adversarial behaviour.

In looking at the attitude plot on the actual occurrence factor chart, it will be noted that in the first year of any employee involvement programme there will tend to be a sharp increase towards a more positive attitude, followed by a steep decline toward the end of the first year. This rapid increase and decline is generally due to the fact that the parties, despite warnings to the contrary, have developed an unrealistic expectation about an improved relationship. In essence, the sharp decline on or about the one-year mark is simply brought on by the parties' realisation that the relationship is not as good as they have led one another to believe and the curve plot will reflect a true levelling out. The one-year level in an employee involvement programme is a most dangerous period with a high potential for a programme collapse. As the parties suffer a sharp decline in the attitudes curve, the concept of a will on the part of the parties will come into play. As labour and management exhibit a will to change and to struggle forward together, the programme will resurrect itself and start a positive incline in the second year. If there is no will on the part of the parties, the employee involvement process will most likely collapse at this point. It must also be noted that between the second and the third years of the employee involvement programme, the attitude plot will suffer a slight dip. This dip should be characterised as a political dip brought on by events such as renegotiations of labour contracts and the election of new union officials. *

The fourth test revolves around the fact that the employee involvement programme is *not a replacement for collective bargaining* but is actually a supplement to the process. It is very important to realise in starting the process, that the union will be concerned about its existence. It is very important to make

---

* In the USA labour contracts tend to be negotiated every three years as opposed to the annual bargaining which characterises South African industrial relations.

sure that the union understands that its existence is protected and that the process will not be used to replace it.

We must now address the *traditional roles and politics* factor. Historically the institutions of management and labour have been adversaries where management jealously guarded its rights to run the business and the union did not have a large interest in running the business, but attempted to secure its future by bargaining wages and fringes from business profits. The employee involvement concept changes this basic assumption and places employees in positions of suggesting and making decisions that have historically been reserved for management. The people most resistant to the employee involvement process tend to be the first-line supervisor and the union shop-steward. The supervisor approaches the process from the position that any employee input to decision-making will be an erosion of his/her power to run his/her area and as a result, resists vigorously. On the other hand, the union shop-stewards will resist because the historic way that they settled employee problems was through the negotiating grievance procedure and now they have had a second dimension added for employee problem solving, i.e. problem-solving teams. Union shop-stewards in many cases have viewed this new process as a threat to, and distraction from, the traditional grievance procedure.

The last area of concern is *training and education*. A strong training component is necessary when attempts are made to bring two distinctly different groups together for co-operative purposes when their history has been one of adversarialism. Employee Involvement training needs include:

1. Team Building Fundamentals
2. Group Problem-solving Techniques
3. Report Preparation & Presentation
4. Communication Techniques
5. Interpersonal Skills

6. Effective Feedback Methods
7. Positive Reinforcement Techniques
8. Current Needs.

The following factors must be considered when planning a training component for the employee involvement process.

- Training must be conducted for employee involvement participants as close to the time as possible when they will be required to use the skills.

- The parties should avoid training massive numbers of people over a short period of time and concentrate on training small groups of people as programme needs require.

- Training needs may be met through formal or informal means.

- Train with the thought in mind that employee comfort levels must be maintained.

The three purposes of the above-mentioned training components are as follows. First, through training, a new, neutral problem solving methodology must be installed which will allow the adversaries to operate in a round the table mode rather than the familiar across-the-table mode. Secondly, the training modules must prepare both parties to communicate more fully within and outside the employee involvement process and in addition, provide a way for ideas to convert to action steps. Lastly, the training must address the compilation, understanding and utilisation of data within the employee involvement process.

There are three exclusions to be noted in order to insure that the employee involvement process is not a threat but an enhancement to the collective bargaining process. The parties must be able to feel free to be honest with one another without a fear of retaliation. Thus, the following exclusions are necessary:

1.   Current Grievances
2.   Negotiations
3.   Legal or Quasi-legal Forums.

The parties should agree that all current or any future *grievances* once they become an official part of the contractual procedure remain there. This will protect the function and integrity of the contractual grievance procedure. It is also recognised that the employee involvement process should allow for the solution of problems before they become formal grievances, thus possibly cutting the official grievance load.

The parties should agree that the employee involvement process is *not to be used to negotiate a change to the current contract*. There may be times, however, when the parties in an employee involvement process discuss mutually beneficial changes which can be accomplished only through contract language. It is suggested that these recommendations be forwarded to the parties respective negotiating committees for any action. Thus the two processes are kept separate.

The parties should agree that any conversation held within the employee involvement process not be used by one side against the other in any *legal or quasi-legal forums*—i.e., NLRB hearing, arbitration, contract negotiations, and a court of law.

THE DEVELOPMENT OF STRUCTURES FOR THE
EMPLOYEE INVOLVEMENT PROCESS

As stated earlier, the structure outlined here is only one of many and it is important to understand that there is no one perfect structure that meets all the needs of all organisations. Structures should evolve out of organisational needs. The development of a full employee involvement process is discussed below.

Stage one: Development of the steering committee

Stage one is the development of the steering committee. There are several factors to consider when developing the steering committee.

1. The role of the steering committee will evolve from one of problem-solving to one of overseeing and guiding the process. This will happen after about four years.

2. The steering committee members must be union and management individuals who have the authority to make decisions for their respective groups.

Steering committee membership sources

Management	Union
1. Plant Manager	1. Local President
2. Personnel Director and/or Industrial Relations Director	2. Shop Chairman
3. Quality Control Director	3. Union Member*
4. Superintendent	4. International Representative
5. First-level Supervisor*	5. Steward

*Rotating seat

3. In some cases the process will not develop beyond the Steering Committee stage and many parties have been quite satisfied with this development.

The procedural aspects of the Steering Committee include attention to such issues as:

1. Number of People—Rotating Seat
2. Time Frame

3. Use of Contract
4. Future Expansion.

In determining a workable *number of people* on the steering committee, the parties must consider cost and control. It is suggested that the steering committee consist of no more than four or five members on each side. In the beginning the process is very difficult, so it is not advisable to involve too many people at any one time. The committee should allow one team position on each side to be a designated rotating seat. This allows for the union and company to bring a supervisor and union member from the same department to each meeting to discuss problems that affect them and to in some small way increase the number of people participating.

The *time factor* must now be reviewed. The steering committee should meet once a month for a period of no more than two hours in length unless the parties agree otherwise. The meetings should be during working hours and scheduled at least for a period of no less than six months in advance. Once these meetings are scheduled, they should not be cancelled. This is a part of the commitment on the part of the parties to each other.

As previously mentioned, the *separation of the traditional contract mechanisms* from the employee involvement process is very important. This includes grievances within the contractual grievance procedure that must remain there and contract negotiations that must be conducted outside of the employee involvement process.

The steering committee members have *training needs* that must be addressed. This is important because the two parties solve problems differently within their own structures and are used to an adversarial method when working together in collective bargaining. The following training areas must be addressed:

- Problem-solving techniques—i.e., consensus, brainstorming, pareto and cause and effect charts.
- The hows of operating within a structure which is not your own—i.e. Union/management vs employee involvement.
- How to conduct a meeting in a non-adversarial atmosphere.
- Data presentation techniques.

The *role of the outsider/facilitator* must be defined so that it is effectively blended with the process. It usually includes the following:

1. Chair the Meeting
2. Take and Maintain the Minutes
3. Prepare the Agenda
4. Expedite the Discussion.

It must first be emphasised that the role of any outsider is not, under any circumstance, a permanent one. The parties to an employee involvement project are the owners of the project, not the outsider. The outside facilitator will leave at the point when the project is working well and the parties themselves can manage it.

What is involved in the outside facilitator's role? First, he/she will chair the meetings of the steering committee, which allows for the elimination of an adversarial environment. Secondly, he/she will take and maintain the minutes of the committee's meetings. This is done in part due to a lack of trust that may exist between the parties. As this trust is established, this function will be turned over to the parties. Thirdly, the facilitator will prepare the agenda from items listed by the parties that they would like to discuss. The facilitator will take great care in monitoring the items to be discussed to see that current grievances and items to be negotiated do not get into the discussion. The facilitator may flip a coin to see who will present their item first and will then rotate items from union to management to union, and down

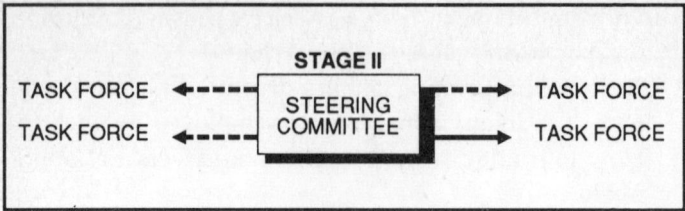

FIGURE 4.4
Creation of the task force system

the agenda. Fourthly, in the beginning the facilitator has a strong role in expediting the discussions. This is due in part because the parties to this process are only one step removed from the adversarial relationship and will find it very easy to revert back to. This role also helps being under control the tensions that might be there.

As the employee involvement process expands, the next step in the process is embarked on.

Stage two: The creation of the task force system

The task force is not a permanent part of the structure although some task forces will have a life-span greater than others depending on the nature of the problems to be solved by them.

The task force is set up to work on problems that have an effect on the organisation as a whole and for which the steering committee does not have the time necessary to explore in depth. The task force structure allows for the development of a core group of employees, both union and management, with experience in working in the employee involvement process. The task force is a creation of the steering committee and is set up to work on problems referred to it by the steering committee. The task force's mission is to develop recommendations on problems referred to it and to

---

Section 1

EMPLOYEE ACTION TEAM NAME: . . . .
Date: . . . .
Name/Dept: . . . .
Phone: . . . .
Initial evidence of problem: . . . .
ate initial problem-solving effort completed: . . . .
SKETCH:

Section 2
IDENTIFY PROBLEM

What is affected? . . . .
What are the symptoms? . . . .
Where is the problem? . . . .
When does it occur? . . . .
How many are affected? . . . .
Define problem: . . . .

Section 3
ISOLATE AND CONTAIN PROBLEMS

What can be done to prevent the problem
from reaching the consumer? . . . .
. . . .
. . . .
Identify key persons/areas involved: . . . .
. . . .

COLLECT AND ANALYSE DATA
List methods of gathering data . . . .
. . . .
Attach all tests/analyses that were done . . . .

Section 4
CORRECT OR REDUCE THE PROBLEM

List possible solutions. . . . .
. . . .
. . . .
What is the best solution? . . . .
. . . .
Who implemented the solution? . . . .
Who verified the solution? . . . .
. . . .
MONITOR AND DOCUMENT CHANGE
What documentation was issued? . . . .
. . . .
When was documentation issued? . . . .
Who was the documentation sent to? . . . .
What follow-up is needed? . . . .

BOX 4.1
Problem-solving report form

present these recommendations, which will include timetables and responsibilities, to the steering committee.

The task force meets for two hours in company time every other week with a prepared agenda and minutes to be kept and distributed to all employees. The task force *operational procedure* is as set out below:

Step I: Brainstorming—discuss items that effect quality, cost and work environment.

Step II: Fill out sections 1 and 2 of the Problem Solving Report Form.

Step III: Gather data to prove whether the problem is real or not—fill out section 3 of the Problem Solving Report Form.

Step IV: Fill out section 4 of the Problem Solving Report Form (see Box 4.1).

The task force reporting procedure to the steering committee is as set out below.

The reporting format to the steering committee is as follows:

Step I: List problem.

Step II: List proposed solution.

Step III: What will the proposal do?

Step IV: How much will the proposal cost? (approximately.)

Step V: How long will it take to complete? (approximate time.)

Step VI: Who is responsible?

Step VII: Follow up—outline procedure.

The task force structure faces many problems in its quest to become functional. First, both sides tend to be in an adversarial mode. Secondly, most employees do not know how to translate their knowledge into solutions to problems. Thirdly, most employees don't know how to read or understand organisational figures—i.e. financial statements, etc. Fourthly, most employees are unable to reduce their thoughts and ideas to writing. Fifthly, most employees do not know how to prepare and present data. Sixthly, most employees have a problem with making a presentation to the steering committee; there is a fear factor that must be overcome.

The employee involvement process can now advance to the next stage.

Stage three: setting up the department structure

At this point in the evolution of the employee involvement process which is at or near the three-year level, the final phase should be started.

This final phase involves taking the process to the shop floor itself. It involves the final phase of involving all employees in the process. It is at this point that the role of the steering committee starts its transition from a problem-solving forum to a forum to oversee the total process.

It is important that in moving to the department level the area with the best chance for success is picked; one that possesses good leadership on both the union and management sides and where there is a concentration of previous task

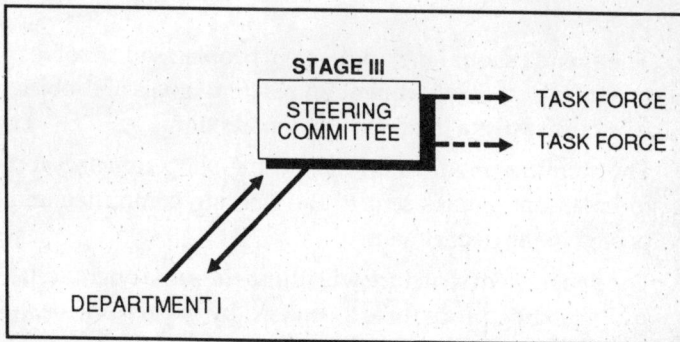

FIGURE 4.5
Setting up the department structure

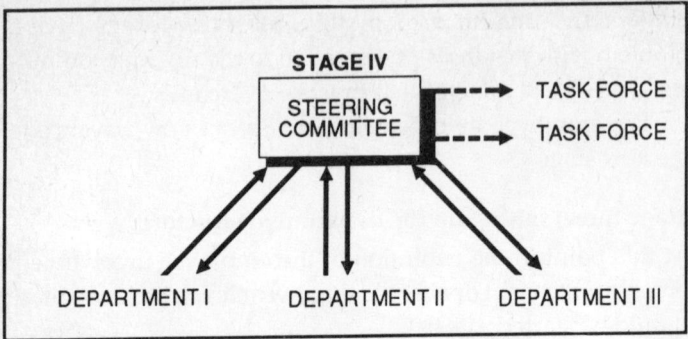

FIGURE 4.6
Completion of the Department Structure

force members. The department committee would function as follows:

- They should meet for one hour each week or for two hours once a month.

- The meeting should be chaired by the department foreman and union shop-steward.

- The parties must develop a system to determine what it is that the people would like to discuss.

- There should be a mini-agenda prepared in advance and posted.

- The agenda should include current problems to be solved, progress of the department on reaching goals and objectives and lastly, a general comment section.

- The minutes should be kept by the shop-steward and foreman and copies sent to the steering committee and posted in the department.

- The department structure will utilise the same operational and reporting procedures as utilised by the task forces.

The training components for the department sections should include problem-solving techniques, communication skills and the hows of conducting a meeting.

Stage four: completion of the department structure

This stage of the employee involvement process will bring to a completion the transition of the steering committee to a true overseer of the process.

Stage four is to complete in all departments the process started in Stage three, that being the extension of the process to all employees. A very important consideration in this final step is the cross-communication problem between the various types of problem solving groups. These problems can be reduced to a minimum by scheduling all department meetings within the same week, where possible, and by scheduling the steering committee one week in advance so that they can co-ordinate any problems beforehand. All agendas and minutes are cross-exchanged so that there is no duplication of effort.

SPECIAL PROBLEM AREAS

There are some areas that involve special problems that one should be aware of in considering an employee involvement process:

1. Communication System
2. Company Suggestion Systems vs. Task Force
3. Employee Involvement Programme Introduction Procedure.

It is very important to note that the programme will be destroyed if a good system of communication is not developed. It is important that all of the employee involvement proceedings are public and nothing is hidden from view.

It is suggested in addition to the various minutes that are kept, that a newsletter be published. This newsletter should be jointly written and published and mailed to all employees' homes. The content of the newsletter should, in a simple and concise manner, inform all about the affairs of the employee involvement process.

A very serious matter that should be explored when setting up an employee involvement programme is the relationship between a company suggestion system, if one exists, and money saved as the result of a task force system. The parties should ask the following questions of themselves: Should we route task force ideas through the suggestion system? Thus, what about the following questions:

1. The employee who joined the task force just prior to project completion?
2. A member who transferred out of the task force two weeks after the project was started?
3. A member left the company altogether at some point in the analysis?
4. The 'expert' called in to assist briefly?
5. The supervisors included in the task force, and are they covered by the suggestion system?
6. Assistance that was received by another task force?
7. Situations where an employee is at the same time working on the same problem.

If these questions are not addressed, then the parties face the possibility that employees can make more money by staying out of the task force system as contained within the employee involvement process.

It is important that before starting any employee involvement programme that it be introduced properly to all employees. This must involve a presentation to all employees explaining the intent and structure of the programme. This will allow the employees to review the programme in advance and have their concerns addressed.

As we assess the potential impact of the employee involvement process on American business and the American Labor Movement, it is quite clear that our economic survival is dependent upon such a process. We must proceed with caution, however, as we acknowledge that the parties may not be ready to abandon the old adversarial system and allow true co-operation to take place.

5

Frank M Horwitz

EMPLOYEE
FINANCIAL PARTICIPATION:
A COMPARATIVE PERSPECTIVE

INTRODUCTION: THE STUDY OF FINANCIAL PARTICIPATION

An analysis of comparative systems of employee participation in general, and financial participation in particular, is subject to two difficulties. Firstly, the use of common nomenclatures to describe phenomena which are substantively different may occur. Secondly, there is a need for a conceptual framework which is both valid and reliable. These two methodological questions are important if an analysis is to move beyond mere description to be critically evaluative and penetrating. An understanding of financial participation must be rooted in an analysis of socio-historical patterns of industrial relations in a particular society and an examination of the goals or rationale for participation at both societal and organisational levels. These two variables require rigorous analysis if a proper understanding of the scope and particularly the processes of legitimation of financial participation schemes, is to occur. The actual content of participation schemes—their structure, benefits, administration and (trusteeship) control also requires examination. Finally, associated with the question of legitimation is the process of employee participation in the formulation, implementation, policy management and control of financial participation schemes. This refers to the level of influence employees and their representatives have—the extent to which their participation in the development and control of the scheme reflects processes of unilateral employer introduction, joint consultation, negotiation, or co-determination.

A framework for analysing employee participation is proposed based on the work of Poole (1988) and Salamon (1987) (figure 5.1). This framework suggests that prevailing managerial and labour ideologies, economic and legislative variables, coupled with the balance of power and internal industrial relations (IR) climate, represent a complex set of interrelated factors. These affect strategic choices and the extent to which financial participation schemes, occur.

COMPARATIVE TRENDS IN INDUSTRIAL RELATIONS

An overview of comparative financial participation schemes should be seen against the background of the interrelationship between industrial relations developments and changes in managerial and trade union power, state ideology and strategy. In the United States, the United Kingdom and to a lesser extent other European countries, as well as in Australia and New Zealand, certain important IR shifts have occurred during the 1980s. Firstly, the moves towards greater decentralisation and organisational flexibility have seen a corresponding focus on the decentralisation of industrial relations, especially collective bargaining and IR policy, in the United Kingdom, Australia and New Zealand. Direct forms of participation such as Employee Share Ownership Schemes (ESOPS) and indirect forms of participation other than collective bargaining, such as joint consultation, have become more prominent in Britain, the United States, Japan and Australia. At the same time the introduction of new technology, changes in work processes and job design, have also been accompanied by a shift away from heavy smoke-stack manufacturing industries in the United States and United Kingdom, towards higher employment and growth in the service and information sectors. This has also been associated with demographic changes in population, with a move of large segments of the populace in these countries towards the Southern states/counties. Managerial strategies have become more assertive, seeking a breakdown of traditional job demarcation and regulation towards greater flexibility and skills diversity. Job control/fragmentation has become more prominent with a decline in union membership in Britain of some 25% to approximately 40% of the economically active population, and a more dramatic decline in the United States to less than 15% of the private sector work-force. Union density has declined marginally in West Germany, Israel, Australia and New Zealand. Changes in union membership have an important bearing on the persistence of particular IR institutions. In particular, an alteration in power balance towards employers seems to have also been associated with employer initiatives seeking greater decentralisation of IR policy and bargaining procedures in the context of state policies of deregulation and privatisation aimed at economic revitalisation. Managerial ideologies are also important variables in understanding the contemporary emphasis on financial participation. The reassertion of the ethic of individualism in most Western societies (although varying in degree) is an important factor ideologically underpinning managerial strategies, which seek decentralisation, business unit autonomy, personal commitment and identification with organisational goals. These strategies have been criticised as reflecting a more sophisticated, paternalistic form of unitarism aimed at union marginalisation or exclusion. Employee participation, comparatively, can therefore be seen as a difficult balancing act between managerial control and employee opportunity, requiring sensitive judgements and sometimes awkward trade-offs.

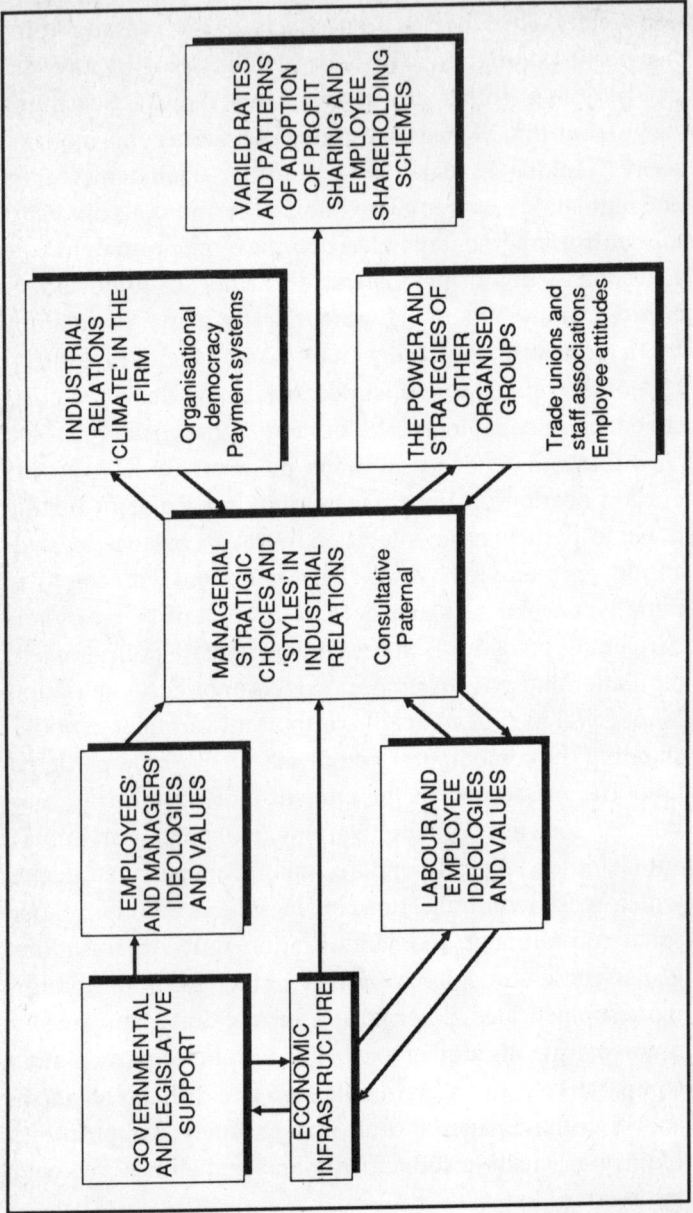

FIGURE 5.1

PARTICIPATION OBJECTIVES

It is important that a considered analysis of both the goals of employee participation and the requirements of its legitimation, occur. The economic or financial participation of employees may take various forms, such as profit-sharing, individual and group bonus incentive schemes, and share ownership schemes. These schemes are not, indeed, new in many companies. Their recent popularity does, however, reflect a comparative trend in several Western industrialised economies towards devolution of financial participation to lower levels of the organisation.

The goals of employee participation are alleged by some to reflect managerial strategies aimed at the co-option of workers into a management ethos—an ideological goal, using participation and sophisticated management techniques to seduce commitment away from the pursuit of class interests and trade unionism toward the organisational goals of productivity and efficiency. Proponents of this view argue that it is simply a manipulative form of managerial control aimed at humanising capitalism and its work processes (Maller 1989, Nicol 1989, Horwitz 1988).

A second goal of employee participation is that of the stakeholder thesis; that is, employees are given a genuine stake in the prosperity of the business and are likely to benefit substantially by its success. Whilst the stakeholder argument could be criticised as similar to the management ideology thesis, it can reflect a pluralist conception of industrial relations (IR), recognising inherent conflicts of interests between capital and labour and acknowledging the importance of collective bargaining as a primary process for wealth distribution. The rationale of the stakeholder thesis is however, different. It focuses mainly on facilitating wealth creation by linking organisational commitment to rewards. Research findings in the United States indicate that financial stakeholding through ESOPS is frequently considered as an employer method to prevent potential takeover bids, as employee shareholders are more likely than outside ones to support the company's managers against a hostile takeover bid (*The Economist* 1989). International comparative studies have shown that the stakeholder thesis in general, and financial participation in particular, are more likely to work successfully, where the trade union movement is strong and is able to influence the type and implementation of these schemes (Poole 1988). In most Western industrial societies, as well as in South Africa, it has been argued by employers that financial participation, such as share ownership, reflects the employer's right to deal directly with employees to enhance their stake in the organisation and is therefore a separate matter from that of collective bargaining. Since wealth generation has its origins in the labour process of employees, it is difficult to see how the essentially substantive (IR) interest issue of wealth distribution can be separated from collective labour relations processes.

This raises the third objective of employee participation: the question of employee influence in policy and strategic business decisions which affect their interests. This is a question of power. Financial participation is an individual-based form of participation based on the willing consent of an individual employee. It has little to do with the de facto distribution of power in and governance of organisations. Representational or collective forms of worker expression are a necessary prerequisite for industrial democracy. Financial participation has little to do with the idea of industrial democracy, since workers' influence is generally limited as minority shareholders.

Yet increasing numbers of employers are taking employee participation seriously. It can be asked whether their goals are primarily economic/productivity ones, whether they seek humanistic/ethical reasons for participation, or whether they have a sincere intention to explore the precarious path towards industrial democracy. In most Western societies, such as the United States and Britain, an interrelated ideological goal of enhancing the commitment to a free market economy, and achieving added wealth through organisational commitment, seem to be the main motives for the popularisation of ESOPS and profit sharing. That many employers seek to reduce polarisation and enhance employee commitment, motivation and identification is an important statement of intent. The need to achieve these goals is seen as fundamental to wealth creation.

However, unless the primacy of a plurality of interest groupings having a common stakeholding and yet paradoxically competing for scarce resources is acknowledged, financial participation risks being perceived as an ideological threat to collective employee organisations. Research in the United Kingdom suggests that share schemes are introduced mainly to encourage workers to identify more with the aims of the firm, as well as for tax advantages. Motivational effects are seen as a consequence of achieving greater congruence of interests (Dewe 1988).

Given the legitimacy of the labour movement in representing Black workers in South Africa, processes for both reducing polarisation, and facilitating a relative balance of power in labour relations require vision and sensitivity. It is understandable, therefore, why trade unions frequently tend to be wary if not hostile to financial participation. Comparative international trends suggest that financial participation is viewed alongside an array of employer strategies, state policy, structural economic changes, shifting values, and broader transformations in IR institutions, as reducing the power of trade unions in many Western economies (Poole 1988, Cohen 1987, Martin 1987, Kochan 1987). Yet in South

Africa trade union membership is increasing against these international trends, and South African society continues to reflect broad attitudinal and structural divisions. It is in this context that the perceived legitimacy of financial participation schemes is most important.

Given the requirement of voluntarism of financial participation schemes, unlike negotiated representational forms of participation, financial participation is a form of individual, direct, personal involvement which may be described as participation by consent (table 5.1).

CONTEXTUAL FACTORS IN FINANCIAL PARTICIPATION

The current idealisation or romanticism of financial participation as a new-found panacea for organisational problems must be considered contextually. The social regulation of conflict by institutional means such as collective bargaining, reflects a preference for the dominance of a pluralist ideology. Although this latter interest-based model denotes a greater acceptance of a pluralist ideology, acknowledging the inherency of conflict in industrial relations (IR) and independence of interest of the parties, certain recent developments suggest a strengthening of sophisticated, paternalistic forms of unitarism in several Western countries.

Given that industrial relations may be considered as a sub-system of a wider socio-political system, developments in workplace representation as previously noted, reflect a decline in private sector trade union membership during the 1980s in several Western countries, for example, in the United States, Great Britain and in European countries such as Italy,

TABLE 5.1
Comparison of two models of participation

Item/Type	Participation by consent	Participation by negotiation
Motivation		
1. Employers	• Solicit co-operation on opinions • Unitarist 'Managing without union' ideology • Advice on operating new equipment • Reducing 'them & us' polarisation • Changing work organisation for higher productivity • Wealth creation Efficiency goal (Australia, Japan, USA, UK, New Zealand) • Improve motivation organisational loyalty and commitment • Tax advantages of financial participation (USA, UK) • Legitimising free enterprise • Competing with union for 'hearts and minds of employees'	• Acknowledge need to have independent employee leadership • Legislated direction (Australia, Belgium, France, Netherlands, West Germany) • Acknowledge participation on wider social economic issues
2. Unions	• Often opposed and try to contest or limit it (RSA) • Or silent observers initially (UK) • Or passive supporters • Cautious support (TUC in UK)	• Democratisation of society (W Germany, Netherlands, Scandinavian countries) • Institutionalisation of employee *rights* • Protection of employee's interests
3. Employees	• Often supportive (USA, Japan, UK, Australia) • Depends on union's position, power and relative influence of *other* key issues (e g living wage in RSA) • Basis for involvement is voluntarism and individual consent (e g financial participation, QCs)	• Unionised employees ambivalent or supportive • Risk of alienation between rank and file and representative bodies • Possible decline in union membership

France and Spain. This decline can be attributed to the following:

- Technological and structural change in the economy—for example, a growing white-collar workforce in many Western countries.

- Changes in worker attitudes and needs—trade unions may be seen as less instrumental than in the past for improving working conditions in some advanced industrial countries.

- New employer initiatives such as financial participation and strategies denoting a stronger focus on human resource management (HRM) and union marginalisation or even exclusion.

- Broader transformations of IR institutions.

- Shifting socio-political trends, which reflect, for example, policies such as privatisation and deregulation aimed at addressing economic crises in free market economies. The notion of 'people's capitalism' in Britain and the United States has become more prominent in this context.

Rather than one single factor predominating, a combination of these factors may be associated with changing patterns of union membership. These may in turn be associated with the nature and extent of financial participation. In developing African countries for example, the organisational development of trade unions has been stunted by state corporatism eroding trade union independence by executive intervention and central wage fixing and control over dismissal decisions, as, for example, in Zimbabwe and Mozambique. In contrast to developed industrial societies, trade union density in some developing countries is increasing, (for example in Namibia and South Africa) with industrial relations policy choices reflecting a strong ideological content. Unitarist ideologies in the latter context can be associated with employer responses to political conflict and the extent of polarisation in the so-

ciety, with organisational manifestations in lower commitment, the strong prevalence of instrumental attitudes to work,
and poor labour productivity. However, financial participation in both developed and some developing countries such
as South Africa is, perhaps for different reasons, sometimes
associated with practices and strategies which seek to achieve
the following:

- Seducing employees away from collective forms of indirect or representative participation, towards individual,
  consensual forms of direct involvement, such as financial
  participation and quality circles. For example, the general
  secretary of the National Union of Mineworkers in South
  Africa, Cyril Ramaphosa, has described the Anglo American Corporation's offer of shares to its employees as 'political and economic blackmail to try and seduce workers
  away from unionism and socialism' (Ramaphosa 1987).

- Provision of a personal, economic stakeholding in the
  organisation through financial participation, for example,
  employee share-ownership plans, profit-sharing and per-
  formance-related incentive schemes. This seems generally
  to be the case in Australian and British companies.

- De-emphasis of interest-based models of collective bargaining in favour of decentralised joint consultation, problem solving, strike-free agreements and single union
  agreements, such as those in the United Kingdom entered
  into between the Electrical, Electronic, Telecommunica-
  tions and Plumbing Union (EETPU) and employers such
  as Hitachi, Irlandus, Nissan, Sanyo, Sharp, Shotton Paper
  and Xidex (Basset 1989).

The somewhat persuasive emphasis of financial participation
on achieving organisational and particularly managerial objectives, belies the pluralist conception of organisations. The
latter approach views organisations as comprising groups
with common and competing interests with various coali-

tions of power, given that pluralism itself represents an ideological form.

TYPES OF FINANCIAL PARTICIPATION

Comparatively, the following are four main types of financial participation which occur:

- *Profit sharing* is most prevalent in Australia, New Zealand and the United Kingdom, occurring at all organisational levels. Profit sharing is considered by many employers as preferable to share ownership schemes, as effort and reward are considered more measurable, especially if short-term rewards/returns are offered, based on measurable performance in particular sectors (eg batch manufacturing, and retailing). In the United Kingdom over 20% of companies have profit-sharing or share ownership schemes (Poole 1988). The share of profits fluctuates with the economic performance of the firm. Profit-sharing may not, therefore, provide a stable level of income over time.

- *Employee share ownership schemes (ESOPS)* are popular at various levels in the United States, United Kingdom and South Africa. It is estimated that at least 11 million employees, (10% of the workforce) in the United States are on an ESOPS-type scheme. Current estimates in the United Kingdom are that over 50% of publicly quoted companies have some type of financial participation scheme (Poole 1988).

  The sector which has the most 'all employee' schemes (both for ESOPS and profit-sharing is the financial sector (50%). However, evidence of a link between ESOPS and improved worker performance has proved elusive (Dewe 1988). Based on a poll of 350 United States companies, those with ESOPS were found to have had a sales growth 40% higher and job creation 46% higher in ten years than those without ESOP schemes (Crainer 1988). Whilst legislation in the United States creates tax advantages for ESOPS, research into the relationships between ESOPS and economic performance is fraught with methodological difficulties. Rival causal or intervening variables may account for superior performance and not ESOPS, for example, productivity increases in large companies may occur independently due to the impact of other factors such as particular economies of scale, technical innovation, sophisticated human resource management together with other forms of participation. Changes in organisational culture and structure, such as the devolution of decision making down to the lower levels in the organisation, and the associated autonomy, are also factors in productivity improvement. There is an indication, that in wholly employee-owned firms in the United States, the mix of ESOPS and other forms of participation can be linked with growth and productivity improvement, as for example in Austin Industries and Wyatt Cafeterias. Studies at the University of Michigan have shown that (wholly) employee-owned companies are more profitable than non-employee-owned companies (Henry 1989).

Research in Australia and New Zealand suggests that the correlation between top executives' performance and that of the company is more observable, but the relationship is less distinct further down the hierarchy (Martin 1987). Taxation incentives have been introduced in the United Kingdom (in the 1978 and subsequent Finance Acts). Australian companies do not receive much encouragement to implement ESOPS. The American tax incentives are such that they cost the government an estimated $13,3 billion between 1977 and 1983.

• *Group financial/bonus incentive schemes* occur largely in the manufacturing sectors including unionised firms in the United Kingdom, Scandinavian countries, Northern Europe and Australia. Unions, whilst remaining wary, are more likely to negotiate a group productivity bonus scheme than an individual performance-based scheme. The main purpose of bonus incentive schemes is to enhance economic performance and motivation by financial reward.

• *Individual performance incentive payment schemes* occur in non-union or partially/weakly unionised firms at all employee levels, predominantly in the United States. Elsewhere they occur mainly at executive management levels and for sales functions.

COLLECTIVE REPRESENTATION

An important issue relates to the relationship between financial participation and the collective representation of employees. According to Poole (1988) the modern development of financial participation schemes at employee levels is connected with managerial 'styles' of industrial relations. Poole argues that the weakened position of trade unions in several Western countries has enabled managers to actively promote financial participation, rather than being constrained to accept extensions of collective bargaining or board-level union representation. In unionised firms, Poole's research indicates that financial participation schemes tend to be part of a consultative process and are less likely to be unilaterally introduced than in non-unionised firms. His findings also suggest that there is a consistent tendency for companies with financial participation schemes to be more likely than those without, to have various other types of employee participation.

Stated differently, the *evolutionary* approach to participation posits that there has been a progressive expansion of many types of participation during the twentieth century, and that financial participation is merely part of a continued expansion and advance of more enlightened and 'democratic' management–employee relations practices. What limited research there is on defining the organisational context for successful financial participation, tends to support the evolutionary position. The second approach is the *cyclical* position which envisages participation as most likely to develop in eras of economic growth or unrest, or conversely when an individual organisation is in decline. Anecdotal evidence is, however, quite strong for the thesis that ailing organisations may often resort to participative initiatives to try to surive (for example, Chrysler Motor Corporation, Eastern and Pan-American Airlines). In these organisations, share ownership was negotiated with agreements on wage cuts and interim job security guarantees. At Eastern Airlines, salaries were reduced by 18 to 22% in return for a 25% share ownership, whilst employees at Chrysler forfeited $585 million in pay increases over three years for equity of $165 million. Pan-American employees took a 15-month salary freeze and a 10% pay cut in return for $35 million in shares.

In sum, where consultation and joint decision-making is part of the 'culture' of industrial relations in a firm, it is likely that these processes would be invoked in respect of the introduction of financial participation, and that this is more likely to be the case with stronger trade unions. This raises the important issue of the compatibility of direct participation and existing collective bargaining arrangements. It seems likely that legitimated financial participation is more an outcome of harmonious and co-operative industrial relations than its cause. Preconditions for the legitimation of financial participation schemes have been referred to by Horwitz (Horwitz 1988).

TRADE UNION RESPONSES

In Western European countries such as West Germany, and in the social democracies of Scandinavia, unionism tends to

be acknowledged as a societal value and as part of the democratic process. Through their support of legislation or basic
agreements, effective joint consultation in the period between
annual collective bargaining occurs. Worker representatives
are thus empowered. An important underlying assumption
in the social democracies of Western Europe is the societal
(corporatist) institutionalisation of the basic rights of freedom
of association, the right to organise and to bargain collectively. The extent to which pluralist industrial relations principles
and policies are internalised as a pervasive societal value may
limit the expression of sophisticated forms of unitarism.
Whether or not this may be a valid assumption about financial
participation schemes, they have not made the same impact
on employees in unionised firms in Northern Europe and
Scandinavia.

This raises important questions regarding trade union
responses to perceived sophisticated but paternalistic neo-
unitarist strategies. Depending on the extent to which pluralist values and inherent conflicts of interests and rights are
institutionalised, unions tend to regard managerial practices
of direct employee involvement, as undermining the independent nature of collective representation and the power
base derived from collective mobilisation. Attendent responses include: a direct rejection and vetoing of the introduction
of financial participation initiatives; active subversion once
introduced (this has occurred in some Australian companies);
malicious compliance and subtle forms of protest; grudging,
passive acknowledgement (eg the Trade Union Congress in
the United Kingdom, which has endorsed financial participation schemes provided that they materially improve their
members' standard of living; exerting union influence beyond collective bargaining by a reconsideration of participation in other forms and levels of both direct (for example, the
EETPU in Britain) and indirect participation; and influencing

corporate strategic decision-making centrally, for example, pressure from trade unions such as the Chemical Workers Industrial Union on multi-national oil companies in South Africa for participation in decisions on social responsibility programmes, disinvestment and alternative forms of investment.

COMMON VALUES

The process of seeking the attainment of homogeneity or mutuality of organisational values may be unrealistic in the context of viewing organisations as pluralist societies. While a shift in the direction of commonality and convergence of values and objectives is desirable for optimisation of organisational performance, and reduction of attitudinal polarisation, it raises important ethical and ideological questions.

There are sensitive issues regarding the methodology of formulating and implementing specific values desired by a particular interest group. The organisational expression of particular value systems, requires perceived and institutionalised legitimacy. The imposition of a value system considered alien and possibly hostile to prevailing values poses significant problems in respect of legitimacy and the defensive protection of interests. The 'values issue' cannot be oversimplified. Prevailing and often competing value systems, multi-cultural environments, subcultures and even countercultures within organisations reflect the diversity and complexity of modern organisations. Financial participative processes therefore require careful consideration, planning and contextual sensitivity.

While there are overlapping and common interests between different groups within organisations, the pursuit of complete identification by employees with the company and its values reflects a paternalistic unitarist ideology or a dominant human relations orientation. The notion of a plurality of common and competing interests, values, diversity and sub-cultures, suggests that the organisational promotion of over-lapping values and goals, accommodation of diversity and the regulation of conflict may enrich organisational experience and effectiveness. The notion of freedom of organisational association and the attendant employee rights in respect of trade union affiliation, would be considered as an anathema to the somewhat utopian managerial goal of the complete identification of employees with the company's values and ethos. An understanding of power, and its distribution at various organisational levels, is not prominent in financial participation literature. This might imply a blindness to the role of trade unions in providing a degree of balance in the exercise of economic authority. The much-valued idea of an equal partnership between management and employees can only start to become relatively meaningful in the context of a near power balance between these interest groups at a collective group level.

MANAGERIAL INITIATIVES

Assessment of the effectiveness of employee ownership schemes tends to be defined in terms of profit improvement and growth, for example in Weirton Steel and the Vermont Asbestos Group in the United States (Rosen & Quarrey 1987). Employee share purchase schemes have often been introduced in circumstances of financial crisis and when jobs and union membership were under serious threat, for example, the United States motor industry, as previously discussed.

Participative goals may tend to be managerially defined in efficiency terms, for example, quality circles. Collective or representational participation in the governance of organisations beyond the level of individual jobs is not adequately addressed in most financial participation schemes. The increasing popularity of direct employee involvement, whilst having important advantages for management and employees can mask a deeper underlying distaste for unionism. Attendant managerial strategies seek to formulate more 'effective' techniques for humanising the work environment, gaining co-operation and competing with the union for employee support. It is in this ideological context that formal employer–union recognition and practices may not always successfully regulate conflict.

Management constantly seeks to enhance its ability to exercise choices. While the effectiveness of financial participation in seeking to optimise co-operation and organisational loyalty varies comparatively, being most successful in the United States, the question of participation as a method of control, in the unitarist sense, implies that a strong ideological orientation is required. Taking the initiative, the exercise of managerial choice may, however, occur on either an ad hoc or strategic basis, and the degree of informality in IR may facilitate incremental changes rather than sharp shifts such as union de-recognition in the United States (Marginson 1987).

Although union membership has declined in the United Kingdom and to a lesser degree in European countries, many IR structures and institutions have endured. The latter are indeed developing in certain African countries in the absence of broadly acceptable political rights structures and on occasion, either in spite of, or in conjunction with, participative practices and strategies.

Similarly stated, there is, in several Western market economies, a threat or erosion of interest-based or pluralist models by participation strategies, ideologically trying to 'win the hearts and minds' of workers. This is evidenced by a shift of focus, away from interest-based centralised relations towards flexible and decentralised management and direct forms of employee involvement. This has been a factor in the erosion of unions as public parties in most advanced Western countries and, with corporatism as a form of regulation declining, a neo-conservative and micro-level regulatory model has begun to develop (Muller-Jentsch 1987). In developing African countries, however, the opportunities for developing centralised corporatist regulation have not been adequately explored. Employers are mainly concerned with facilitating decentralised, organisation-level improvements in economic/productivity objectives by defusing employee polarisation and enhancing commitment to organisational objectives. Employee financial participation schemes have therefore assumed greater managerial prominence. This shift of managerial strategies to the decentralised-level seeks to reduce the adversarial relationship patterns of collective bargaining and enhance co-operation and trust by direct involvement of employees and union avoidance policies. In this sense, trends in developing countries show similar patterns.

A fundamental question in this regard concerns the feasibility of the coexistence of both interest-based (social regulation) and co-operation (wealth generation) models. It is perhaps unrealistic in both developed and free enterprise-orientated developing countries to expect trade unions to accept an exclusively co-operative role at organisational levels for an indefinite length of time. The potential for coexistence and de-emphasis of the ideological role of financial participation is to a large extent a function of variables affecting prevailing power realities, including economic factors, changing values, technological advancement and labour market patterns.

FINANCIAL PARTICIPATION AS A COMPONENT OF MANAGERIAL STRATEGY

Both economic and political crises have led organisations to consider greater flexibility in the management of financial, material and human resources. It could, however, be misleading to exaggerate the impact of financial participation and decentralisation as a dominant feature of current trends, with the possible exception of the United States. In Britain and Europe there do not seem to be dramatic changes to industrial relations structures and institutions, although there does seem to be an increasing shift away from collective towards individual relations. Where this shift occurs, it is often associated with managerial initiatives such as financial participation and 'sophisticated' neo-unitarist human resource management practices which may reflect preferences for challenging union legitimacy, marginalisation or even exclusion of trade unions.

The shift towards decentralisation of decision-making processes, and plant- or enterprise-level participation, does not necessarily reflect a profound change in the levels of power and influence in organisations. As organisations decentralise, they may tend to centralise certain managerial and industrial relations policy and control functions. In general, it would seem that policy development is formulated centrally, but greater freedom is being granted regarding operationalisation of policies, and values, at lower levels (Treu 1987). Similarly, broad policy parameters and monitoring controls, may tend to be centrally formulated even in operationally decentralised and diversified organisations (Purcell 1988).

CONCLUSIONS

The critique that financial participation trends reflect a determination to impose new forms of managerial control, facilitated by power imbalances created by political, technological and socio-economic change, could indeed carry some credence with pluralists too, with the latter's support for interest-based models of institutionalising conflict through social regulation. This ideological viewpoint of financial participation is perhaps an open question given the voluntary nature of direct forms of participation or employee involvement in most countries, and the belief that various types of participation can evolve pragmatically at all levels of an organisation. However, the intent, intensity and zeal of contemporary managerial initiatives seems to reflect strong ideological overtones. Yet shifting power relations, and variations in trade union density comparatively, cannot be explained solely by reference to financial participation developments and ideological motives. New forms of individual consensual participation are, however, different from participation by negotiation. Strongest resistance to participative practices which seek greater loyalty, commitment and motivation is more likely where unions are still developing and workers have strongly positive views about the instrumental and ideological benefits of union membership. A strong, powerful and established trade union movement is less likely to see these managerial approaches as potentially undermining their traditional role according to Poole (1988). Unions in these circumstances may indeed be willing to consider alternative forms of participation in a more favourable light, given the durability of existing collective bargaining institutions and structures.

The ideological view of financial participation as a 'sophisticated' form of managerial control is compelling, though its explanative value regarding shifting trends varies comparatively. There is also a re-emerging debate in Western Europe and Scandinavia on the notion of democratising capital through *collective* capital formation as a means of socialising, rather than nationalising control in organisations. Such control can pertain to several institutions such as pension schemes and employee investment funds, though it does not necessarily disturb prevailing property relations (Mathews 1989). The theory of collective capital formation sees trade unions as major participants in this largely long-term transformative process. The Histadrut trade union movement in Israel is a vivid example of social ownership and control providing employment in union-owned business. The definitional and contextual understanding of financial participation does, however, require a reconceptualisation of its assumptions about employees and structures in organisations. This requires a review of the exclusive managerial definition of the work milieu, towards a more global, eclectic perspective.

Co-operative activities seek a reduction of coercive forms of control, although they can be seen as introducing a different form of control. Greater participation of employees in decisions affecting their interests may complement the distributive processes of collective bargaining and procedural resolution of labour relations disputes. Hence, the contextual co-presence of both interest-based social regulatory structures and processes, and co-operative, participative interventions within the same organisation, can be explored. The extent to which either becomes predominant and a potential threat to the other, rather than the maintenance of a functional and strategic balance, raises difficult ideological questions and poses significant dilemmas for management and labour. Prerequisites for their coexistence might include the following:

- Internalised acceptance of the principle of freedom of association by management.
- A mutual acceptance of both the interdependence and independence of management and organised labour.
- A relative or near-balance in the distribution of power.
- The legitimation of managerial authority at shop-floor level.
- Formalisation and proceduralisation of mechanisms for regulating conflict.
- Mutual trust between the parties.

- Participation of employees and trade unions in the design and control of financial participation schemes.

There are no instant solutions to the complex task of managing in turbulent times. Innovative management approaches are, however, more likely to be facilitative of enduring change, if the propensity for adopting the latest fads were to be avoided. Soundly principled, relevant developments based on building from past experience and current research, may offer both unique opportunities and realistic goals.

REFERENCES

Basset, P *Strike Free* London, Papermac 1989.

Cohen, D 'Employee Share Ownership: When Incentive is Diluted' *Financial Times* 14 August 1987.

Crainer, S 'ESOPS: Fables no longer' *Personnel Management* January 1988 pp 27–8.

Dewe, P 'Employee Share Option Schemes: Why Workers are Attracted to them' *British Journal of Industrial Relations 20 (1) 1988*.

Editors 'Give the Workers Shares' *The Economist* 20 May 1989 pp 14–15.

Henry, J W 'ESOPS with productivity Payoffs' *Journal of Business Strategy* August 1989 pp 32–5.

Horwitz, F 'Ownership Issues' *Finance Week* 10 February 1988 pp 27–8.

Kochan, T 'Recent Developments in Workplace Representation' Paper presentedd to Second European Regional Congress on Industrial Relations, Herzlia, Israel, 13-17 December 1987.

Maller, J *ESOP's Fables* Johannesburg: Labour Economic Research Centre, 1989.

Maller, J 'Worker Participation: Response to Martin Nicol' *South African Labour Bulletin* 14(1) 1989 pp 97–103.

Marginson, P 'Managerial Strategies & Industrial Relations' Paper presented to second European Regional Congress on Industrial Relations, Herzlia, Israel, 13–17, December 1987.

Martin, B 'Benefits in Giving Employees a Share' *Rydges* July 1987 pp 36–44.

Matthews, J 'The Democratisation of Capital' *Economic and Industrial Democracy* 10, 1989 pp 165–190.

Muller-Jentsch, W 'Industrial Relations Theory and Trade union strategy' Paper presented to second European Regional Congress on Industrial Relations, Herzlia, Israel, 13–17, December 1987.

Nicol, M 'Promoting Participation in ESOPs' *South African Labour Bulletin* 13 (8) 1989 pp 94–99.

Poole, M *Industrial Relations: Origins and Patterns of National Diversity* London: Routledge & Kegan Paul, 1988.

Poole, M 'Factors Affecting the Development of Employee Fenancial participation in Contemporary Britain' *British Journal of Industrial Relations 20 (1) 1988 pp 33–5*.

Purcell, J 'The Impact of Corporate Strategy on Human Resource Management' Templeton College, Research Paper 88/11, December 1988 pp 29–40

Ramaphosa, C quoted in 'Capitalism and Socialism' *Financial Mail* 4 December 1987 p 51.

Rosen, C & Quarrey, M 'How well is Employee Ownership Working?' *Harvard Business Review* No 5, October 1987.

Salamon, M *Industrial Relations: Theory and Practice* New York: Prentice
    Hall International, 1987.
Treu, T 'Social Concertation: A Comparative Outlook' Paper presented to
    second European Regional Congress on Industrial Relations, Herzlia,
    Israel, 13–17, December 1987.

6

Loet Douwes Dekker

POTENTIALS FOR ORGANISED EMPLOYERS AND LABOUR AT A SOCIAL POLICY LEVEL

In the first section of this paper the nature of social and economic policy is discussed in relation to the potential utilisation of the industrial relations system. This potential is dependent on capital and labour using the self-governance principle of bilateralism and distinguishing, as a matter of strategy, between political and industrial citizenship as mutually reinforcing goals. The second section discusses, from an industrial relations perspective, the current South African situation. The factors shaping the IR system are considered in order to reveal the scope for bilateralism. The last section discusses some of the tough choices facing federations of unions and federations of employers' associations in negotiating compromises to their preferred socio-economic, and hence political, order.

SOCIAL POLICY

The nature of social policy

Berenstein (1982) proposes that an important stage in the evolution of a country's social policy is acceptance that the rights of man include:

- protection of what an individual has already acquired, i e *static property rights*; and

- assistance to the individual to alter his situation and help him acquire something he does not possess, i e *dynamic social rights*.

No country making conscious efforts to develop these parameters of social policy starts off with a 'clean slate'. Inequities are structured by history, industrialisation and urbanisation. If property rights are maintained for the individual, then social welfare rights constitute the best trade-off to negotiate the mix of the economic system. Hartman's study of Sweden suggests that sole emphasis on political rights as the means of overcoming inequities is insufficient. He concludes that civil, social and economic rights require conscious protection. (Hartman 1979). The emphasis in the USA on individualism and lack of support for socialism amongst the working class enabled the Reagan administration to 're-trench' social rights. This experience suggests that political rights alone cannot help the working people and the poor.

The social rights promoted in mixed economics in exchange for maintenance of property rights include:

1 *Procedures to regulate employment relations*. These are best achieved through basic national agreement on the rules of the game, e g recognition agreement procedures and codes for behaviour requirements and articulation of values.
2 *Collective bargaining* and the right to strike, lock out, picket, etc, with as little State interference as necessary.
3 *Forms of worker participation*.
4 *Social and health insurance*.
   (a) Pensions or Provident entitlements;
   (b) Workmen's Compensation; Sick Pay
   (c) Unemployment benefits (family and child insurance, medical aid or medical benefit schemes,other contingencies against loss in income);
5 *Education* and continual training and re-training.

6   *Public housing and public transport.*

7   *Environmental concerns.*

8   *Other dimensions* resulting from trade-offs reflecting that country's history and returns of industrialisation.

The differences and interdependence between social and economic policy

A further stage in a country's development is reached when the tough choices arising out of the dilemma of the interpretation by key interest groups of the difference and interdependence between social and economic policy is faced (Dembinsky 1984). Social rights have to be funded and the State cannot abdicate its role.

The difference between economic policy and social policy is highlighted when the relations between the role of the State, requirements of the producer (capital) and needs of the householders (labour) are related to: (i) the cost-price dimension, (ii) values negotiated and (iii) instruments of measurement. Unions bargain in the workplace for their members but should also support householders' needs at a national level, i e have a wider community consciousness. The consumer will not automatically agree to the goals of labour.

Economic relations involve equivalent exchanges in which money is the common denominator; i e a cost *and* price are involved in goods produced and services rendered. Certain goods and services, however, have a cost but no price; i e they provide a public (common) good for society, such as national security (defence force), justice, culture promotion, social welfare protection, etc. In these social relations the services or goods have no price because monetary value does not provide a standard and there is no rational market mechanism which could result in that good not being bought. The country has to have a legal system to ensure justice and a social security net for the poor.

Because economic relations rely on rules of equivalent exchange certain producers will not survive if they cannot in terms of price remain in the market. Householders are not subject to these constraints of being forced out of existence in their demand for social welfare. Yet in the household are some workers and members who can earn some income in the informal sector. The products bought by the consumer are produced in terms of economic relations.

The efficiency of economic policy is instrumental—the only principle guiding its operation is efficiency. Equity and social justice are the principles guiding social policy.

The efficiency of economic policy can be measured. The measurement depends on value targets of economic goals stressed by a society, e g balance of payments; rate of inflation, or growth; increase in exports or reduction in imports; privatisation; deregulation; etc. Social policy can only be measured in terms of volumes of resources it uses, e g the in-principle decision by society that no poor are denied free medical treatment implies a cost, namely the running of state hospitals. Inputs can be measured by money but a monetary yardstick cannot be used for social policy output, e g if there is a budget one cannot decide half-way during the year that the State hospital budget has been spent and no more patients will be treated.

Social policy and economic policy limit each other's scope because of minimum standards as well as rising expectations *and* availability of resources respectively. Hence the need for tolerance by those promoting those policies. Not all aspects of economic life can be deregulated but similarly not all needs can be met by the State.

In a market economy the State can only indirectly influence behaviour and choices made by actors. These include for producers: money supply; volume of money in circulation; tax burden; cost of welfare benefits; nature of contract of employment; authorised rate of depreciation; introduction or abolition of price control; tariff barriers; control over imports; risk protection for exports; etc.

The above overview highlights the difference between the capitalist who wants an economic policy promoting wealth creation and the socialist who wants a social policy for wealth distribution. The reality of development requires hard and messy negotiations between the respective interest groups as to priorities and what is affordable.

The complementarity of political citizenship and industrial citizenship: Two circuits of civil order

Offe (1985) proposes that the machinery of democratic representation polity consists of two circuits. The use of the word 'polity' and not 'politics' emphasises that the process of civil order requires, in addition to parliamentary decision-making of political parties, interest groups such as independent unions and employers' associations, who can control their own affairs to pressure government agencies. Periodic elections, political parties, manifestos and parliamentary governance constitute the central elements of the machinery of democratic polity but need to be complemented by structures which allow major organised interest groups through self-governance to bring order to their relationship, and to influence the nature and implementation of social policy and economic policy. Changes required in laws and regulations might also arise out of trade-offs made during negotiations. For example, a negotiated package might include limits on unemployment benefits (the worker) in exchange for improvements in health-care (all householders) and an accord between the federations whereby a certain percentage of increases are to be productivity-linked (the producer) but in exchange for the peace obligation and industrial action as a last resort instrument (State).

The industrial relations subsystem of a society, when activated at all levels, provides the crucial structural base through which procedural and substantive agreements are achieved by means of collective bargaining and through which trade-offs are made on the parameters of social policy by the labour market parties. This constitutes the 'second circuit' referred to by Offe (1985) which activates industrial citizenship for both workers and employers. It would appear that, if the federations of capital and labour decide voluntarily to control their own interaction and accept self-restraints in return for negotiated trade-offs, then the State will have little or no justification for interfering in their affairs or imposing constraints on them. The State's role of intervention to protect public interest is then confined to what the procedures agreed to require of it. Is such an imposition on the State desirable?

American people struggled and sacrificed to achieve political citizenship but at present only 45 % of adults vote in national presidential elections, and in other elections the percentage is lower still (Converse 1989). American citizens, because their trade union movement is poorly developed and has no national role, do not enjoy effective industrial citizenship rights.

The poor use of the political democratic process is a consequence of:

• superficial levels of public information about what occurs in or should shape a nation's public life; and

• pressures on people most of the time to attend to 'doorstep problems' of eking out a living (paying the bills); keeping a job; caring for the extended family; fighting government bureacracies and legal snares; etc.

In Western European countries the voting percentages for parliamentary elections are higher. But even if the social-democratic-orientated party wins, the workers as members of unions still influence government policy. The union federations together with employers' association federations in most of those countries influence social policy. This is necessary because once in power a political party has to adopt economic policies.

Unions and employers, because of their indirect representational structure, assist in introducing people to the democratic process and thereby overcome some of these problems. Because unions pay more attention to democratic processes, careful thought is given to how they aggregate, through various levels of the union structure, policy preferences. Experience in and scope for pressure through industrial citizenship complements the right, provided by political citizenship, to vote for party candidates. Industrial citizenship is more collective than political citizenship and hence the complementarity of both in maintaining a balance between conflicting interests of capital (primarily economic policy concerns) and labour (primarily social policy concerns).

Employers have to consciously decide if they will exercise their right to associate in employer bodies in order to make *industrial democracy* a reality. In Western Europe, bilateral agreements between the labour market parties and joint bodies such as a labour market council perform the role of a formal lobby.

Utilisation of the space and time potentials of the industrial relations system

Different organisational expressions of capital and labour manifest themselves at five different levels of the industrial relations subsystem of a society (figure 6.1). At all levels procedural agreements are needed to guide the interaction of the parties. Collective bargaining with the right to strike or lock out takes place at the lower three levels while for levels 4 and 5, trade-offs are entered in terms of preferences of the parties for socio-economic and political order. Technically, collective bargaining for substantive agreements on minimum wages and working conditions can be negotiated at levels 1, 2 and 3, but collective bargaining will concentrate on one of those levels depending on the preferences and power of capital and labour. The second or conglomerate level has recently emerged in most countries because of high concentrations of economic power. The conglomerate level prefers the informal route of lobbying directly with State agencies, and 'captains of industry' tend to find the employers' association route cumbersome and time-consuming. The preference for action at this second level can frustrate if not block the utilisation of the higher levels of the industrial relations system. In other words, the boards of conglomerates have to *consciously* decide to use industrial citizenship and make employers' associations professional organisations rendering meaningful services to affiliated companies.

The extent to which capital and labour in their organised form are active on all levels is dependent on:

1   the legitimacy which workers obtained through the struggle for unionism in that society;

2   support by capital of employers' associations (conglomerates in particular); and

3   support for socialism amongst the working class.

A number of other factors can be listed which influence the utilisation of all levels: cohesive national federations, propensity of both the federation of employers' associations and the federation of trade unions to consider trade-offs on the nature of the socio-economic order; extent of enpowerment by legislation or basic agreements entered into on level 4, of the expression of capital and labour on the first levels, e g co-determination rights for worker representatives on company boards; powers to require management to consult unions on decisions; relationship between labour market parties (the federations) and political parties; levels at which

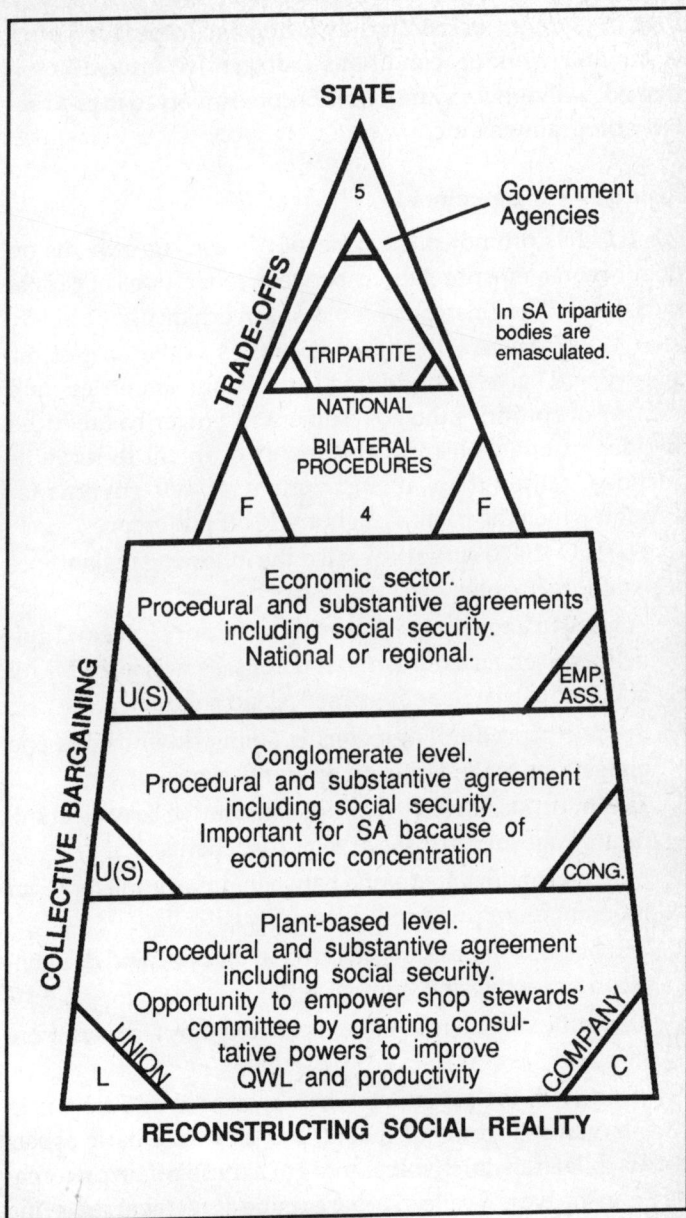

FIGURE 6.1
Levels of industrial relations subsystem in society

trials of strength (strike and lock out) for improvement in wages and working conditions (substantive issues) is expressed; willingness by unions to become involved in productivity programmes, etc.

Basic bilateral agreements

The ILO has promoted the concept of basic agreements on labour-management relations between federations of capital and labour. These instruments of self-governance had already emerged in Western European countries at the turn of the century and have been adopted in various countries. In a number of countries the government in power has reduced the idea of bilateralism to statements of intent to serve its purpose, rather than an instrument of self-governance through which the parties might trade off preferences.

The ILO (1983) survey revealed the following major types of basic agreements:

1   Framework agreements covering basic principles and guidelines to govern industrial relations, as well as codes for good industrial relations practice and conduct.
2   Specific procedural agreements laying down rights and obligations for an issue, e g apprenticeship.
3   Minimum standards to control substantive issues—minimum wage levels or social security benefits.
4   Macro-economic trade-offs between union and employer federations on preferred systems.
5   Tripartite structures which bring in the State and its agencies as an active *or* dominant actor.
6   Tripartite statements of intent promoted by a government in power.

As suggested, the processes whereby capital and labour in their organised forms of federations conclude basic agreements (bilateralism) involves more of a trade-off on preferences than the typical collective bargaining agreement reflecting a compromise on substantive matters, although the procedures guiding those latter negotiations might be, in part or whole, contained in a basic agreement. A bilateral agreement can be an implicit or explicit statement to the State and its agencies to adopt or implement its decision, e g new public holidays, or minimum disclosure of information requirements. In other words, the tripartism archetype is an ever-present reality.

The State is a ghost at the bilateral forum at which national issues are discussed. This statement can be:

1   *negative*; the self-governance route is to prevent interference from the State, specific procedural implications of the basic agreement being a self-restraint on conduct and behaviour; or

2   *positive*; the 'negotiated order' achieved through trade-offs represents a requirement on the State to act in terms of the agreement. This can range from grants in social security benefits to regulations to prevent workers being exposed to dangerous substances, etc.

It is significant that Spain's dramatic change from an industrial relations system controlled by the State to one of trade-offs between all three actors (from fascism to democracy) was achieved through the use of both tripartite accords and bilateral basic agreements (Annexure A). In 1989, after nine years of participation in tripartite deliberations, the socialist union federation withdrew from the tripartite accord but continued the system of basic agreements with employer federations. The communist union would not participate in either from the start.

SOUTH AFRICA—POTENTIALS FOR BILATERALISM

Factors shaping the Industrial Relations System

The following broad statements provide a perspective on factors which have, and still do, shape the industrial relations system in South Africa.

Capitalist–Socialist duality

Black people have experienced a society with severe restrictions on freedom: very limited scope for business activities; no freedom of association; control over where to live, work and permissible education and training; no political rights; and sparse social welfare benefits. Since 1979 this "socialism without benefits approach" has been reformed to varying degrees, but the outcome for the black and white working class is not clear.

Wassenaar (1977) analysed the South African economy from his perspective of the importance of private enterprise principles, and argued that it had progressed far down the road of nationalised production and services. Writing in 1977 he listed the following as state controlled: railways; postal services; telecommunication services; electricity (taken over from municipalities); radio service; television; *and* control over industries through the Industrial Development Corporation (IDC). The IDC central companies are: Iscor (steel); Sasol (coal and gas); Metkor through which Iscor has controlling interests and its interests in leading steel companies; Alusaf (aluminium); Foskor (phosphate); and all investment companies of the homelands. Wassenaar observed that this 'creeping socialism' is also reflected in requirements that insurance investment be held in government and other public-sector stock.

'Because of its approach to life-insurance, the socialist tendency of the RSA Treasury is far greater than that of even the Labour Party in Britain.' (Wassenaar 1977, p 54)

Within a decade the accusation by Wassenaar of the 'assault on private enterprise' appears to have been heeded. Privatisation of some parastatals has been started even if all the implications have not been understood.

The black unions regard the government's strategy of privatisation and deregulation, as well as the 1988 amendments to the Labour Relations Act, as part of a comprehensive strategy to weaken their goals of socialism. But once socialism finds expression in a society it is not easily eliminated. In the 1930 decade the State stepped in to tackle the 'poor white' problem. The recent mooted role of the IDC and Development Bank in tackling the financial and infra-structural problems of township development, *and* the role of the Regional Services Councils in redistributing (correctly so as a goal but dubious in its authoritarian execution) financial resources from white to black areas, represent socialist tendencies. While capital directs itself to bringing earlier ventures (which it felt at that time were too risky to enter) into its fold, the State by sheer pressures of needs and threat to order in demographic society, has to step in with assistance and negotiate compromises. The negotiations between the Soweto People's Delegation and Transvaal Provincial Administration regarding the Soweto rent boycott debt and need for a one-city base, represent reality-testing developments. The Government reform process has impinged on the quality of life of the white people. The post-1973 Natal strikes period witnessed increased erosion of institutions of white society: press freedom, judicial independence and subjugation of parliament by the security system. The white unions in the post-World War II period relied on the Government's social policy to provide their social needs. Hence their participation in tripartite bodies as 'their' political party was in power. They did not have to consider utilising national bilateralism to set parameters for social policy.

The white people have experience of a parliamentary democracy and the benefits of a market economy. But the costs were that the 'invisible hand' of marketing regulation was distorted through a symbiotic relationship between capitalism (requiring docile black and co-opted white labour) and the State (requiring revenue for both planned economic activities and apartheid ideology). Can basic agreements open up an additional fourth level in the industrial relations system?

Sound IR principles

The 1924 Industrial Conciliation Act and subsequent legislation established some sound industrial relations principles including an early distinction between conflicts of interest and conflicts of rights (peace obligation) and self-governance in terms of industrial councils as sectoral bipartite forums providing for negotiation of procedural and substantive agreements as well as apprenticeship committees. The 1950 decade witnessed the emergence of tripartism as the Department of Manpower promoted statutory institutions, e g Unemployment Insurance Board; Vocational Services Councils; and National Productivity Institute.

However, both the output as well as subsequent outcome of these various institutional mechanisms were racially biased and created privileges for the white working class.

The establishment of the industrial court as part of post-1979 labour law institutionalised the principle of fair labour practices and due process. The increased membership of the black union movement resulted in the growth of bilateral recognition agreement procedures and wage negotiation at the workplace, a neglected level of the IR system. The fact that industrial justice and fair employment practices were achieved in the workplaces without State influence or support strengthened the relevance of bilateral self-governance as an indirect form of democracy (industrial citizenship).

The job colour bar and exploitative colour bar

The Government's positive response to the 1979 Wiehahn Commission recommendations provided the basis for industrial unionism to counter and increasingly supplant craft unionism, which had been tainted by racism as part of the strategy of controlling entry into jobs. In 1988 the last vestiges of legal job reservation were removed from statute books but the social colour bar remains, primarily because of legislation perpetuating apartheid, i e from Group Areas; Population Registration; own affairs requirements affecting education, health, welfare, etc. The 1979 Riekert Commission recommendations were intended to address 'community' problems but within the 'separate development' framework. The Government's overall response to the recommendations was also negative. Hence the exploitative colour bar discriminating against black people remains.

The conglomerate factor

'However measured, whether by asset concentration within companies quoted on the stock exchange; by turnover controlled by all enterprises; by gross assets of economic entities; or by ownership of shares of public companies (6 companies control 84,5 % of total market capitalisation), the degree of concentration of production and centralisation of capital in the South African economy is very considerable' (Savage 1987, p 8).

This concentration of economic power in conglomerates impacts on utilisation of the industrial relations system. These conglomerates employ legal and industrial relations consultants, who can facilitate *or* repress the development of sound relations with unions. The divisions of the Barlow Rand Group (which has signed over 500 recognition agreements) pursue a policy of decentralisation in regard to collective bargaining at the lowest level of the operation or 'profit centre'. This strategy threatens the potential utilisation of the industrial relations system and implies the weakening of employers' associations. If Barlow Rand Group companies were to disaffiliate from SEIFSA, the engineering industry employers' association, this would reflect a strategic decision not to use the right to associate and, because of the prominence of the Group in the manufacturing sector, endanger industrial democracy. By definition this would lead to the Group using informal lobby pressures on State agencies to put forward and promote its preferences for social policy, including industrial relations, and economic policy. Unions believe the Group already pursues this approach. However, the boards of other conglomerates have continued to support a role for employers' associations: AAC, AECI, SAB and Western European multinationals. The possibility for the complementarity of functions and activities between third and first levels of the industrial relations system is emerging. However, the financial resourcing of employers' associations remains a crucial concern for the 1990 decade.

Industrial unionism

The emergence of unionism for black unskilled and semi-skilled workers in the 1970 decade implied, as it did in other countries, particularly the USA, a challenge to the exclusive strategy of craft (white) unions. For example, those who did not change had to disaffiliate from the International Metalworkers Federation. The consolidation of membership of COSATU and other metal unions into NUMSA resulted in it replacing the craft unions as the key bargaining agent in the annual negotiations for that industry (level 3).

Workplace and community dynamics

The intended and unintended consequences of decades of separate development based on the assumption that the urbanisation process of the black people could be not only halted but reversed (by 1978 as Verwoerd promised) created an unprecedented gap, not only in housing but community facilities from shopping complexes to schools, clinics, old-age homes, welfare services, and recreation and meeting halls. Employers increasingly face demands from unions to address community issues. One employer with 13 000 workers faced the following issues and formulated with the union responses with reasonable outcomes: community facilities—creches; halls, housing, land, social welfare services, drug and alcohol abuse, evictions, transport problems and routes of bus companies, police and defence force actions, and detentions of union members.

It is evident that some of these arise out of immediate needs but others are results of repressive features of State response to rising expectations regarding the reform era and its lack of sufficient fundamental change. The State's privatisation route as perceived could endanger provision of social rights. The question is whether employers can afford to fund and be involved in the provision of all neglected community needs. Will their involvement not bring the realisation that they cannot afford the costs as the driving demand for equity increases expectations, particularly of conglomerate social responsibility programmes?

Emasculated tripartism

The Department of Manpower operates, in terms of various labour laws, a number of statutory institutions which are tripartite in composition (Annexure B). Black union federations have refused to nominate potential candidates for these bodies; they refuse to give legitimacy to a structure set up by a government which denies them citizenship in the land of their birth. The outcome of the decisions of those bodies cannot be said to be adequate or reflect normative consensus even though they are administered by Directors from the Department who are dedicated to offering the best service. Bilateralism (level 4) could provide a structural step to facilitate the continued operation of those bodies until such time as black union federations agree to serve on them.

National security system

An analysis by Swilling and Phillips on State strategies in the 1980s suggests that a programme of dual objectives was developed to maintain security through repression while at the same time promoting welfare amongst black communities (Swilling 1988).

The repressive measures included: press restrictions; mass detentions; vigilantes and death squads; forced removals; rent boycott evictions; army occupations; and restricting extra-parliamentary organisations. These repressive measures were co-ordinated by the National Security Management System (NSMS) and were complemented with programmes attempting to 'win the hearts and minds' of the people (WHAM). The lifeblood of the NSMS was the network of more than 500 national, regional, district and local Joint Management Centres (JMCs). These organs brought together military, police and civilian officials usually under the chairmanship of the ranking military officer in the area. The trade union movement was also a victim of arbitrary action in terms of detentions of union leaders and restrictions placed on COSATU.

The 'welfare' objective was needed to meet at least some of the demands that the now crushed civic associations articulated during the first years of the 1980 decade. A combination of strategies were identified under WHAM: infrastructural upgrading; housing development; local government reform; scrapping of influx control; legitimation of state structures; and populist co-option in squatter camps.

It appears that some of the community needs which social policy should address could be attended to by these programmes.

But would a 'Wham programme' 'fit' in relation to the anger of the youth and the proposed street committee structure stated to be the preferred system of local governance? Is it hoped that with the help of conglomerate social responsibility programmes a middle class will emerge to provide a stable buffer zone?*

International impact

The disinvestment strategy gained serious attention from the international Western community from early 1970, consequent upon sports boycott successes *and* South Africa's withdrawal from the ILO as it could not accept international employment practice standards. The EEC and Sullivan codes of conduct were a response to that strategy.

Black unions from 1970 onwards received, and continue to receive, moral and financial support from the international union and national union organisations. Union resolutions attempting to reduce reliance on international financing reflects concern about the need for independence; it empowers them but can interfere both in deciding what is appropriate action and when, and creates a wrong sense of organisational strength to sustain programmes and actions.

The international campaign to isolate South Africa forced employers to redefine SACCOLA's role from an international voice to a body of internal relevance. The role of the national body of employer interests was forced onto it by the power tactic of the three-day stayaway in 1988 in response to amendments to the Labour Relations Act. Will SACCOLA become a

---

* The courageous and fundamental changes introduced by President FW de Klerk include placing the NSMS under the Cabinet. It is hoped these developments will have as a consequence the elimination of such state corporatist activities.

well-funded professional body to seriously represent employer influence on organisations where social policy is set?

The above list of factors shaping the industrial relations system reflects the reality of different tendencies at work during the transition period which South Africa is undergoing. Lawyers had warned that proposals for the 1988 amendments to the Labour Relations Act would shift the balance of power between capital and labour in capital's favour. The three-day June 1988 stayaway against the proposed legislation brought the black union federations and the federation of employers' associations to the table. Although the legislation was enacted, reinforcing the authoritarian tendency, the joint letter sent by the federations of unions and employers created awareness that the fourth level of the industrial relations system presented an opportunity to influence the State.

In the following section the scope for bilateralism strategy by unions and employers to promote the democratic tendency is discussed.

BILATERALISM TO PROMOTE DEMOCRATIC TENDENCIES

As noted above, economic and social policy are interdependent. But how is that interdependence to be guided?

As the 1980 decade draws to a close there is evidence that the South African State is transforming fundamental aspects of its economic policy. Privatisation and deregulation are taking place in order to promote economic development. Other economic policy requirements arising out of the four summit conferences held between business representatives and the Government during the 1980s are being considered. There is no guarantee that social policy implications are being taken into account nor that democracy will be reinforced.

Democracy is not a necessary condition for economic development.

Hence the importance of achieving expression of industrial citizenship through cohesive federations of unions and employers' associations and promoting bilateralism as a mechanism for establishing the parameters of social policy. South Africa has a tradition of bilateralism. Industrial councils have operated in important manufacturing sectors and the black unions promoted the procedures of the recognition agreement. However, the magnitude of the problem of the backlog of social services and community infrastructures requires significant bilateral trade-offs at a national level. The following four action areas illustrate what could be covered in such negotiations:

Basic agreement to safeguard self-governance.

If employers and trade union leaders are serious about industrial democracy, the possibility for SACCOLA and COSATU and NACTU entering a basic national agreement could be considered. The following broad categories could be included:

1 endorsement of the three freedoms of association rights and concomitant civil liberties;

2 minimum basic pro-forma procedural agreements containing the best (in terms of fairness, due process and empowerment of unions) from the experimental decade of negotiating and operating recognition agreements;

3 sectoral agreement on the complementary nature of third level collective bargaining for minimum wages and working conditions, and plant-level negotiation including *productivity* agreements; and

4 procedures whereby both organised capital and organised labour can be represented on statutory institutions of the Department of Manpower and others such as the National

Housing Trust and Economic Advisory Council, *and* the issues a Government in power has to refer to such bodies.

Current industrial relations issues

The above basic procedural agreements would constitute a grand trade-off to set basic rules of the game. At any time specific issues of national importance could arise which are also best negotiated on a trade-off basis. The following current industrial relations issues serve as examples:

1   Industrial action in the form of union-endorsed strikes, stoppages by workers and lock-outs by employers have received haphazard attention in terms of procedural requirements. Both sides want to retain the power of uncertainty, but each party suspects the other of using it either unfairly or for 'hidden agenda' purposes. The legislative provisions were previously followed but with the 1988 amendments to the Labour Relations Act (LRA), the need for renegotiating the dispute procedures of procedural agreements has arisen.

2   The right of workers to regard overtime as a voluntary decision, and the determination of employers, for purposes of flexibility, to regard it as an employment condition, has been fought at supreme court level with conflicting judgments being passed. This problem suggests how important it is to seek industrial relations solutions and not legal ones to issues which affect the quality of life of people.

3   The mediation and arbitration services of IMSSA have doubled in usage each year since 1985. The issue which arises is who should direct the affairs of that organisation Should the major users through their federations serve on the Board of Trustees or the professionals who supply the service?

4   Workplace intimidation amongst workers and by managers on workers has emerged as an important concern. The multi-racial nature of the workforce in key industries (mining, motor assembly, steel and engineering) makes discussion imperative on the 'why' and the 'how' of avoiding or 'eliminating' circumstances promoting it. Violence has been a feature and will remain a characteristic of the workplace, but it can be contained. The attempt by the National Union of Mineworkers and the Anglo-American Corporation to negotiate a code of conduct represents a challenging approach to this issue to built-in self-restraint in behaviour.

5   The developmental thrusts of reconstructing industrial relations have moved from the workplace to other levels; union resources are increasingly focussed on achieving entry to sectoral level. The shop steward system in a number of organised companies is endangered through lack of clear definition and resourcing of the role, in particular for the 'period in between' collective bargaining. The vulnerability of the shop steward can be protected and his role performance enhanced through negotiated empowerment, space, time off, facilities, and special protection against dismissals and disciplinary actions, etc. This threat to shop stewards is not necessarily a consequence of ill-intent by management. Thus, unless OD techniques and intervention programmes are 'IR-driven' they can easily result in alienation of shop stewards from membership (Douwes Dekker 1990) (Annexure C). Shop stewards' rights require a formal procedural endorsement and a basic national agreement is the best way of achieving this.

Quality of Life

A very serious backlog in development of community infrastructure for black townships and the consequences of racially discriminatory State expenditure on education, pensions, health, and welfare are being identified. Unions, in addition to the living-wage demand, have placed on the union-management agenda items reflecting the following categories:

- housing and land needs;
- old age provisions;
- social welfare needs; and
- educational needs.

The use of provident funds to provide financial assistance to union members for their housing needs, represents an experimental approach. Union long-term goals require the State to be more responsible for low-income housing but the 'provident fund route'—besides providing an incentive for union membership—will uncover the other obstacles to housing provision: land availability; township declaration hold ups; site-and-service schemes potential; and town-planning options.

As noted, social policy requires that the disadvantaged are assisted, a dynamic component to compensate for retention of the principle of property rights. The revised ANC guidelines support property rights but land and excessive accumulated wealth are issues. The specifics of the dynamic assistance can best be identified if involvement in current blockages is unravelled. What are appropriate institutional mechanisms to reveal the 'how' of eliminating discriminatory practices in housing and community facilities and enhancing the quality of life of the working people?

Focused debate

The following institutional mechanisms are suggested as specific examples of bilateral instruments and focus the debate of this paper so that the persons involved from COSATU, NACTU and SACCOLA and the wider community can respond. Institutional mechanisms are required to provide a forum for trade-offs and achieve a balance between economic and social policy needs.

Labour Market Council (Annexure D)

The establishment of a Labour Market Council (LMC) provides an institutional mechanism to tackle the historical reality of a dual economy in South Africa. This duality is being strengthened by the current promotion of an informal sector and deregulation to encourage small businesses. In mixed economies co-ordination is achieved between (public) labour market policy and (private) collective bargaining. But this co-ordination expresses itself in various degrees of effectiveness depending on institutional arrangements for:

(a) active labour market policy to ensure effective utilisation and training of labour in terms of strategies formulated through a Labour Market Council; and

(b) passive labour market policy to establish parameters of social security funds and benefits.

These considerations about joint control over the labour market illustrate the major argument of this paper and would imply that:

(a) The parties can—in terms of their interdependence while respecting their independence—sufficiently articulate the scope of their respective interests to direct and control market forces affecting manpower resources. This gives the parties the capacity to establish a Labour Market Council (LMC) for an economic sector or the national economy (bilateralism). That LMC provides an opportunity to debate most of the Department of Manpower statutory institutions: training, vocational services, unemployment, occupational health and safety, workers' compensation, etc (Annexure B).

(b) The negotiations by the parties on the LMC in terms of their respective interests as reflected in the variables of Annexure D, can transform the present ad hoc arrangements through plant-based negotiations and enhance restructuring of social reality at sectoral and national level through trade-offs. The nature of agreement achieved would reflect the consensus of negotiated order as manpower and productivity as well as flexibility needs of employers are accommodated, as are the needs of workers for job security and protection of employment standards.

(c) The parameters of consensus would be negotiated on the LMC and require *inter alia*: information, resources, cash grants and administrative support from the Directorate of Training. The employers' associations' representatives on the tripartite National Training Board (NTB) would be required to transmit the consensus of the parties achieved at LMC level and thereby affect the decision-making process of the NTB. The LMC could also investigate the scope for assisting State agencies to utilise the annual allocation (over R250 million) for 'public works' activities to provide temporary work and training opportunities for the unemployed.

Investigation into principles and operation of the Economic Advisory Council

The relationship and differences between economic policy and social policy are easier to suggest on paper than to unravel from ongoing programmes and historical realities. However, to date economic development in South Africa has been the focus of State allocation of major financial assistance, with, of course, the indirect consequence of employment creation at the same time and subsequent 'spin-offs' as other industries which might have emerged. The fact that it is not called a social *and* economic council reflects this reality. What concerns and trends are emerging in the transition period?

1   The Government has embarked on a programme to privatise parastatals (divest its holdings).

2   Black unions have stated their preference for a planned economy.

3   White unions are, according to recent editorial comment, concerned about privatisation plans in regard to health care.

4   Business has articulated its preference for 'unfettered' free enterprise.

How are these trends to be understood and the magnitude of the forces identified? Does the 'transition period' not offer an opportunity for gaining insight into what is occuring? The invitation for the Chairman of SACCOLA to serve on the President's Economic Advisory Council presents an opportunity for that federation and union federations to set up an ad hoc body to examine what that institution concerns itself with. This ad hoc body, assisted by experts, could for a two-year or longer period investigate the reports and recommendations of that Council and debate the scope for transforming it into a Social *and* Economic Council.

Regionalised community negotiations

The rent boycott by township residents became and remains a significant power tactic. It:

1   demonstrated the anger of the residents over the denial of their political rights, and their refusal to accept arbitrary actions, e g increases set by local councils;

2   brought awareness that the people be allowed to exercise the right to protest against authorities;

3   revealed the complexities and inadequacies of township finances;

4   identified how CBDs of major cities attract revenue for white residential areas;

5   brought home to management the township conditions to which workers are exposed;

6   forced employers to take a stand against the government's attempts to make them 'collectors of arrear rental';

7   revealed the significant role of civic associations in mobilising action;

8   demonstrated the scope for employers from different sectors to form associations for the purpose of tackling jointly community problems in townships which supply their labour;

9   revealed the important role provincial authorities play in black communities' affairs.

The important dynamic which has emerged is the propensity of the parties in certain situations to seek a negotiated solution. Equally important, when potential negotiations are considered, it brings together the local actors involved in that situation, i e promotes the decentralised focus essential for democracy. This is important, as unions have to demonstrate visibly to their members what they can do for them, how they represent them, and what achievements are likely.

Significant ad hoc negotiations have brought employers (individually and collectively), unions and civic associations together in times of crisis and in consequence of the power tactic of boycotts. Those which received publicity include: Oukasie—forced removals; Empangeni—bus fare increases; various townships (e g Mamelodi, Tembisa and Soweto)—rent boycotts; Alberton Employers' Association—plight of squatters. Some of these interventions and negotiations did achieve a compromise resolution of the issues, but in others, detention of leaders frustrated the potential of compromise settlement. The present transitional nature of South Africa has arisen because of the stated illegitimacy of the white Government. Hostilities arise because there is no accepted superordinate power.

If the federations of capital and labour negotiated, at national level, an in-principle statement with guidance on use of resources and relevant expertise which is available, this would facilitate the emergence of a superordinate reference group or power. Unions make use of service groups such as Planact (town-planning) and LERC (housing and utilisation of provident funds), whilst the Urban Foundation is available to employers as well as those service groups. Such a statement on the importance of regionalised negotiations would also be accompanied by guidance on resource agencies available, legislative provisions and an indication of process aspects distilled from the learning experience gained in other instances to promote decentralised action programmes. The rhetoric of national statements could be focused and directed through localised action programmes.

The in-principle endorsement of regional/local negotiations would also assist capital in the process it must undertake to distance itself from the State and its agencies. That is, by supporting unions and civic associations and indicating the scope and opportunity for negotiations, and of community mediation for deadlocks, it would define what the key parties regard as a rational approach to the settlement of the crisis. The public standing of these negotiations with not only the local authority and in many cases the Defence Force, but also with the Provincial Authorities, will provide forums which can also examine and influence, on an ad hoc basis, the performance of Regional Services Councils in their task of reallocating financial resources.

The emergence of institutional mechanisms to deal with local/regional community needs would acknowledge, in the current South African context, that the IR system is firmly embedded in community dynamics *and* the workplace.

The Rules of the Game

The concept of a second-generation recognition agreement emerged in response to the unacceptable restrictions on industrial action of the 1988 amendments. Thompson (1988) expressed concern that second-generation agreements should reflect a consistent and deep-seated commitment to democratic values. (Box 6.1).

- *a right to strike* without threat of dismissal of strikers by the employer, on condition that the action occurs over an industrial issue, is authorised by the union and supported by the members;
- *avoidance of technicalities*: e g no requirement that dispute procedures of the Act be adhered to; no attempt by an employer to rely on the technical offences created by the Labour Relations Act;
- *a picket procedure* which acknowledges that it is a civil right of persuasion conducted in terms of an agreed set of rules to prevent possible intimidation and violence;
- *the right to conduct wage campaigns* for collective bargaining;
- *introduction of joint decision-making* in a number of other areas, e g pension and housing schemes.

BOX 6.1
Thompson's proposals for second-generation agreements

The idea of second-generation procedures to revitalise the relationship between a union and a company or its employers' association, should be seen as an opportunity to establish self-restraints and not only as a means to avoid the constraints of the Labour Relations Act. The idea of self-restraint on conduct and behaviour is implied in both parties demanding from each other the three rights of freedom of association, namely the rights to organise, bargain collectively and use industrial action. In other words, the manner in which an employer exercises rights should interfere as little as possible with the exercise of the rights by the union, *and* vice versa.

The first recognition agreements transformed the workplace by introducing: due process and job security in regard to dismissal and discipline; collective bargaining to reduce racial discrimination and improve the ratio between unskilled and skilled wages; acceptance of the right to industrial action; retrenchment criteria; private third party intervention; empowerment of shop stewards as representatives of workers. A significant degree of democratic process emerged in quite sudden contradiction to previous practices.

However, important deficiencies crept into those 'first-generation' procedures:

1 Collective bargaining procedures lacked detail particulary compared with grievance and disciplinary procedures. The following aspects were seldom mentioned: collective bargaining units; disclosure of information; industrial action only after deadlock declared; what happens to wage rates when a current agreement expires; and so on.

2 The nature of third party interventions in the event of deadlocks arising from different phenomena was not considered. The possible use of mediation as the best means of settling conflicts of interest (wages, working conditions, etc) was accepted only from 1984 onwards when those services became available.

3 A retrenchment procedure was introduced only when companies wanted to reduce the labour force and experienced work stoppages and demands for fair selection methods and compensation.

4 The rules regarding use of industrial action (strike or lock-out) were and remain, generally speaking, unstated. Each side has some idea how to use that essential right in

the collective bargaining process but the threat of criminal action led to a reliance on provisions in the legislation.

5   Technology, safety, occupational health and job evaluation, as well as related aspects of human resource employment practices, were not seen as critical issues for negotiation between the parties.

6   A procedure to negotiate an end to work stoppages was considered by some parties. Most recognition procedures contain one general dispute procedure which does not distinguish between a strike constitutionally endorsed by the union through balloting and a work stoppage resorted to by workers in response to real or perceived industrial injustices.

7   Shop stewards' rights and obligations to facilitate recognition of their status as the physical expression of the union in the workplace, and their role responsibilities as defined in procedures, were granted hesitantly by some employers. If both sides accept the necessity for annual (intermittent) collective bargaining for improvements in wages and working conditions, then the nature and purpose of their relationship and interaction between those annual events for the life-term of the agreement has to be considered, i e full-time shop steward, empowerment of decision-making through consultation, access to information, time off, etc.

8   The idea of a peace obligation was implied in general sentiments of the 'intent clause', but the limits and scope of that requirement in relation to the right to embark on industrial action (strike or lock-out) were not spelled out. It is assumed to be sufficient that it is stated as a general requirement in the procedural agreement and not also as a specific clause negotiated each year in the substantive agreement.

Second-generation procedures cannot rectify all these deficiencies. The need to ensure development of the industrial relationship in the context of South Africa's political crisis will leave certain areas vague. However, to the extent that the rules of the game can be institutionalised and necessary empowerment built in, uncertainty can be eliminated from procedural requirements which guide actual negotiations between unions and employers at various levels of the system.

CONCLUSION

The tough choices

The influence and power of bilateral negotiations require cost/benefit analysis. Implied or explicitly stated in the output of collective bargaining is the peace obligation for the life-term (duration) of the agreement. Implied in trade-offs on social/economic preferences at sectoral and national level is self-restraint in the exercise of power tactics by the parties. Constituents of the parties face tough choices in entering higher levels of the IR system. What price the ability to influence decisions and shape parameters of social policy besides responsibility for decisions arrived at? The nature of consensus provides some clues as reflected in the following three types:

1 ·A policy is deliberately formulated to reflect conventional wisdom, i e differences of opinion are avoided by trying to reflect in that policy aspects of the middle-ground position and perceived needs. By adopting this unilateral approach, the dominant party hopes to obtain the tacit support of the other (subordinate) party.

2 A policy is arrived at through manipulation of the decision-making process. In this approach the dominant party deliberately evades basic conflicts by excluding certain

issues and/or parties from the argument and negotiations.

3   A policy is arrived at through negotiated agreements between independent interest groups entering that process in near power balance, in terms of tacit or agreed procedures. Commitment to carrying out decisions is a responsibility and, because the policy will probably be administered by agencies, the issue of monitoring must also be raised.

Black leaders have clearly rejected the first two forms of 'consensus'. The third form is not, for national-level issues, easily attained. In certain situations boycotts and the power tactics are easier to sustain or reintroduce if it is believed that the process of political reform is too slow. Can the parties accept that 'working together' is not a sign of weakness nor handing over of power?

The packaging of trade-offs shaped by the negotiating process between the trade union and employers' association at sectoral level and between their federations at the national level depends on the issues deemed important at a particular time. In overall terms, the mixed economy in a social-democratic-type of society, with its combination of social and property rights, forms the broad framework. The trade-offs emerge because of:

1   the union (labour) emphasis on the broad definitions of a living wage *and* removal of discrimination arising out of continuation of the social colour bar in the workplace, *and* continued apartheid laws of 'own' and 'general' affairs in the wider society;

2   the employer (capital) emphasis on private enterprise and its need for certainty in planning (peace obligation for the life-term of the agreement); flexibility in handling change; utilisation of labour with removal of violence and self-re-

straint on the use of industrial action, while demanding state support for privatisation and deregulation.

Do unions and employers want industrial democracy?

Trade unionism is a movement which, in terms of free and effective operation, functions best in a mixed economy and democratically orientated society. The inherent appeal of socialism and worker control articulated most forcibly during the early phase of the organisational development of unionism brings tough choices to the leadership of the union movement. The fundamental question is: 'What incentives keep workers as union members?' The SA Communist Party*, which should be allowed to operate openly in society, also finds support amongst the working class. However, it does not see a role for unionism in its vision of a State. The rights of independent union expression through collective bargaining and industrial action are not part of the society it wants to create. The extent of the influence of the SA Communist Party on and in South African unions is not known. This is one of the challenges and realities of a transition period with restrictions on political party activity, particularly amongst the black people. Will the black demand for socialism accept the drastic reform of that ideology which communist countries are experiencing at present? Are employers in South Africa interpreting those developments wisely? Industrialist Chris Saunders, on receiving the *Sunday Star's* 1989 Emeritus Citation Award, said: 'I have reason to believe the tide is beginning to turn against collectivism, socialism, statism and apartheid, but this turn is locked in the sour fruits of socialistic and apartheid experiences' (*Sunday Star* 3.8.1989). What are the hoped-for implications of world-wide trends anticipated

* Since unbanned.

by the 'captains of industry' whose economic power is as concentrated as that of the National Party? Is the implied assumption that that 'tide' will also sweep aside expectations of the majority of blacks, or that the leaders will accept that they must rethink their ideology, *and* that the SA Communist Party will do so? If South Africa is to 'short-circuit' certain historical developments in communist countries, then captains of industry should be prepared to accept industrial democracy and, for employers this implies active participation in and representation on highly professional employers' associations (and not just trade associations). But are the captains of industry, for instance, prepared to say to Barlow Rand Group: 'Your policy of decentralised wage bargaining and withdrawal from employers' associations is in fact destroying the scope for trade-offs and for establishing the parameters of social policy'?

Transition dilemmas

In the transition period and initially for some time under a black government, market forces will continue to be the guiding mechanism dictating the nature of economic activity, even though forms of planned State economic intervention (a historic reality of South Africa) will assist the plight of the disadvantaged. This possibility will be enhanced if, in the transition period, understanding of social policy has emerged, its parameters identified and the interdependence between it and economic policy understood.

This paper has been premised on the necessity, both in the transition period and after, for unions and employers' associations to be independent of State control over their conduct and behaviour. To the extent that limitations on actions (conduct and behaviour) are necessary, these should be negotiated as self-restraints, not imposed constraints. The instrument of bilateralism has been deemed the best means of achieving those goals as the outcome of the negotiations carries both a union and employer input, but within the context of socio-economic trade-offs.

The issues facing both parties, and unions in particular because they have limited social power, are extremely difficult and the choices hard to make. Risks are involved, not only for labour because of the dangers of co-optation into the current Government's definition of how reform is to be processed, but because of the powerful hold of an 'unfettered capitalism' ideology on business leaders committed to a free market which sees no role for social policy direction in a society. Black unionism re-emerged in the 1970s determined to make good the decades of suppression by both capitalism and a paternalistic/authoritarian State protecting white privilege. The black unions have shown a healthy caution and ability to resist co-optation. Some examples include: their refusal to accept works and liaison committees; in the 1970s their rejection of the State-imposed pension preservation Bill; their refusal to accept the commuter (migrant) distinction regarding union membership; their refusal to accept imposed codes of conduct, in particular the Sullivan Code which initially made no mention of unionism; their refusal to use the Industrial Court without clarity on its scope and impartiality; their refusal to accept the 1988 amendment to the Labour Relàtions Act; their determination to ensure independence through negotiated recognition agreements; their stand on the right to receive funding from overseas; the stature to make employers aware that they should not become rental arrears collectors; and the ability to redefine aspects of the concept of public interest.

The union movement states it is determined to honour democratic processes and to fight present Government tendencies towards totalitarianism. This dimension is supported by leading employers' associations and the boards of those companies committed to freedom of association rights. The democratisation force is powerful but still threatened by the reality of suppression.

Influence on the State and its agencies might take three forms:

1   the intention stage, where interest groups make an issue of certain wishes regarding national policy, but go no further;

2   the consultative stage, where the State invites the interest groups to give their opinion and advice but takes the final decision; and

3   the issue resolution stage, where the interest groups can place before the State their requirements.

The use of bilateralism now with built-in co-responsibility at all levels of the industrial relations system will provide a basis to ensure this third form is relevant in the future.

The concept of industrial citizenship is central to this paper's emphasis on bilateralism as a basis for establishing an equitable social policy. The acceptance of industrial citizenship implies management must support employers' associations *and* unions' members must take care not to allow their mobilisation ability to be used solely for political goals—a difficult task while certain working class leaders with political aspirations cannot operate openly and hence retain their posts.

The experience of industrial democratic process will complement those which political citizenship provides, but ensure that unions and employers have a voice in national affairs other than their respective support for a political party. The institutional mechanism of bilateralism underpins industrial citizenship (i e prevents its 'retrenchment' as in the USA and to a certain extent the UK) and reinforces incentives for union membership whereby its maintenance is assured for union leaders. The system of self-governance resulting from industrial citizenship

1   provides structures for national influence irrespective of which government is in power;

2   ensures that trade unions do not become caught in 'workers' egotism' which is implied in the limitation of operating only on the first two levels of the industrial relations system (as Barlow Rand proposes);

3   forces capital to transform the self-righteous parternalism of social responsibility programmes (established as a front by conglomerates) into joint activities with independent unions;

4   requires assessment of the propensity for organised capital and labour to consider the implications involved in social policy-making and responsibility for its implementation (Annexure E);

5   establishes societal gains for the unemployed and the disadvantaged. Unions, by considering the plight of these people in the trade-offs implied in national negotiations, can avoid being labelled, or becoming, a labour aristocracy; i e by promoting 'welfare property rights' for those whose life chances are blocked by lack of property rights and a job in the formal sector. It is possible for both achieved and ascribed status to be promoted in a post-apartheid society.

In terms of long-term strategy, the pursuit of bilateralism, in the transition period of South Africa 'in-becoming', provides the basis for the winning of public status by the powerful labour market parties through their federations (Annexure F). Public status has to be worked on now by these parties on their own because, if granted by the new government in power, it can equally easily be manipulated, as in South America, to deny the freedoms now being fought for at considerable cost in terms of economic policy requirements.

Considerable responsibility rests with leadership in both the union movement and 'big business'. They, after all, set the tone in defining the nature of the tough choices to be made. As the 1980 decade draws to a close there is evidence of a move from the ethics of conviction to the ethics of responsibility. The decision-making process can be shaped by the components of those dimensions if both sides deliberately appoint facilitators who can remind them in their caucus sessions of these components.

It is possible for the 1990 decade to be shaped by reparation and reciprocity so as to avoid retribution and retaliation (Annexure G).

ANNEXURE A
SPAIN: FROM STATE TO SOCIETAL CORPORATISM

The following explanation of the fundamental change achieved in Spain's industrial relations system provides insight into the strategies adapted by the three key actors in promoting their respective socio-economic preferences. This descriptive analysis is neither comprehensive nor implies that South Africa will follow Spain's pattern of development. But if the unions and employers in South Africa are desirous of achieving societal corporation then similar tough choices have to be faced.

1   During Spain's period of fascism freedom of association rights were suppressed and class differences were denied. Even employers could not establish their independent organisations. The unions were forced to go into exile.

   The system of representatives was hierarchically controlled by the State for the goals of unity, order and nationalism. The structure brought together at local (15 000), provincial (1 400) and national (28) levels syndical groupings which consisted of social (worker) and economic (employer) components. The administration of these syndical groups was in the hands of state agencies.

2   But Spain realised it should become part of the Western world ànd benefit from membership of the International Monetary Fund. Hence the period 1958–1975 was characterised by liberalisation of the economy and a willingness to allow collective bargaining. However, the procedures were cumbersome and any agreement had to be ratified by the State.

   The process of controlled change was accelerated by pressure through the international union movement.

3   Although the ILO recommendations to change legislation were not incorporated in 1971 statutory amendments they became a reference point for the demands from the exiled

socialist union (UGT) and the underground communist union (CCOO). The latter had developed a membership base by infiltrating the works council system the State had introduced. The period 1975–1979 was one of transition, with internal awareness that Spain wanted to return to democracy. In 1976 UGT held a conference and gained worker support.

The unions became aware that rivalry would emerge and it was agreed that election to works council posts would provide them with an opportunity to test their support among workers. Spain ratified the ILO conventions on freedom of association (No 87 and No 98) in 1977. In the first free elections CCOO gained 34,5 % and UGT 21,7 % of the votes.

The move from economic liberalisation to democracy was accompanied by attempts to establish pay and employment policy norms. The government took the initiative but in the 1980s the federations themselves entered into bilateral agreements or contracts besides trilateral pacts with the State.

The following brief overview of these various social contracts and central agreements provide perspectives on achievements and subsequent problems.

1977–1979

In 1977 the political parties signed a social contract with the employers' association and the socialist union. The communist union refused to be a party to it.

The main purpose of the social contract was to tackle the high inflation of 30 %. A *voluntary* wage norm of 20 % as the target for negotiations was agreed to in exchange for tighter monetary policy to restrict the growth in the money supply. The result was positive. Inflation dropped to 19,8 %.

Where unions were representative in a company collective bargaining took place within the agreed norm of pay limits. This became the national strategy for the next decade. The parties could negotiate a wage increase above the lower limit. It was hoped it would be linked to improvement in productivity.

For the year 1978/79 further attempts toward a social contract were made. The parties refused to participate. The government set a wage norm of between 11 % and 14 %. Actual wages increased by 14 %. Inflation dropped to 15,5 %.

1980

In 1980 the two employers' association federations—one for small employers—and the socialist union signed a bilateral agreement with the following features:
1   voluntary (to avoid the threat of a statutory incomes policy) wage increases between of 13 % and 16 % (the subsequent negotiated average was 15,6 %);
2   wage re-opener clause;
3   guidelines for reducing working time and absenteeism;
4   peace obligation and productivity clauses;
5   rationalisation of collective bargaining—removal of State interference.

The communist union refused to sign because the scope for collective bargaining was seen as limited and favouring capitalism, and furthermore job creation measures were excluded. Commentators characterised this decision as a strategic mistake for CCOO and of advantage to UGT in terms of priorities and willingness to compromise by its members.

1982

In 1982 the Government, employers association and *both* union federations entered into a national employment contract whereby the State allocated finances to employment creation programmes.

Other trade-offs agreed to were:
• public sector wage increases of between 8 % and 9 %;
• private sector wage increases of between 9 % and 11 %;

- increase in social welfare and security provisions;
- check off for union dues.

1984

The tripartite *and* bilateral agreements entered into were innovative and more comprehensive than the previous social contracts. The emphasis was on both economic and social reforms.

The tripartite agreement signed by the Government, two employers' associations federations and the socialist union federation provided for:

1 tax incentive for investments;
2 fixed allowances for low-income earners;
3 plus/minus 160 000 jobs for the unemployed to be created in the public sector;
4 reduction in the proportion of social security contributions paid by employers;
5 labour reform commission to be set up;
6 health and safety at work to be attended to;
7 vocational training to be attended to;
8 structures for union participation in nationalised industry to be established;
9 progress or monitory commissions to be established.

The bilateral agreement signed by the employers' associations federations and the socialist union federation provided for:

1 wage increases to be negotiated between 5,5 % and 7,5 % (inflation expected to be 6 %). A joint committee to be established to monitor implementation;
2 joint effort to improve productivity: (i) measurement criteria and obstacles to be removed; (ii) profits to be used to create jobs through investment; (iii) wages to be productivity-linked provided unions were granted information; (iv) wage guarantees during changing work patterns, etc;
3 levels of absenteeism to be reduced;

4   overtime to be replaced by recruitment;
5   multiple employment (one worker with two jobs) to be reduced;
6   rationalisation to achieve sector-level bargaining to be introduced;
7   voluntary mediation and arbitration services to be set up;
8   joint national committee to monitor implementations to be established.

The communist union federation refused to sign because:
1   not enough funds were set aside for job creation;
2   pay reviews should be on a six-monthly basis, not annual;
3   amendments to dismissal and redundancy procedure were necessary.

However, that federation demanded representation on various committees set up under the above two agreements. This demand was refused.

As mentioned, the union federations used elections of their members to works council positions as an indication of support. The following pattern emerged (expressed in percentages):

	1978	1980	1982	1986
Communist unions	34,5	30,9	33,4	34,5
Socialist unions	21,7	29,3	36,7	40,8
Other federations	43,8	37,8	29,9	24,7

NOTE: A total of 300 000 delegates were elected by 5,7 million workers in 1986.

1987

The following report highlights how the parties prepared for the 1987 central agreement:

'The main Spanish employers' organisation, and the two principal union confederations have opened separate discussions in an attempt to negotiate a new central agreement for 1987.

The Government has already indicated that it will not intervene although it will give legal backing to any agreements reached at the bargaining table provided that a request to do so is submitted by employers and unions. It also considers that pay should not rise above 5 %, the percentage figure corresponding to its forecast rate of inflation for 1987.

UGT and CCOO both believe that pay should rise above this rate, and CCOO insists that the Government should take an active part in central negotiations. (EIRR, 158, 1987)

The socialist union believed that there should be on-going negotiations with the Government before policy decision on social protection, tax, etc were taken.

The communist union wanted to bring pensions into line with a minimum wage and greater employment security. It wanted bilateral negotiation with employers on purchasing power, labour units, reduction of systematic overtime, productivity pay and profit sharing.(EIRR, 156, 1987)

CEOE circulated a memo to its sector-level organisations recommending rises of about 5 % from January and has also had interviews with the Ministers responsible for the economy and for labour for them to explain their position. The themes of most concern to employers labour market flexibility, reductions in social security contributions and pending tax reforms. Meanwhile, the unions began to present joint claims, as, for example, in the case of the Barcelona province metalworking agreement one of the largest sector-level agreements   for which they demand a 7 % pay rise.

The Ministry of Labour proposed an increase of 5 % in the Spanish national minimum wage. CCOO registered a firm objection to the proposal insisting instead on a 10 % increase and a six-monthly revision of the rate in view of what it saw as systematic underestimates of the projected rate of inflation' (EIRR, 156, 1987).

It is of interest that a project-type pressure group called the Employers' Circle published a document which called for decentralised collective bargaining, adding that this would aid the competitiveness of Spanish industry following entry into the EEC. The employers believed that central agreements with wage norms had been appropriate but should be replaced with flexible arrangements. Each sector or company should negotiate pay rises in line with their own particular situation. Although this system could increase the number of labour disputes, the group felt that that risk had to be taken.

However the 1987 attempts to establish a new central pay agreement collapsed. The key reason for the failure of the negotiations was disagreement over the level of pay rises. The employers were unwilling to concede above 5 % while the socialist union refused to go below 7 % and the communist union below 8 %. Wage negotiation at work-place and regional or industry level were concluded and the average pay increase was 7,6 %.

1988

The strains emerging from trade-offs required by bilateral and tripartite negotiation caused a breakdown in the 1987 attempts to establish a central pay agreement. In 1988 the relationship between the socialist union and the socialist party in power became the focus of attention. No central agreement was concluded. In fact the parties did not come together.

The proposals put forward included the following positions:

1   The Ministry of Labour stated that negotiations on one of the most fundamental issues—the extension of the cover of unemployment benefit—would not be resumed. The Government would approve the reforms contained in its last offer to UGT and CCOO, the two main union confederations. The reforms, which had been rejected by both confederations, would extend unemployment benefit to cover around 200 000 long-term unemployed aged above 45 who had exhausted all other forms of benefit.

2   The main employers' organisation proposed there should be negotiations designed to reach a framework agreement, lasting three or four years. The employers were concerned that, over the previous two years, during which there had been little bargaining, there had been an increase in the

number of industrial disputes and a paralysis of the process of industrial restructuring. The employers wanted a two-year agreement which, besides setting a wide band for pay increases, would also include discussions on labour relations and social benefits.

In December 1988 the socialist and communist unions called a 24-hour general stoppage to protest against the Government's economic policy, especially on the youth employment plan.

This youth employment plan was aimed at Spain's 1 158 200 unemployed people under 25 years of age 800 000 of whom had no work experience. It was envisioned that over a period of three years 800 000 young people would be taken on by participating companies at the statutory minimum wage for periods of between six and 18 months. Employers would be exempt from paying social security contributions with respect to these employees, with the exception of those covering occupational diseases and accidents and unemployment.

Opposition was articulated by a joint platform of unions, youth and political organisations, which rejected the plan as 'an attack on the constitutional rights of the young'. The main objections were that the plan encouraged discrimination on grounds of age, subsidised a low standard of employment out of public funds and was unconstitutional as it undermined the principle of 'equal pay for equal work'.

The main employers' confederation stated that the plan would rejuvenate the workforce and help young people into the labour market.

A barely noticed step was taken. The long proposed Economic and Social Council was finally to be established and become operative at the beginning of 1989 as a tripartite consultative and advisory body on socio-economic and labour affairs.

The 24-hour general stoppage received a high degree of support with around eight million workers (approximately 90% of the working population) taking part. After the strike the Prime Minister agreed to shelve the controversial youth employment plan and proposed a tripartite dialogue on the subject. The unions, however, did not accept that employers should take part in discussions on the issue and the matter remained unresolved.

1989

The series of negotiations for 1989 central pay agreement which followed the successful general strike collapsed after six weeks.

The negotiations broke down over the following mattes: the refusal of the Government to concede to the unions' demands that at least 48 % of registered unemployed be eligible for unemployment benefit; and the fact that the Government's 'final offer' for an improved social package— spread over two years to cover increased pensions and unemployment benefits—represented only 40 % of the amount the unions were demanding.

The collapse of the talks was expected to lead to a further rupture in the historically close ties between the socialist union and the governing Socialist Party. The Party's leadership threatened to terminate the system whereby party members automatically became members of the socialist union. The collapse also placed a question mark over the continuation of the social contracts and central agreement on income policy.

However, the collapse should also be judged in relation to the achievements of 10 years of social contracts and the scope for identifying new priorities and power alignments.

Both union confederations believe the Government has become preoccupied with economic growth and inflation control and have ignored the social dimensions of development. Unemployment in Spain in 1989 was 18 %—the highest in Europe. The eight million people who heeded the one-day stayaway call in December 1988 rejected that Government policy. The communist and socialist confederations agreed in 1989 on joint proposal of demands aimed at securing a social dimension for the Government's rigid monetarist policy. The four main areas are:

1   employment creation via tighter controls on temporary contracts, a shorter work week, overtime controls, early retirement and training for young people;

2   improved social benefits such as extended unemployment benefits, a social security net and health care services;

3   redistribution of income and wealth such as inflation-linked increases for public servants, more progressive taxation;

4   participation and negotiation rights for employees including collective bargaining rights for civil servants, extended health and safety rights, improved rights of disclosure and participation in company decision-making, the formulation of a code of practise for the autonomous regulation of collective and individual conflicts and a procedure to determine minimum essential service requirements in the event of industrial action without prejudicing the right of strike (EIRR No 190, 1989).

The above description draws attention to the scope and challenges of bilateral and trilateral national negotiations. The parties continued to face tough choices about the input requirements for the relationship as well as output comprises and outcome responsibilities. South Africa will follow a different route. Unionism was rebuilt on the shop floor but the public status of the federations is still to be granted. Mediation and arbitration services are in place and representivity has been achieved in many sectors.

ANNEXURE B
STATUORY INSTITUTIONS AND DIRECTORATES OF THE DEPARTMENT OF MANPOWER

1   Advisory Council for Occupational Health

Function: To make recommendations to the Minister, or advise him on request or own initiative. To obtain and process technical information.

Tripartite structures: Yes

Scope for bilateralism: Black unions have criticised the Act for not promoting the role of unions in the plant-based Safety Committee. A number of recognition agreements contain a procedure to overcome this. The crucial issues are: expertise and information on technical matters and negotiation on priorities involving cost. The parties can negotiate guidelines on sectoral level.

2   Unemployment Insurance Board

Function: Collect and make available monies and control its disbursement to: unemployed person; dependants; and for other beneficiaries.

Tripartite structures: Yes

Scope for bilateralism: Black union federations have been critical of the operation of the administrative services and inadequacy of the benefits. The recognition agreement has been used to improve maternity benefits and provide supplementary benefits. However, national bilateral agreements between federations are more appropriate.

3   National Training Board

Function: To co-ordinate, facilitate and promote training of manpower and advise the Minister on policy matters. To accredit training schemes run on sectoral level and approve financial assistance.

Tripartite structures: Yes

Scope for bilateralism: Black unions are increasingly concerned about training opportunities for their members. Unions and employers' associations at sectoral level can set up training activities and obtain the necessary funding from the Department. This could be a subcommittee of the proposed Labour Market Council.

4   National Manpower Commission

Function: To monitor and analyse the manpower situation, to evaluate application and effectiveness of legislation and conduct research.

Tripartite structures: Yes

Scope for bilateralism: The Wiehahn Commission recommended the establishment of this body. A number of State Agencies are represented on it and hence black union federations do not want to participate. For ad hoc problems and issues pertaining to these functions, bilateralism could be used on national level. The successful outcome of any decisions taken is difficult to predict, e g to prevent legislation being passed.

5   Industrial Court

Function: To resolve issues involving conflict of interests and conflict of rights.

Tripartite structures: No

Scope for bilateralism: The credibility of the Industrial Court has been questioned by both parties at different times. The increased use of the Court is indicative of its relevance in endorsing aspects of freedom of association and due process in employment practices and in establishing what are unfair labour practices. A conference held in 1987 identified a number of crucial areas of concern regarding access to and operation of the Court. The labour market parties could effectively negotiate principles to guide the functioning of the Court on issues such as: role of legal representatives; when a party facing a Court action should be advised on preference for private arbitration; some agreed principles of unfair labour practices; etc.

6 Wage Board

Function: To investigate wages and conditions of employment in sectors, and submit reports and recommendations to the Minister.

Tripartite structures: No

Scope for bilateralism: Black unions have not made use of this body. Where employers do want to do so to prevent unfair competition, they should initiate discussions with unions on the wages and working conditions for that sector.

7 Workmen's Compensation Commissioner's Office

Function: To insure workers against financial loss in cases of accidents at work.

Tripartite structures: No. Proposals have not been implemented.

Scope for bilateralism: Unions have specific concerns about not only the administration of the Fund but the process whereby diseases, due to occupational hazards, are certified; access to and nature of rehabiliation services; medical services rendered; extend of compensation for accidents suffered; etc.

As the Fund absolves employers from direct liability for negligence, the two parties could improve on the functioning of the service through bilateral negotiations on national level.

8 Vocational Services and Placement

Function: To establish career counselling. To collect and distribute information on manpower and unemployment.

Tripartite structures: Not active

Scope for bilateralism: The human resource function of companies and consultants are involved in these issues. Unions are concerned that those activities emphasise only efficiency and effectiveness needs and not democratic needs. Bilateral agreements at sectoral level could address these issues and lead to establishment of a Labour Market Council.

9   National Productivity Institute (NPI)

Function: Not administered by the Department but in receipt of a financial grant. It promotes awareness of productivity and offers consultancy to companies.

Tripartite structures: Yes

Scope for bilateralism: Black unions have questioned the method of operation of the NPI and accused it of not ensuring job security when productivity programmes are instituted. Bilateralism would provide a means towards ensuring sound workers' participation and negotiated quality of work life.

10   National Occupational Safety Association (NOSA)

Function: Not administered by the Department but in receipt of a financial grant. It promotes awareness of the need for safety and offers consultancy services.

Tripartite structures: No, only employers and the state.

Scope for bilateralism: Black unions regard NOSA, as well as the NPI, as management-orientated. The concern of NOSA with accident-free rating is perceived to emphasise only management needs. This body has neglected occupational health protection of workers. A bilateral approach could to a certain degree prevent all safety and health becoming confrontational issues.

ANNEXURE C
THE CONTRACT OF IR DRIVEN OF INTERVENTIONS DURING THE LIFE-TERM OF A WAGE CONTRACT

Bolweg recommends that any project such as a quality-of-working-life programme be formalised through contract. The items or clauses in such a contract would include:

1   the objectives of the project;
2   guarantees on resulting wage, productivity and employment levels;
3   composition, rights and responsibilities of the project's steering committee;
4   the project's budget;
5   experimental period of the project and discontinuance of the project's steering committee;
6   periodic evaluations of the project by the parties;
7   the dissemination of information;
8   conflict regulation, including the possibility of submitting conflicts arising from the project to binding arbitration;
9   protection against dismissal of persons involved in the project (e g in the Netherlands the same legal protection that work council members enjoy may be given);
10 special provisions for older workers or for those who do not want to participate on a voluntary basis;
11 selection and position of external consultants;
12 organisational change and research methods to be excluded (e g sensitivity training, questionnaires);
13 updating of job description and job classification as the project progresses, including the use of 'broad banding';
14 procedures and proposals on how to deal with the positive financial outcomes of the project which can be expressed in terms of total net savings per employee (e g the introduction of some form of profit-sharing or productivity bargaining could be in order here);
15 monitoring and enforcement of issues.

ANNEXURE D
LABOUR MARKET COUNCIL

South Africa post-apartheid will have a mixed market economy. Even if individual business leaders support 'unfettered' free enterprise, historical realities and export needs imply continued State direction. If organised labour is involved in both these socio-economic dimensions of labour market policy formulation then this will mould and be moulded by the wishes and preferences of membership.

In order to promote and protect their respective interests, both capital and labour have a keen interest in controlling the labour market. The craft union strategy of controlling entrance to the market has been replaced by the industrial union strategy of controlling exit from the labour market. Hence the emphasis of the latter on plant-based procedures to ensure due process and protection against victimisation as well as unfair practices in regard to discipline, dismissal and retrenchment. Training technology and job fragmentation are also eroding the craft unions' hold over apprenticeship and hence their ability to create a scarcity of artisans and journeymen to ensure a wage drift over minimum negotiated rates of industrial council agreements. Capital, in order to cope with technological innovations and to explore export opportunities, requires flexibility in the use of labour. The scope for trade-offs in joint control by directing aspects of the labour market, which exemplifies the interdependence of capital and labour, are considerable.

Offe's distinction between two strategies whereby persons are included in, and excluded from, the labour market is highly relevant to current choices facing capital and labour in South Africa. Both parties want to exclude persons from the market, either temporarily (e g pregnant women) or permanently (white immigrants and black workers from Front-line States). Both parties want to include certain persons, e g the unemployed, by reducing the working week and through occupational and regional flexibility, outwork arrangements, etc. To achieve these differing objectives, the supply and demand considerations have to be weighed up against each other. The following schedule juxtaposes these strategies in relation to the scope for positive and negative sanctions. The parties can recreate the social reality of the labour market if negotiations and trade-offs are made. In fact, these issues are already part of plant-based negotiations through the recognition forum, but in a fragmented form. Do the parties want to continue 'sniping' at each other at that low level in the industrial relations system and achieve small but isolated gains with no pay-offs towards lasting stability in the workplace and the sector? Or do they recognise the relevance of national negotiations on basic principles to prevent atomisation of demoralised workers? When such concerns become agenda items, the industrial council structure can be revitalised. If capital strengthens its third form of expression through employers' associations, it has the opportunity to be pro-active, bearing in mind its representation on the National Training Board of the Department of Manpower, which has proposed decentralised control over training by the parties in an economic sector.

STRATEGIES OF LABOUR MARKET POLICY INTERVENTION		
	POSITIVE SANCTION (INCENTIVES)	NEGATIVE SANCTIONS (PENALTIES)
EXCLUSION STRATEGY To reduce supply to market by excluding persons or providing them at certain time periods with legitimate means of non-participation	DEMAND SIDE	
	Early retirement and other social policy schemes, e g subsidise self-supporting households (youth, elderly, women, men)	Prohibit child labour. Prohibit employment of illegal immigrants
	SUPPLY SIDE	
	Paid maternity leave (1 year) Incentives to encourage migrants to go home (those from outside the republic) Subsidies for small business.	Raise school-going age.
INCLUSION STRATEGY To integrate labour into the market by increasing the chances for persons to find employment	DEMAND SIDE	
	Wage cost subsidy Short-time allowances	Quota for youth
	SUPPLY SIDE	
	Further training Occupational flexibility Subsidise regional mobility	Outwork (for export industries) at reduced negotiated rates Subsidised work for unemployed Limited benefits for 'work-shy' unemployed Worksharing

The examples merely illustrate the nature of the two strategies.

In fact the relevance of negotiations is that creative sanctions will be identified by labour market parties. For example, union federations would want to stop white immigration, while employers' associations would want flexibility in using employees across job categories.

ANNEXURE E
MATTERS AFFECTING THE PROPENSITY OF ORGANISED CAPITAL AND LABOUR TO NEGOTIATE THE PARAMETERS OF SOCIAL POLICY

ORGANISED LABOUR   ORGANISED CAPITAL

Willingness

Factors which will influence the 'willingness' dimension are: similar interpretation of events as constituting a crisis, even though for different reasons; concern about State interference; experience of trauma and concern about survival; acceptance that industrial democracy is the best way to protect own interests. These thrusts create tensions.

The tensions created will emphasise the different tendencies in the organised labour movement in regard to the issue of entering into trade-offs with organised capital.

Conglomerates will resist implication that certain industrial relations activities will be directed by employers' associations.

Ability

The unions experience manpower, resource and infrastructural problems. The process of mandating is crucial to ensure leaders can explore options and test acceptability of trade-offs. This requires protection of civil liberties.

Employers' associations experience resource problems

ORGANISED LABOUR   ORGANISED CAPITAL

The negotiating style of union leaders and management representatives will be eased from confrontational emphasis to 'working together' if tangible improvements in quality of life of workers occurs and workers can believe that there is a future for their children.

Resources

An examination of the issues in Annexure B suggests that outside expertise or commissioned research is required. Assistance from international unions is to be welcomed.

Industrial relations events have taken more time than was planned. Costs of consultants

Controlling process and monitoring outcome

Union federations, in particular, are concerned that once they step out into any joint activity with capital, they will be committed to a direction which is irreversible. Both sides need to build into any negotiations, for even ad hoc issues, the question of how monitoring and implementation is to be handled. These constituents of both sides should watch the situation carefully and 'test' its relevance with early rejection and questioning of its appropriateness.

The scope for decentralisation of an issue and the implementation of agreed programmes is considerable. This decentralisation potential needs to be actively promoted as the involvement of union leaders at those different levels will bring tangible evidence to union members of the benefits of industrial democracy.

ANNEXURE F
NOTE ON PUBLIC STATUS OF INTEREST GROUPS

Organised labour and capital influence the supply and demand side of the market and their actions can stabilise or destabilise social order. Hence state agencies involved in policy-making prefer to control them (negative status) or accede to their demands (positive status). Can the two labour market parties utilise South Africa's transition period and build up a positive public status? Four dimensions of public status assist in determining whether State co-optation–coercion strategies predominate or whether the parties maintain a degree of independence (Offe 1988).

1   Organisational status is achieved through an effective process of mandating and regulation between the executive of an organisation and its rank and file affiliates, whatever form of indirect representation is used. Both federations of unions and employers have to improve this dimension of their public status. To do so they require civil liberties, i e to hold meetings; report back; use balloting process; have freedom to express opinion; and have protection against arbitrary action—particularly against leadership.

2   Resource status is usually provided and facilitated by legislation or the State. Closed-shop arrangements need not be legislated for but can be agreed to in the first instance as procedures in a basic agreement. If too much legislation controls this dimension, it becomes a legislative snare, e g recognition in the USA is dependent on the National Labour Relations Board's accreditation process.

3   Procedural status results from the degree of formal acknowledgement of the organisation's relevance by the political system. A tendency is noticeable in South Africa for representatives on national bodies to be appointed and no longer even selected from a list of nominations put

forward by interest groups as a result of an invitation; an example of this is the President's Economic Advisory Council.

4   Representation status refers to the range of areas in which an interest group may operate, e g manpower, social security, housing, public transport, etc.

By definition the more an interest group is granted these dimensions of public status automatically, the less it becomes accountable to its membership, i e the less the will of the membership guides its actions and accomplishments, ideologies and preferences. Similarly, the voluntary trade-offs on national policy issues between the two labour market parties, with the implied responsibility for self-restraint, will ensure status attribution is positively won instead of negatively granted (and hence threatened by withdrawal) by the State. These considerations clarify the dilemmas that leaders of both parties face in considering how to gain access to national policy-making bodies. Implicit in any demand either party voices to gain influence on national policy issues (or on shaping the socio-economic order) is the degree to which it is prepared to share responsibility for consequences of implementation and ability to cope with crises resulting from operationalising policies.

ANNEXURE G
THE TOUGH CHOICES FACING THE LABOUR MARKET
PARTIES

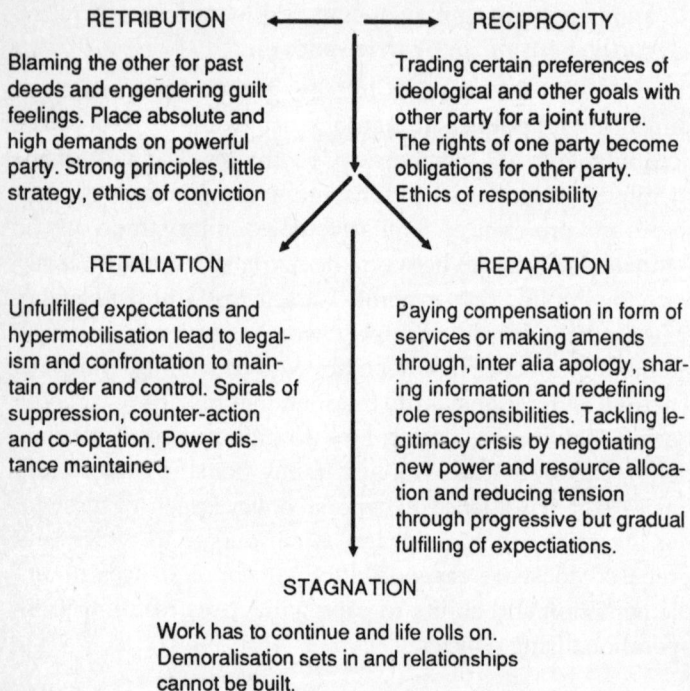

RETRIBUTION ◀━━━━━ ━━━━━▶ RECIPROCITY

Blaming the other for past
deeds and engendering guilt
feelings. Place absolute and
high demands on powerful
party. Strong principles, little
strategy, ethics of conviction

Trading certain preferences of
ideological and other goals with
other party for a joint future.
The rights of one party become
obligations for other party.
Ethics of responsibility

RETALIATION   REPARATION

Unfulfilled expectations and
hypermobilisation lead to legalism and confrontation to maintain order and control. Spirals of
suppression, counter-action
and co-optation. Power distance maintained.

Paying compensation in form of
services or making amends
through, inter alia apology, sharing information and redefining
role responsibilities. Tackling legitimacy crisis by negotiating
new power and resource allocation and reducing tension
through progressive but gradual
fulfilling of expectiations.

STAGNATION

Work has to continue and life rolls on.
Demoralisation sets in and relationships
cannot be built.

REFERENCES

BERENSTEIN, A. 1982. 'The development and Scope of Economic and Social Rights' *Labour and Society* vol 7, no 4.

BOLWEG, G. 1982. 'The Quality of Working Life: An Industrial Relations Perspective' *Proceedings of the 33rd Congress of the Industrial Relations Association, USA.*

CONVERSE, P. 1989. 'Perspectives on the Democratic Process' *ISR Newsletter* vol 16, no 2, University of Michigan.

DENBINSKY, P. 1984. Economic Policy—Social Policy. *Labour and Society* vol 8, no 2.

DOUWES DEKKER, L. *Industrial Relations for a Changing South Africa,* Lex Patria (In Press).

HAMMAN, J. 1978. 'Social Policy in Sweden' *Labour and Society* vol 7, no 1.

ILO 1983. 'Selected Basic Agreements and Joint Declarations on Labour-Management Relations' *Labour Management Relations Series* no 83.

OFFE, C. 1985. *Disorganised Capitalism* The MIT Press, Cambridge, Massachusetts.

SAVAGE, M. 1967. 'An Anatomy of the South African Corporate Economy' *Industrial Relations Journal of South Africa* vol 7, no 2.

SWILLING, M. and PHILLIPS, M. 1988. 'Reform, Security and the State'. Working paper presented at the 1988 Annual Conference of the Association of Sociology of Souther Africa.

THOMPSON, C. 1988. 'Beyond Recognition: A New Social Contract *Indicator South Africa* vol 5, no 4.

WASSENAAR, A. 1977. *A Thought on Private Enterprise.* Tafelberg, Cape Town.

7

Georgina Jaffee

WORKER CO-OPERATIVES: THEIR EMERGENCE, PROBLEMS AND POTENTIAL

INTRODUCTION

Over the past few years there has been interest shown in the formation of co-operatives from a number of quarters with otherwise divergent positions on issues such as worker participation, apartheid, capitalism and socialism. These organisations include trade unions, community organisations, black business groups and a variety of institutions involved in job creation programs and economic development. Co-operative ventures are funded by local banks, multinational corporations, local capital and foreign donor agencies. Furthermore, in the ANC's *Constitutional Guidelines for a Democratic South Africa*, a co-operative sector is mentioned as part of the mixed economy and supported by the state.[1]

The number of small and medium size co-operatives in both urban and rural areas has increased over the past few years.[2] The most significant of the newer initiatives in co-oper-

1 African National Congress Constitutional Guidelines. Lusaka, 1989.
2 Existing producer co-operative projects include sewing, brickmaking, fencing, T-shirts, furniture production, weaving, auto mechanics, repair work, toys, jewellery and panel beating. There are also a number of consumer and service co-operatives which include gardening and secretarial services. According to a study by Kate Philip, many of these co-ops have been started within the last four years; the majority are craft and sewing co-operatives; there is an average of eleven people working in each co-operative; most ventures are dependent on outside funding; and few provide their members with living wages. A more recent study by M Lupton has shown that there are a total of 96

ative development in South Africa are those co-operatives being developed by unions for dismissed or retrenched membership. Amongst Cosatu affiliates co-operatives started with the Sarmcol Workers Co-operative (Sawco) which was established in 1985 by the National Union of Metal Workers of South Africa (Numsa) for 960 dismissed workers from BTR Sarmcol in Pietermaritzburg. Sawco has five different projects which include both production and service co-ops. The initiative has been followed by co-operatives linked to ACTWUSA (Amalgamated Clothing and Textile Workers' Union of South Africa) which makes a range of clothing; the National Union of Mineworkers (NUM), involved in T-shirts, and block-making, and the Post Office Workers Association (POTWA) which is supporting a building co-operative. A consumer co-operative is being initiated by NUMSA in Port Elizabeth. The National Council of Trade Unions (NACTU) is also in the process of investigating the potential of co-operatives for their unemployed membership.

The development and re-emergence of co-operatives or workers self-management is evident in many western economies. Co-ops have been in existence in many parts of the world since the mid-19th century, having developed in response to the inherent exploitation of capitalism. Co-operatives have sometimes been a critical response to the effects of industrialisation characterised by hierarchical relations at the workplace and worker domination. The present crisis in capitalism resulting in mass unemployment, class conflict, low productivity and job dissatisfaction has seen the re-introduction of worker co-operatives as a potential remedy.

producer co-operatives in the country which have a membership of between 1 600 and 1 800, and that the largest category of co-operatives is sewing, knitting and weaving, with building co-operatives constituting the second largest category and craft production coming third. This study also shows that over 70 % of the co-ops have fewer than 20 people.

Newer co-operatives in the USA and UK have developed through both worker buy-outs of failing enterprises (conversions) or new start-ups for the unemployed. In addition to this, community-based approaches to local economic development have also utilised co-operatives (sometimes referred to as community businesses) as an appropriate form of organisation for a more integrated process of economic and social development. These trends are evident in many under-developed parts of western Europe such as Ireland, Scotland, France and Italy.

Although there are trends towards co-operatives in many different parts of the western world, in most cases (except Italy, France and Spain) co-operatives do not pose satisfactory employment alternatives for large numbers of people. More often than not co-operatives are small-scale enterprises based in marginal sectors of the economy which are characterised by low wages.

CO-OPERATIVES DEFINED

The presence of co-ops in many parts of the world does not imply uniformity in terms of internal organisation and overall structure. The term 'co-operative' has taken on a number of different definitions and has in many parts of the world become synonymous with marketing boards, credit societies and consumer organisations. These organisations differ from the definition of a worker co-operative which was adopted by the International Co-operative Alliance in 1895 and to which most authentic co-operative movements are affiliated.

A co-operative is defined as an enterprise which is collectively and democratically controlled by those who work in it. Members of the co-operative which are also the workers of that co-operative contribute both their labour and (not always) a sum of money. This is done on a voluntary basis with open membership. The management and control of the enterprise is organised on a democratic basis in which members have equal voting rights. There is proportional sharing of benefits which accrue from trading activities and limited interest on share capital.

With different forms of co-operative development emerging in various countries, an international debate has started on the future of the movement. The debate has included issues such as whether collective capital is better than individual stakes; the maximum size of a co-operative for democracy to work, state aid to co-operatives, hiring of managers, and trade union involvement in co-operative development.

Besides control and sometimes ownership of the enterprise being vested in the workers, co-operatives differ from conventional enterprises in the provision made for social goals. Co-operatives are concerned with good working relations between their members, membership education and responsibility to the community at large.

As co-operatives are concerned with bringing both economic and social benefits to their members and the community at large, they are more than a means of creating or saving jobs. The co-operative form is an instrument for both economic and social progress. Consequently, co-operatives have been taken up as appropriate income-generating institutions by organisations concerned with both the economic and social prosperity of communities.

Co-operatives are also committed to participation in socially useful activities. This may involve trying to meet the consumer needs of other workers or engaging in production activities which meet the needs of the immediate community. Co-ops, therefore, are not simply another way of doing business, even though they are subject to the same economic constraints as conventional small businesses. Their manner of democratic working makes them implicitly critical of power structures in broader society, and in societies where a fundamental transition to a different economic order is possible, co-operatives have identified strongly with political and social movements for change.

OWNERSHIP AND EMPLOYEE SHARE OWNERSHIP SCHEMES (ESOPS)

There is an ongoing debate on the consequences of different forms of ownership of co-operatives and this debate has become more complex with the development of Esops.

British co-operatives are characterised by common ownership where all control and benefit rights rest with employees, whereas other forms of ownership may include situations where a community body, outside organisation or even the state benefit from the enterprise through having provided share equity. Whatever the options in terms of ownership, it is accepted within the international co-operative movement that control of all decisions of the co-operative should be vested in the workforce of that co-operative.

It has been argued in some American literature that Esops could represent a transitory form eventually leading to broad-based workers' control. A counter-argument posits an alternative view that even though Esops have some immediate appeal to workers, this form of worker participation only meets worker needs within specified limits. As Leo Panitch, a well-known Canadian economist says 'the framework for Esops is set by managers and owners. Workers often find that their newly acquired power is limited'. Esops are not intended to give control now or in the future to the workers. Empirical data on most employee-owned companies shows that employees seldom own more than 50% of the shares.[3] In South Africa where there are about 140 Esops, employees do not in

3   See debate in *Worker Co-ops*, University of Saskatchewan, Canada, vol 6 No 3.

any instance own more than 24% of shares and the average shareholding of employees is 5%.[4] Therefore, the fundamental difference between Esops and co-ops remains one of who has *control*.

CO-OPS AND THE LABOUR MOVEMENT

In the UK, Canada (English) and USA, unions and labour organisations have treated co-operatives with some skepticism. Developments which result in small, disparate, low-income enterprises, which undercut union wage demands and perpetuate low-wage jobs are viewed with hostility by labour organisations.

In other countries such as Italy and France, worker co-operatives have obtained support from political parties and unions. In these cases, co-operatives have been taken very seriously as institutions which provide broad benefits to their members through democratic structures. They are seen to play a vital role in providing an alternative set of symbols and practices for workers' control and democracy which is of benefit to all working-class organisations. Furthermore, co-ops have been successful in organising groups of people who have either been marginalised by the economic system or are in positions of economic inferiority. These include women, youth, the elderly and the disabled. In this respect co-ops have the potential to broaden the base of working-class struggles outside of a unionised sector.

The recent co-operative initiatives in South Africa need to be understood within current economic and social changes taking place in the country. Worker co-operatives can never be divorced from the societies in which they are being developed. Like any other social movement, co-operatives can mobilise and empower their members for the restructuring of

4   Mallor, J *Esop's Fables* Labour and Economic Research Centre, 1988.

society or they can be part of the reformist strategies of the
state or institutions representing the dominant classes. South
Africa's recent co-op initiatives can be broadly categorised
into both *reformist and transformative initiatives*.

CO-OPERATIVES AS INSTITUTIONS OF ECONOMIC REFORM—REFORMIST INITIATIVES

Large corporations are placing more of their social responsibility investments in community projects, some of which are
co-operatives. These initiatives are tied to the exploration of
ways in which to promote entrepreneurial activities in the
black community and assist in the reduction of unemployment. There is a growing trend by social responsibility programmes to move more seriously into community projects
which have credibility and legitimacy. Both Shell and Mobil
Oil, for example, are setting aside 'social investment' funds
for community projects, some of which are co-operatives. The
attention these companies are paying to community projects
is a result of pressure on the multinationals from two sides.
On the one side the disinvestment campaign has put increased pressure on multinationals to legitimise their role
through contributing towards change in South Africa. This
has forced them to extend the amount of money for 'social
justice programmes', to show the disinvestment lobby that
they are attempting to oppose apartheid. On the other side,
the radicalisation and organisation of the black community
has led to intense debate and discussion on the relationship
between capital and the state. This has forced capital into the
recognition that if it wants to develop a good image in the eyes
of the community, it will have to sponsor projects which are
credible in the eyes of that community.

The growth of community organisation has provided alternative funding opportunities for large corporations. This
is an important area of concern in terms of the overall interests

of international capital in the post-apartheid phase. A spokesperson at Mobil when asked why there is a shift to supporting co-ops said 'it is clear that there are important grassroot alternatives which are making a structural impact and that these must be accommodated—and that we must look at what they are doing and build a coalition with these groups, not to direct them, but to stimulate them and move efforts faster'.[5]

The most overt statement with regard to supporting community co-operatives comes from Shell. In a speech given earlier last year to the Western Province Branch of the Institute of Marketing Managers, the Chairperson of Shell, Mr Wilson spoke directly of broad co-operative endeavours in the black community and called on capital to support these initiatives. He gave examples of SABTA, Tiakeni Textiles, Sarmcol and the Atlantis co-operative as endeavours which have grown within the community because 'they have taken stock of unemployment and are attempting to do something about it'. He noted that 'small business development does not feature in concept, or in the final result, in any of these ventures'. He argued that capital has to meet the challenge which is set by these new co-operative ventures which reveal that the 'black community has standards, protocols and expectations which differ from our norms'. He stated that Shell is prepared to assist 'credible representatives of black constituencies who are in the forefront of initiating projects, covering a wide spectrum of economic activities . . .'.[6] Shell has started supporting small co-operatives in the Western Cape and is presently in the process of drawing up criteria that projects must meet if they are to be regarded as co-operatives.

5   Telephone interview with spokesperson from Mobil Foundation, August, 1988.
6   Speech given by Managing Director J R Wilson to the Western Province Branch of the Institute of Marketing Management, 1988.

Several spokespeople from large corporations have also indicated that, to promote entrepreneurship in the black community they believe it is important not to impose a 'western-style' business ethos. Co-operatives are regarded as an 'African way' of doing business and promoting entrepreneurship, which are not a threat to the present economic order.

Research and discussions within the Urban Foundation and large corporations are arguing that Western styles of entrepreneurship are not that appropriate for South Africa because of the ethic of 'communalism' which exists within the black community. This communalism, they say, is not inconsistent with free enterprise but may bring with it some of the best aspects of socialism. This, interestingly enough, is similar to the explanations given for the potential for stokvel savings to be used as sources for investment.

It is in this context that co-operatives come to be seen as a potential institutional embodiment of 'African entrepreneurial values'. Organisations such as the Urban Foundation are taking the informal systems of finance, support and co-operation in black communities very seriously. There are arguments being made that it is not appropriate to impose a western-style business ethos. This argument is also closely connected to the development and promotion of black business which is based on the self-help model. Wilson's speech refers to this point of view when he speaks of the 'standards, protocols and ethics which differ from our (Western) norm'. Wilson's claim is given credence when members of the black community make precisely the same arguments. Andrew Lukhele, founder member of the National Stokvel Association said in the interview on the role of the new National Stockvel Association.

'There exists a great cultural divide between black and white entrepreneurial attitudes to enterprise. Whites tend to be individualistic, aggressively competitive, goal driven and reward-orientated. Blacks, on the other hand tend to be more co-operative and collectively driven. In fact, in the African economic system one does not speak of competitors but of colleagues'.

This is echoed again by Sisa Kampepe of the Small Business Development Corporation. When interviewed he said

'the community-based organisations want to indigenise business—business has been regarded as an outsider and collaborator with apartheid—business must relate to people on a day to day basis and not be a distant cousin or an enemy.

Co-ops emerging within black business

Legal restrictions on black business development have led to growing frustration within this class. This has contributed to the efforts of black business groups to seek other avenues for entrepreneurial activity. These include the formation of consumer and service co-operatives designed to make up for black business's economic inferiority and disadvantage.

According to spokespeople for these initiatives, they aim to promote self-reliance and create services on a co-operative basis, which benefit the black community. In many instances these organisations are responding to the real needs of the community. The co-operative form lends itself to addressing these needs in a manner acceptable to communities which have become highly politicised and critical of conventional business enterprises. There is a strong emphasis on building independence and self-reliance through co-operation. 'Let us build our own economic institutions, dig our own gold for the betterment of our people, build our own supermarkets.'[7]

Consumer co-operatives will 'serve as a vehicle for consumers to participate effectively in the South African economy' and to 'mobilise consumer power'[8] for the benefit of the black community. Besides this there is also social awareness and

7   Business plan of Sechaba Sizwe Co-operative (unpublished document) 1987.
8   Molotov Bizzah 'Co-operation as a strategy for the creation of employment' (unpublished speech) June 1988.

community consciousness expressed in the intention of funding job-creation programmes as well as providing education and training to the participants.

There are also initiatives to establish credit unions and start-up finance for 'upliftment' projects. Although most of the co-ops appear to be concerned with issues in the broader community, there is a difference in the extent to which some co-operatives are committed to community programmes and job creation. There is also a difference in organisational approach. Some of the co-operatives, for example, are hoping to begin with a large injection of capital while others are more concerned with participants raising their own capital, starting small and expanding over time.

These co-ops appear to be committed to a particular form of social change. This is predominantly expressed through words such as 'economic liberation', where economic self-help and self-management are seen as they key to the process of transformation. They are inspired by an ideology of self-help which is a response to the ongoing restrictions and limitations placed on black business, the limited assistance provided by such organisations as the Small Business Development Corporation (SBDC) and the absence of significant socio-political change overall. The premise on which these co-ops are based is that if blacks have been excluded from the economic system and continue to be, then the only way out is to develop their own economic organisations and institutions. These will not only ensure participation but will also prevent exploitation. 'If a shop or business exploits us by charging high prices, why do we not start our own shop?'

These initiatives must be seen in the context of recent political events as well as material conditions which characterise most townships:

- The consumer boycotts of 1985/86 forced township dwellers into using local shops more frequently. Customers became more aware of the higher prices charged by the local shops as well as the poorer quality of goods compared to the shops in urban centres. A recent HSRC study[9] (commissioned by the Black Consumers Union) on consumer attitudes towards township or city buying has shown that there are many criticisms of township shops. The most frequent and important criticism made is that they have inflated prices and there are great price fluctuations. Other criticisms include shortages of stock, limits on the goods available and lack of concern for expiry dates.

The township retailers are not able to compete with the larger stores in the city for many reasons including lack of purchasing power. They are forced to buy in small quantities from the wholesalers rather than directly from manufacturers. They are unable to establish economies of scale because of lack of space and financial constraints. This leads to higher costs and higher prices of goods.

- Black businessmen have become increasingly aware of the buying power of the black consumer as well as the need to provide cheaper goods to the poorer majority in the townships. The conclusions of the HSRC study on the feasibility of consumer co-ops, are of some use in explaining the emergence of consumer co-operatives. It was revealed in the study that one of the most important motivations for the establishment of consumer co-ops is to provide savings on purchases for the poor. This is something which the African Consumer Co-operative society seems to have accomplished successfully.

- During the height of resistance in the townships small and medium-size businessmen were often singled out if they

9   Franks, P E and Shane, S 'An Investigation of Urban Black Perceptions
     of Socio-economic Needs, Black versus Non-black Business, Economic
     Systems and Co-operatives' *Human Sciences Research Council* 1988.

did not 'co-operate' or participate in political actions defined by the youth and political organisations. In many instances this led to the loss of property, closure of shops and death threats. Co-operatives are seen by the business groups as a way of involving the community in business with the hope that this will diffuse the potential for further polarisation and class conflict. Co-ops fulfil some of the requirements of those people concerned about more democratic practices without being a threat to present business interests or contradicting the present initiatives by capital and the state to sell free enterprise to the black community.

- The increased radicalisation of the youth and working class has also called into question initiatives by capital and small business to promote black entrepreneurship. Co-operatives are seen as a way in which the community can own and control its own activity as well as providing benefits to the community at large. It has become well known that the SBDC has lost credibility because of its bureaucratic procedures and perception of it as a government agency. One recent study of black entrepreneurs argues that 'the perception of the SBDC as a government agency, intent on implementing government's policies of segregation, has led to scepticism regarding the Corporation's ultimate intent; and to an apprehension of being seen by the people as having been co-opted onto a system whose objective is the perpetuation of white domination.[10]

- The consumer co-operative initiatives must also be seen in the context of the formation of several other organisations which are campaigning against on-going discrimination

10 Davies, W J 'Black Entrepreneurial Experiences and Practice in Port Elizabeth' *Working Paper 36* Institute of Social and Economic Research, Rhodes University, 1988.

and restrictions on black business and lack of access to
funding. Examples of these are: the African Council of
Hawkers and Informal Businesses (ACHIB) launched in
1986 to organise this constituency against legal restrictions
on hawkers and high prices paid by hawkers to supplier
companies; and the National Stokvel Association of South
Africa (NASASA) which is attempting to bring together in
one organisation the many informal savings clubs
(stokvels), credit systems (mashonisas) and investment
syndicates; and the Foundation for African Business and
Consumer Services (FABCOS) formed in July 1988 comprising the Southern Black Taxi Association, the National
Black Consumers Union and the Transvaal African Buil-
ders Association. Some of these organisations are reveal-
ing a combativity which has not existed previously within
black business groupings. They have threatened boycotts
and demonstrations and show hostility to both white
business and the government.

Although support from the interest groups discussed above
could be used effectively to promote community-based co-
operatives, the overall intention of these initiatives is to promote co-ops as part of a reformist strategy. This strategy is
concerned to incorporate the disadvantaged into the economy, promote growth, decrease unemployment and curb
social and political problems arising from conditions of mar-
ginality. The projects which these groups support and the
initiatives started by black business will only serve the interests of the majority of people if there is pressure from a
co-operative movement to abide by the internationally accepted aims and principles of co-operatives.

UNION-LINKED CO-OPERATIVES— TRANSFORMATIVE CO-OPS

The growth of the trade union movement, community organisations, youth groups and service organisations has provided an organisational base on which to promote co-operatives. The 1987 Congress resolution of Cosatu—pledging support to the National Unemployed Workers Co-ordinating Committee (NUWCC)—is illustrative of this. The NUWCC was formed when a number of unemployed groups came together in 1987. In this resolution, Cosatu committed itself to

'systematic support of the recently formed National Unemployed Workers Co-ordinating Committee to achieve a national organisation and build a co-operative movement that serves the interests of the working class'.

In practice however, the NUWCC has not managed to organise co-operatives for the mass of dismissed workers. Co-operatives have nevertheless developed within various other Cosatu affiliates where they have received support from individual unions. As a result of this the 1989 Cosatu Congress adopted a resolution to support the 'growth of democratic co-operatives within the framework of international co-operative principles'. These include 'democratic control of the co-operative by the members; no discrimination on the grounds of sex, race or religion; fair distribution of profits; limited interest on share capital; co-operatives shall co-operate with each other; co-operatives shall encourage the ongoing education of their members'.

Defensive and offensive strategies of co-operative development

There are two assumptions that underlie this recent union-linked co-operative initiative. The first is the assumption that co-operatives are able to maintain the unity of the working class at a time when working-class struggles are characterised by mass dismissals. The promotion of co-operatives is seen as assisting in building links between the employed and unemployed, and as a defensive strategy for those expelled from the workplace. One aim is to prevent scabbing or the formation of vigilantes by organising the unemployed around activities which may include co-ops.

The overall objective is to maintain the unity of the working class—especially important at a time when increasing social and economic divisions are emerging between employed and unemployed. Co-ops are also potential arenas of working-class control and power in the broader community. This perspective is advocated by those involved in building organisations for unemployed workers. Proponents sometimes assume that co-operatives can mop up unemployment on a wide scale. The Cosatu resolution attempts to dispel this myth by saying

'Co-ops cannot provide jobs for all. To do this we need the political power to restructure the economy, and to use the wealth of the nation to serve the needs of the people as a whole'.

The second assumption underlying this co-operative initiative is that co-operatives can be an offensive strategy on behalf of the working class. Co-ops have the potential to give workers and trade unions some experience in workers' control and democracy. Experiments in workers' self-management are seen as very important for the trade union movement in promoting the principles of workers' control of production and distribution. Co-operatives may be linked directly to union activities and of mutual benefit. They play a supportive role for the working class on the shop-floor and strengthen the unions and working class in the community. The labour movement in turn plays a critical role in the development of co-operatives because of its familiarity with workplace organisation, the production process and the struggle waged to democratise the workplace.

In the short-term, co-operatives allow workers to develop appropriate skills in self-management and extend workers' control. In the long-term it is believed that all forms of working-class organisation will contribute towards working-class hegemony within the struggle for social and economic transformation. This position recognises the limitations of co-operatives in the present economic system and recognises too that co-operatives cannot, on their own, prefigure a new social and economic order.

Co-operatives in South Africa are occurring in a politically and economically hostile environment. Both these defensive and offensive strategies of co-operative development face enormous practical and organisational difficulties.

PROBLEMS FACED BY UNION-LINKED CO-OPERATIVES

The problems faced by South African co-operatives are no different from co-operatives in other parts of the world. The major problem facing all co-operatives in a market economy is that they are forced to measure viability in terms of market competition and not in terms of social utility. In South Africa co-ops are being set up within a highly developed capitalist economy. In order to be successful, they must find a suitable and viable gap in the market so as not to remain marginal enterprises. In most parts of the world except where the state has played a significant role in promoting co-operatives, barriers to co-operative development include lack of access to start-up finance, shortage of business and managerial skills, problems of marketing and lack of efficient support and training institutions. There are two general areas where difficulties are being experienced by the emergent co-operatives. The one area can be defined as technical, the second organisational.

Technical problems

Finance

Co-ops are traditionally undercapitalised. Financial problems not only include access to start-up grants or loans but problems associated with financial controls. The inability to secure low interest financing from conventional lenders (because co-ops have no security) such as banks or development agencies, means that co-operatives are forced to go elsewhere for funding. In situations where grants are given, they are often not enough to cover the start-up requirement. Furthermore, alternative money given to development projects sometimes does not require financial accountability and this can affect attitudes towards financial control. The recognition that it will be unlikely that large amounts of funding will be secured from formal institutions in the short-term is forcing co-operative initiators to explore other sources of funding. This may include the use of retrenchment packages, pension and provident funds.

Shortage of business and managerial skills

This is particularly acute in the SA situation. Apartheid has generally retarded the development of black business skills and until recently black workers have remained on the lower rungs of the industrial hierarchy. Dismissed workers wishing to form co-operatives are mostly unskilled. They therefore bring with them very little experience on which managerial skills could be built. This situation poses a serious dilemma for co-operative development. Some co-ops may in the short-term have to use managers from conventional capitalist enterprises but in the long-run co-operative development programs will have to find appropriate training for co-operative managers. Capitalist management cannot be simply repackaged for co-operative usage as these techniques are reflective of a hierarchical and authoritarian world and are in the long-run inappropriate for co-operative development.

Support organisations

Co-operatives in other parts of the world have been far more successful when there has been access to local support organisations which have been linked to national support organisations. One recent study entitled *The Role and Impact of Local Co-operative Support Organisations* carried out in Britain in 1985 reveals that local co-operative support organisations have been a major factor in the growth of co-operatives since 1980.

In South Africa there are very few serious support organisations for co-operative development. Even though there has been a growth of interest in co-operatives, much of the work on co-operative development is being done by academic researchers and little is being done to provide practical assistance for co-operative development. Unions are forced to hire their own consultants, who are trained in conventional business management, or they are forced to encourage personnel and co-operative development agencies from outside the country to assist with these developments. Limited funds place a ceiling on the ability of unions to hire appropriate professionals or organisations.

Unions are being forced into the position of becoming development agencies. This is extremely difficult in the light of scarce resources, formal union activities, lack of skills and other demands placed on unions due to the political crisis.

Education and training

Education for worker co-operatives requires more than production skills necessary for the job. Education in co-ops must include areas which enable workers to learn how to become economically self-governing within democratic structures. This is fundamentally different from education for capitalist production. Democracy requires education in decision-making skills, debating, analytical skills as well as skills which enable each member to understand the entire process of production. Even if specialist management is hired by the co-operative, each member will have to be given an opportunity to understand the way in which management recommendations are made. This is the essential ingredient for democratic practice. Education in literacy and numeracy are also an essential part of co-operative development and prerequisites for the working of democracy.

It has been shown by international co-operative experiences that where general co-operative education which teaches the philosophical side of co-operative development is lacking, co-ops have tended to degenerate into capitalist enterprises. Co-operatives in South Africa will be forced to take advantage of the numerous training and business education courses available to small businesses. These will not be sufficient to be able to provide co-operatives with all the training necessary for co-operative development. This economic training will have to be complemented with education programs which teach the history and principles of co-operative organisation and the differences between co-operative and capitalist management.

Organisational problems

There are numerous organisational problems which characterise the present union-linked co-operatives. As the unions have begun initiating co-operatives predominantly as a defensive strategy, there is tremendous pressure from below to get started. This means that projects sometimes get implemented *without proper feasibility studies or business plans.* This occurs so as not to lose contact with the dismissed or risk loss of support because expectations cannot be met. Furthermore, *lack of efficient and sufficient welfare* in South Africa exacerbates this problem. Co-ops set up in this way are destined to be temporary alternatives which either fail or collapse when membership finds other job options.

With the union initiating these projects, co-operatives' members tend to see the union as the new employer and develop a *dependency relationship* on the union. This does not assist with the long-term aims of co-operative development. Dependency on the union is also encouraged by unions wanting in some cases to both own and control these initiatives. The challenge facing unions in this regard is to assist in the development of co-operatives in such a way that they become financially and managerially independent and self-sufficient. Unions will have to think through the most appropriate structures in order to develop a relationship where the co-op and the union can be of mutual use to one another in the struggle to establish industrial democracy.

Links to the union also pose problems on decisions about wage levels. The union requires that there be some consistency between wages demanded in the sector and wages paid in the co-op. However, this places the union in a position of controlling the internal structure of the co-operative and therefore provides the potential for division between the co-operative members and the union.

One of the most difficult problems facing the unions, once the projects start up, is how to decide on who gets incorporated into the project initially and what criteria are used for this. It is very difficult to start up co-ops with large numbers of dismissed workers when there is limited funding. Having to choose a limited number of people could lead to divisions within the unemployed.

CONCLUSION

Although co-operatives face enormous difficulties and barriers to their short-term success, these recent initiatives begin to place worker co-operatives on the future political and

economic agenda. Experiments taking place at present will
clarify what is required from various support organisations
and what models are appropriate for co-operative development in South Africa. In addition the present experiences of
building co-operatives will also bring to the fore what recommendations should be made in the short-term and long-term
to secure support for co-operative economic development.
This development will succeed in the long-run only if it
genuinely empowers people. Maintaining the broad principles of the international co-operative movement will assist in
this process.

8

Glen Cormack

THE SACTWU* CO-OPERATIVE

INTRODUCTION

This paper attempts to detail the background to SACTWU's (South African Clothing and Textile Workers Union) entry into the co-operative segment of the economic market; the debate within the union surrounding the issues of worker control and skills; the structures within the co-operatives and its relationship with the union; the formation of the co-operative itself and a view of a future role for co-operatives in a more democratic environment.

BACKGROUND

As within most unions in South Africa, the debate on worker control of the production and distribution processes, is an ongoing one. ACTWUSA (Amalgamated Clothing and Textile Workers Union of South Africa), an affiliate to COSATU, was a result of a merger between three unions operating in the clothing and textile industry, viz, the National Union of Textile Workers, the National Union of Garment Workers and the Textile Workers Industrial Union. The merger was a move

---

* ACTWUSA initiated the co-operative described in this chapter, but subsequently merged with GAWU to form SACTWU. Although it is now correctly the SACTWU co-operative, ACTWUSA will be referred to where appropriate for purposes of historical accuracy.

towards creating one union covering the sector of textile, clothing and leather industries.

Subsequently ACTWUSA has merged with Garment and Allied Workers Union (GAWU) to form the South African Clothing and Textile Workers Union (SACTWU). Its membership of approximately 200 000 ranks it amongst the three largest affiliates to COSATU—the others being the National Union of Mineworkers and the National Union of Metalworkers of South Africa.

ACTWUSA, through one of its founder unions, the NUTW, had a highly documented and often extremely militant history with the Frame Group of employers—the largest employer in the Southern African textile industry. The history includes major strikes and legal actions, often setting precedents in the developing industrial relations arena.

What brought these debates to a head within ACTWUSA was the discovery by the union in September 1988 that Frame intended to retrench a massive 3 000 workers from its workforce of 22 000. This was after an undertaking by the Frame executive that it had no intention of retrenching any more workers after a large retrenchment exercise in the first half of 1988. In negotiations with Frame, ACTWUSA then secured a promise of a further cash settlement of R2,5m which would be used to start a job creation project for retrenched members, run by the union. This settlement was over and above the individual severance packages negotiated by ACTWUSA for its members already affected by retrenchment.

WORKER CONTROL IN INDUSTRY

ACTWUSA now had an opportunity to take the debate on worker control further. The leadership structures within the union debated the role of workers in a new society—one with a democratic government. What role would the workers take in the economy, which would still be in a developmental stage, requiring vast inputs of capital to accommodate a growing workforce? Was it not possible that workers would still remain units of labour dominated in the workplace by the owners of capital? How could workers take meaningful control of their work processes?

These debates led to the issue of co-operatives. Through union-run co-ops, members could learn the skills of running a business whilst starting to take control of a portion of the industry in which they worked. If successful, the co-operative movement could grow and take advantage of the vast developmental aid resources that could emanate from a government more dependent on the working class. The funds now available to the Homeland Development Corporations such as the KwaZulu, Ciskei and Transkei Development Corporations, as well as the Development Bank, could be channelled to more democratic organisations such as trade union co-operatives with a track record of successful management of substantial businesses.

The current decentralised schemes run by the government are more job-relocation exercises than job-creation projects. They have a history of corruption and exploitation, whilst also tending to last only as long as the state subsidies and incentives—funded by the taxpayer—last. This may be an unfair generalisation, but it is made to highlight that these state and quasi-state funds could be utilised more effectively to develop the co-operative sector of the economy. This sector has even received special mention in the ANC's constitutional guidelines, and would certainly 'fit' into a mixed economic environment—going a long way to creating a meaningful control of the economy by those participating in it.

Strengths and weaknesses of existing co-operatives

Once the decision to explore the possibility of entering the co-operative field was taken, the strengths and weaknesses of democratic co-operatives in South Africa were debated. While this is still a relatively small segment of the market, the following factors tend to apply:

Strengths
- Willingness of all the participants in the co-op to work for its success;
- Common goals throughout the structures of the co-op;
- Development of skills and self-empowerment;
- Creates jobs with less capital investment through minimum overhead costs;
- Democracy works.

Weaknesses
- Slow 'getting off the ground';
- Under-capitalised;
- No access to finance through customary channels;
- Become dependent on donors;
- Lack of experience in skills of finance, marketing and general management;
- Very little experience in decision-making in a co-ordinated factory environment;
- Employs small numbers of people;
- Normally does not increase in size;
- Benefits only the people involved in the co-ops;
- Makes no attempt to change the 'system' re capital and labour.

If co-ops could be formed effectively, they could initiate benefits to the workers involved in them, as well as workers generally, which could include:
- adding to the process of exercising greater influence over the process of production and distribution by gradually taking ownership of a meaningful slice of industry;
- creation of job opportunities in the absence of these being created by big capital and/or the government—under-

standing that it is for a government to create the environment that will foster industrial growth;
- creating the environment where democracy in the workplace becomes a meaningful reality;
- development of skills and self-empowerment for a far
  larger segment of the Black population than just a relatively small number of entrepreneurs.

SKILLS AND CO-OPERATIVE STRUCTURES

Again after further debate within the union structures, the
mandate was given to the National Executive Committee
(NEC) of the union to start a co-operative. Ways of overcoming the weaknesses inherent in the co-operative movement
were discussed and the decision was taken to employ persons
with the skills required to start a co-operative. Obviously such
persons would have to work in a democratic manner and with
a very clear brief to develop skills in those workers with the
potential to learn them.

Persons with skills in general management, marketing
and sales, and finance and production respectively were selected and employed. The issue of salary levels was and will
be a problem amongst skilled staff. Persons with the willingness to work for increased democracy for reasons other than
self-enrichment still need to be attracted to the co-operative
movement.

Criteria for selection of the actual workers to participate
in the co-op were set as follows:
- Applicants must have been union members before being
  retrenched from the Frame Group (initially membership
  was restricted to this group because the initial funding
  resulted from the negotiations between the union and
  Frame);
- union activists dismissed by the Frame Group for their
  union activity prior to NUTW gaining recognition;

• dependants of deceased union members where there was
  no breadwinner in the family.

The criteria on retrenched workers was subsequently wid-
ened to include any compulsorily retrenched member regardless of which company they had worked for. However, 90%
of the workers are ex-Frame. If applicants met the above
criteria, they underwent an eye and hand co-ordination, as
well as a colourblindness test. The successful applicants then
started a 10-week retraining course, while some of the unsuc-
cessful applicants were offered unskilled jobs, eg, cleaners,
packers, folders, etc. A total of 275 workers have been given
employment.

To train the workers in sewing skills, 10 people with
supervisory skills in the clothing industry were employed.
They underwent training in instructional techniques, and the
workers were then phased in 60 at a time. This process began
in March 1989 and is now complete.

Training took place on site, in the building rented by the
co-op in the industrial site of Jacobs. The building, 3 500 m²,
has now been rented for 10 years. Substantial alterations to
the building had to be made, amounting to costs of R500 000.
This was mainly to improve air-flows and lighting.

The structures in the co-op interact with the structures in
the union, thus ensuring a maximum participation by workers in the running of the co-op. These structures and their
inter-relationships are best depicted in figure 8.1.

The issue of discipline is a difficult one. Management in
the project does not have the right to dismiss workers. A
worker code of behaviour is in the process of being compiled,
together with workers' views of sanctions applicable. Once
consensus on the code and on sanctions is reached between
management and the workers, then discipline will be undertaken in terms of such code. Appeals against disciplinary
decisions can be directed to the Board of Trustees.

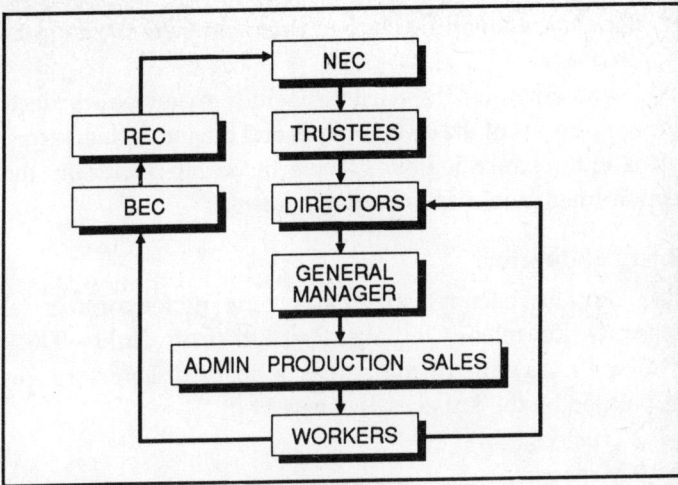

FIGURE 8.1
The structure of the SACTWU Co-operative

The National Executive Committee (NEC)

The NEC is comprised of the National Office bearers of the union, and the Regional Executive Committees from the respective regions. It is the highest decision-making body in the union. The NEC appointed a Board of Trustees to oversee the co-op, and a Trust Fund was established, viz, the Actwusa Employment Trust.

The board of trustees

The board comprises the following appointees:

- The President of Actwusa;
- The General Secretary;
- The National Organiser.

The following trustees were then elected from within the NEC:

- The Regional Secretaries (4);
- The Chairman of the Pinetown Branch (where the majority of the co-op workers were previously employed);

- The Chairman of the Durban Branch (where the co-op is situated).

Decisions taken by the trustees include major policy decisions; approval of the co-op budget and business plan; future plans ie the strategic issues facing the co-op, including the appointment and dismissal of managers.

Board of directors

The co-op has been registered as a company for commercial reasons—Zenzeleni Clothing (Pty) Ltd (from Zulu—'Do it Yourself'). As with all companies, a Board of Directors was appointed by the Trustees. It consists of:

- 2 Trustees;
- 2 Managers;
- 2 Senior shop stewards.

These three parties represent their respective interest groups, eg the shareholders, the managers, and the workers. Decisions taken at this level include the best method or plan for carrying out the strategic decisions made by the Trustees. Monthly reviews of trading accounts, etc are undertaken by the directors, which facilitates the full disclosure of financial and market environmental information.

Management

Again as with any other company, the normal management structures of general, sales, financial and production managers exist. They carry out the normal daily tasks of management, taking very short term, less risky decisions. Workers influence these decisions through their elected shop stewards, if such decisions affect the workers in their immediate workplace. The normal management/shop steward relationship applies, but is obviously not as adversarial as in other companies. The maxim 'We are in this together', really applies.

Management behave in a leading, coaching manner, as opposed to a control, instructional one.

Shop stewards' structures

Workers elect shop stewards to represent their interests on a departmental basis. The Committee then elect a senior and vice-senior steward—these two being appointed to the Board of Directors. The senior shop steward is also appointed to the Branch Executive Committee of the union. He/she can be elected by the BEC to represent the Branch at the Regional Executive Committee. Likewise, he/she can be elected by the REC to represent the Region at the National Executive Committee.

As stated, the NEC elects the Board of Trustees, who in turn appoint the managers, and the lines of control become clear.

THE MARKET AND THE FUTURE

The decision to enter the clothing industry was taken within the reality of the need to participate in a labour intensive industry; the natural alliance a textile and clothing union has with the industry; the promise of the Frame Group, a major supplier of clothing material, to treat the co-op on a preferential customer basis; and the relatively low cost of machinery-to-labour ratio.

A survey of the clothing market was commissioned, which highlighted the pitfalls inherent in the market for a newcomer. In examining what competitive edge the co-op could capitalise on, it was natural to align ourselves with the market in which what the worker wears, is paramount—hence workwear. Likewise, the decision to make T-shirts for the union market was relatively easy to arrive at.

The logo 'Made for the workers—by the workers', was developed and will be the major marketing vehicle the co-op will use. A 'Union' label will highlight this logo, which hopefully will develop a pull effect on our sales drive.

In addition, emphasis is placed on quality and service, with the garments carrying a 3-month guarantee on workmanship. Ten workers have been appointed as quality examiners, and are undergoing training in quality control through the Industry Training Board. The co-op will computerise its production and financial information systems and again this will create skills development opportunities.

With the development and branding of the 'Union' label, it is feasible that this may develop opportunities for entry into the manufacture and distribution of other consumable items for the working class segment of the market.

THE ROLE OF THE FRAME GROUP

This paper would not be complete without including the role the Frame Group of companies has played. The initial undertakings by the Frame executive included:

- an 'up-front' payment of R2,5m;
- material supply agreement which included preferential pricing and delivery arrangements;
- favourable credit facilities covering both credit ceiling and period;
- assistance with marketing problems.

the project started on these undertakings—machinery was ordered at a price of R1,1m and changes to the building were commissioned. They insisted on phasing the payment to the union over an 18-month period, which would meet the cash flow needs of the project. The phasing would be as follows:

R600 000 in February 1989;

R200 000 in June 1989;

R600 000 in July 1989;

R500 000 in January 1990; and

R600 000 in July 1990.

In addition they would guarantee a R500 000 overdraft facility covering the period May to September 1989.

The immediate result was the fact that the machinery, which was already delivered, could not be paid for. Zenzeleni had to raise a commercial loan, at prime rates, to pay for it. Then Frame started delaying material deliveries, and in fact did not supply the first two months' orders causing the project to have to buy material to premium prices for cash—making a bad cash-flow situation worse.

After changes in the Frame Executive took place, the situation worsened. The overdraft facility has still not been granted,* nor has the July payment of R600 000 been paid in full. While the union would prefer the matter to be settled amicably, it has let the current Frame executive know that if the situation is not rectified, it will be forced to take some form of action to safeguard the project.

CONCLUSION

SACTWU's entry into the field of co-operative organisations should be seen as an evolving one. It is a meaningful attempt to come to grips with the management of business, to learn the lessons inherent in such a process whilst simultaneously fighting to bring about change in the greater socio-economic arena.

This change will include greater control of the production process by workers, and these lessons cannot be left to be learnt only after a more democratic government comes to power.

SACTWU has started with this process, knowing full well that it must retain a certain amount of flexibility so as to cater for the democratic nature of co-operatives and union structures. On-going attention needs to be given to the aspect of

* As at August 1989.

education of members in the objectives being strived for, as well as the skills required to realise such objectives.

The question of wage levels within co-operatives will also be a focal point in the immediate future, especially if one considers the need to utilise profits to create further co-operatives and more job opportunities. With success will come growth, and there will be a need to explore the export market so as not to threaten the local job market of other participants in the clothing industry.

While co-operatives may not create enough jobs to overcome the growing unemployment problem in South Africa, Zenzeleni's experience, although limited, indicates that jobs in co-operatives could be created at a third of the cost of that of jobs in the current government's decentralisation schemes.

Finally, democratic workplaces should complement democratic government and democratic unions. Unity between these three organisations could address a major share of the problems facing the people of this country.

9

Brian Smith

VOLKSWAGEN'S HOLISTIC APPROACH TO WORKER PARTICIPATION

I make no claim to be an expert in Industrial Relations. At a recent VW seminar overseas, run by Tom Peters (who wrote *In Search of Excellence* and the book which is very appropriate in South Africa, *Thriving on Chaos*) he stated that there is no such thing as an expert in the world today. Things are changing so quickly that anyone who holds himself up as an 'expert' needs to be seriously questioned. This is especially true in labour relations in South Africa today, because what was the right answer yesterday is not the right answer today, and what is the right answer in one place might not be the right answer in another place. So I certainly do not present any recipe for labour peace. What is happening at our plant today (strike action) proves that. My company is, however, committed to a process of worker participation despite the pitfalls along the way, and we have addressed it on two levels: the industrial relations level, involving the trade union, and more recently on the shop-floor level, in the area of direct worker involvement with programmes which address the worker as an individual or in his work group, rather than as part of a collective relationship between management and union.

This paper will describe some of the background to Volkswagen SA, some of the difficulties we face, our philosophies and visions and, lastly, some practical examples of what we are trying to do in the people field. The first part of the address will in the form of an introduction to Volkswagen—because if anyone is going to look at worker participation and ask

'Could this work in my company?' they need to know a little bit about the background of the company in which it might be working or the company in which things are being tried.

A PROFILE OF VWSA

The company employs 8 300 employees, mostly situated on one large site in Uitenhage. That in itself does not make life easy—to run a large factory on one site and to co-ordinate over 8 000 people. In South African terms we unfortunately always have to look at the racial situation. As much as we like to wish it away—it exists. Some 29 % of our total work force is white, some 25 % so-called 'coloured' people and nearly half of the workforce is black. The black workforce comprises mainly young workers. Volkswagen grew tremendously in the late 70s and early 80s with the introduction of the Golf and phenomenal market growth in the last few years has again led to rapid growth in employment. As a consequence a lot of new labour has been hired—young people—and VW now has a mix of workers who were brought in, in the early 80s—the schoolboys hardened on the unrest of 76, and more recently another group of youngsters hardened on the unrest of the early 80s. The company has a very low labour turnover, and as a result a very stable workforce. Many people have been with us for a long time.

Two trade unions operate at the plant—NUMSA (the National Union of Metal Workers of SA) and the SA Iron Steel & Allied Industries Union, representing only white workers. NUMSA, a non-racial union, has three white part-time shop stewards and a number of white members in the plant. I believe it might be the only plant in South Africa where there are white part-time shop stewards representing NUMSA. Roughly 80 % of the workforce is unionised.

VW has progressed through a number of *phases of industrial relations*. Up to about 1979, employee relations at Volk-

swagen were characterised by management dominance. In
those days, wages were hardly negotiated, they were largely
granted, based on the fact that we were behind a subsistence
level as indicated by the EEC Code. Additionally, we were
influenced by our American colleagues in Port Elizabeth—
Ford and General Motors in those days, and as the HSL or
MSL moved, in terms of the Sullivan code, with great paternalism we handed out more money to the workforce. No real
negotiation—if anyone gave us any trouble, we showed them
the gate and out they went. My production colleagues, I am
sure, think back on those days with fond memories of how
they could spend the whole day worrying about production
and very little time worrying about labour relations.

In 1980, Volkswagen had the now famous three-week
'Living Wage' strike. Starting with this 1980 dispute, VW
entered a phase of real union–management conflict, and although the dates are not definitive, between 1980 and about
1986 labour relations at Volkswagen was characterised by
strike action. I think of our advertising slogan of today, 'Isn't
that what you'd expect from Volkswagen?'—in those days
people expected labour unrest!

From about 1986, the situation started to improve mainly
as a result of a clearer philosophy of where we were going,
and through greater worker participation and involvement of
the union. The company entered a phase of greater institutionalisation of conflict. A phase where more emphasis was
placed on negotiation and there developed an acceptance of
the mutual interdependence between management and
union. This does not mean that today labour relations on the
shopfloor is easy. It is still punctuated by industrial action.
The environment of Uitenhage and the Eastern Cape has
never been easy, but it has certainly moved away from the
very destructive conflict of the mid-80s period. Of course the
difficult factor remains political issues and political conflict. I

believe our current labour problem was certainly sparked by a wage issue, but there is no doubt that it is linked to the political climate as we run down to the 6th of September 1989 (General Election Day). From a purely company labour relations point of view, we have come a long way, but we still operate in an *environment of political instability*.

Locally, the Eastern Cape townships remain highly politicised. It is well-documented that the growth of black political expression and black political thought developed here in the Eastern Cape. For example, the tragic shooting in Langa of twenty people took place in Uitenhage. The first necklace murders in South Africa, took place in the township of Kwanobuhle in Uitenhage. Some of the most influential black political figures in the country come from this region. In Uitenhage we have a very conservative white work force. There is a very good chance that the Conservative Party could capture Uitenhage as a seat in the coming General Election.* So on the one hand we have a politicised black work force, and on the other a conservative white work force. As a result of the concentration of heavy industry in the Port Elizabeth/Uitenhage area, it was always a very strong base for NAAWU in the early days and today, of course, for COSATU. The president of NUMSA is employed by a factory in Uitenhage, and VW's chief shop steward is a vice-president of COSATU. So COSATU and NUMSA have a strong power-base, particularly in Uitenhage.

Obviously, Volkswagen being a wholly-owned subsidiary of VW in Germany, we have to be mindful of the *international political environment*. I do not need to tell anyone that South Africa is a very sensitive subject overseas. The situation has improved a lot recently with the move of Namibia to independence, and better relationships with our neigh-

* The CP subsequently did win the Uitenhage seat.

bours, but South Africa remains a sensitive issue. At the moment we are involved in negotiations surrounding the IG Metall/IMF minimum standards or Fourteen Points for German companies, which I think is a very positive development, and could lead to some positive trends in our labour relations. And of course as Brian Robinson, my colleague has explained (Chapter 3), at Volkswagen in Germany, the president of the IG Metall—the massive German Metalworkers Union, is always a member of the Volkswagen Supervisory Board. So obviously, there is a certain sensitivity about Volkswagen's operation in South Africa. Not that we are ever told how to run labour relations by our colleagues in Germany. They want to be kept informed, but they do not tell us what to do.

Another factor is our *labour relations history*. Volkswagen, and the other multi-nationals in the Eastern Cape, have a long history of formal labour relations. Volkswagen and companies like Ford recognised trade unions representing black workers in about the mid-seventies, which means we have some fourteen or fifteen years of experience of dealings with them. It also means that longserving unionists in this area are very experienced. It was only in the early 80s that unions representing black workers really emerged in most companies in the Transvaal. In 1979, a group of VW shop stewards and managers toured VW and Audi factories in Europe to look at the labour relations systems in those factories. Coming out of that visit, in 1980 we introduced the concept of full-time shop stewards. In recent years in South Africa, this has become quite an important demand at a lot of negotiating tables. As a matter of interest, a number of our shop stewards are still the original people who became full-time shop stewards in 1980, so they are very experienced trade unionists, and in fact in the early eighties, that crisis period I have mentioned, were far more experienced than many of us managers. Today, I think both sides have become a lot more professional.

Enough about the background to Volkswagen South Africa and some of the influences on our labour relations. I shall now address some of the developments and systems which have helped to create the current climate of greater worker participation at VWSA.

NEW VISION

In 1986, we started to crystallise our thinking on where we needed to go as a company. In the early eighties, Volkswagen was riding the crest of a wave. We had about 20 % of the market. By 1984 our share of the market had dropped to 10 % as we were, quite frankly, in a very desperate situation. We really needed to do something urgently. We spent a lot of time as a management, under the direction of Peter Searle, our MD, trying to focus on where we were going and what we stood for. A lot of time was spent developing *a company mission statement and core values*. Our core values are: outstanding quality, total commitment to customer service, and trust and respect for the individual. This may sound trite and simple, but a great deal of work was put into discussing and communicating those core values. Clinics were held, and a lot of actions were built around ensuring we would live these values. They did give the company a lot more focus and direction, in all areas, including labour relations.

At the same time we spent a lot of time talking about an *industrial relations philosophy*. Basically, Volkswagen subscribes to the pluralist model of industrial relations, which acknowledges that management and workers will pursue different interests. However, we believe these differences can be resolved by a system of collective bargaining that will allow some balance of power or equilibrium to be reached. This model recognises the legitimate role of the trade union in helping to resolve the natural conflict in a constructive manner. For the system to work effectively, negotiations must take place between strong and representative groups who have the ability to honour agreements and build relationships of mutual trust.

I believe the last part of this philosophy is very important: *negotiations must take place between strong and representative groups, who have the ability to honour agreements and build relationships of mutual trust.* Here, I don't want to be influenced by our recent strike experience, but I suspect that as a result of the political environment in the country over the past eighteen months, even some of our big, strong trade unions are experiencing some confusion in direction and consequent loss of control over membership in the honouring of agreements. I think it is something that the trade union movement is going to have to give some thought to in a changing South Africa. Perhaps clearer strategic direction is required, but far be it from me to give advice to experienced trade unionists.

INDUSTRIAL RELATIONS AT VWSA

What characterises industrial relations at Volkswagen? In trying to make our pluralist philosophy work, we have attempted to adhere to certain basic principles of industrial relations. The system is built on a very *high level of shop steward involvement.* Volkswagen has seven full-time shop stewards, and approximately thirty part-time shop stewards from both unions. These shop stewards, through a system of committees and other mechanisms, are very involved in the business of the company. The shop stewards are involved with just about everything that happens in the company, based on a *system of prior consultation.* For example, when we bring in a new model, the workers and the shop stewards are told about this; when we reorganise the factory, we have presentations by engineering people to the shop stewards; explain to them

what we are doing, why we are bringing in different processes, etc. We have also, over the years, developed an approach of *negotiation and compromise*. Sometimes it is quite
difficult for the management side to understand that everything needs to be negotiated and there is probably a thin line
between compromise and capitulation. But I believe it is
important, if you are going to have a pluralist philosophy, to
understand that negotiation does involve compromise. If you
look at the situation in Namibia, and Angola, I think the South
African government has really learned there. Even the military authorities have learned, what real negotiation and compromise is all about. If you are going to get to lasting solutions
you have got to have hard negotiation and there has got to be
some compromise on both sides. White management in South
Africa often has a real fear that compromise is capitulation.
We have got to overcome that fear.

Related to this is a need for an understanding of the *power
reality*. Again I am not saying that we must become like a
rabbit when faced by a snake, viz that we believe the union is
all-powerful and just freeze. On the other hand, there are
many examples, tragic examples, of companies that have not
really thought through the power reality. Labour relations,
like politics, is all about power. If you don't understand
power, you don't understand politics or labour relations. I
think it is very important that companies clearly assess their
own power realities and the power reality of the union. I
believe that South African managements have a much more
healthy relationship with COSATU and NACTU unions
today, where both sides have power and they are prepared to
use that power. No-one is ashamed of it. It is a play of
power—as long as that power does not become really destructive, and we do not destroy the system in the process. That is
the important thing to watch out for as, in the long run,
management and unions need each other and this interde-

pendence is going to grow more important in a changing South Africa.

Finally, a *procedural and structural base* is needed to make the system work. It has got to be based on negotiated procedures and some sort of structure. For example, procedures which set out how shop stewards will operate, how grievances will be handled, etc. They should be clear but not totally rigid. They must be understood by everyone and, for the system to work, they must be applied consistently to everyone. One of the strong points in our company system is that, because the shop stewards have been there such a long time, they have been involved in negotiating all the procedures. They understand them and participated in their development. They sometimes have some difficulty getting the workers to stick to procedures, but I believe the union is basically committed to them.

We need to address the *worker as in individual* because he comes to work as an individual, with a lot of individual problems, but we also need to address the worker collectively. In my experience, at different times, a worker approaches a company as an individual, he has individual crises—a death, a funeral, he needs transport, he needs housing assistance, he has legal problems, and there he is looking for, and wants, individual help from his company. However, in the event of a mass dispute, he is not interested in that. *He is part of a collective organisation*, which is very strong, very motivated, because that is the only place where he gets any collective power. His only power lies in his labour and his growing purchasing power. He does not get it through the ballot box. So we have got to address these two issues—the worker as an individual and the worker as part of a group, i e the union.

At VW we are trying to develop, together with our pluralist labour relations philosophy, certain basic people philosophies or values. We see this as part of a holistic approach to IR issues. Things like *trust and respect for the individual*. These are not easy to obtain in South Africa. For over 40 years, we have lived apart, we have been schooled apart—we have done everything apart and been socialized to accept this as normal. Now at VW we come and talk about trust and respect. We must trust each other; we must respect each other. It is against difficult odds, then, that we at VW we are trying to work towards a system of trust and respect for the individual. Of course in South Africa, that has got to go hand in hand with non-racialism and equality of opportunity. Again, easy things to say, but not that easy to achieve, given 40 years of social engineering designed to keep us apart and to create mistrust.

Another issue is *people empowerment*. By people empowerment, we do not necessarily mean we are going to help people to bring on the revolution sooner, as the CP seems to believe. We really mean involving people, training people, developing people. Empowering people to take their own decisions, to do things for themselves, and that comes through a process of sharing information, delegation, training and allowing people to become involved. Allowing people to grow and develop to their full potential.

We are also striving for a *a common vision* of the future and some sort of shared set of values. This is not easy. We have spent a lot of time trying to build or develop this, and it is not easy in South Africa. But at company level and also at the national political level, we have got to develop such a vision of the future that everyone can say: 'I share that vision, and I can move forward with that vision.' At VWSA we have started programmes through which we hope to be able to develop some sort of common vision.

At the centre of this vision is the concept of a *VW family*. It may sound paternalistic, but I think it is a powerful uniting force if used properly. Recent research we did in the company shows that the average worker really buys into the concept of a VW family. He says, 'That is something I can identify with; I like that concept'. It does not mean he is renouncing his membership of the union or that he has now capitulated and is selling out to management, or something like that. It appears to have support among individual workers, particularly the concept of: 'I come here, this place is my home, people help me here when I have a problem.' Together with the pluralist philosophy, we are trying to build up a set of values of this kind in the company. This philosophy must not, however, be used to undermine the union.

SOME PRACTICAL STEPS

I would now like to outline some of the projects that we are undertaking in this area. They are aimed at worker empowerment and building the VW family around a common vision. Most of these projects are run by line managers with their own people.

1   In every area major production of the company we have *Information Centres* where the advertising that goes with the product is displayed. The product is displayed there for workers who want to come and look at a new model—for instance on our Microbus Kombi line the new Syncro 4-wheel-drive bus would be displayed—a finished vehicle for workers to look at. Also included in these areas are pictures of the foreman, the shop stewards, pictures of operators who have had a birthday, etc, and all sorts of information on quality, productivity, company performance and events. The purpose is to share information with production workers, information about people, production, products and so on.

2   Another tool we are using is the whole issue of problem-solving groups. We call these *Achievement Groups*. We have an active Achievement Group programme which includes training in problem-solving techniques and these

groups select and solve problems. A number of staff groups, are in place and we are slowly getting more hourly groups involved.

3   We recently introduced a number of *Recognition Events and Awards*. As Tom Peters says, 'you need to celebrate, share and recognise people', and the idea is to give to workers who have done good things, small awards, small functions with the emphasis on recognition, letters of congratulation, etc. Supervisors organise a bit of a get-together where people can have a few drinks and get to know each other. It really works and I do not believe that the trade union feels threatened by this. They tend to have taken a neutral stance in a lot of these things, and say: 'We will not interfere with it, as it is not a threat to us.' I think they know the company is not trying to undermine the union by doing any of this. If it were management's intention to undermine the union with these activities, they would be dead before they started; the union would see to that.

4   Another activity we have introduced—and are starting to introduce on all our assembly lines, is the Japanese concept of *Jidoka*—the ability to stop the line. On the side of the line there is a button where the worker, if he has a problem with parts or quality or a part that will not fit, can push the button and that will stop the production line. If he stops the line it will flash up onto a big board, showing what work station he is at and what the problem is, and a team will go in there and assist him with the problem. I can assure you that in a motor company, to let someone stop the line is a major step forward. In the old days if someone stopped the line and he was not the superintedent on that line, he was fired; there was no question about it. This is again a new way of doing business and it is a major step forward and another exciting area of change we are moving into. Obviously it is tied up with our

commitment to total quality. If you really are going to build quality, and something will not fit, rather than forcing it or doing it incorrectly, stop the line. Very importantly, it gives people power over their own jobs; it says, We trust you, we trust your judgement enough to allow you to stop the production line. It requires a new management attitude and commitment to worker empowerment.

We try to give as much *feed-back* as possible to all employees. We have recently built an auditorium at the plant where we hold regular information sessions, regular feedback talks; we send out a quarterly 'state of the nation' letter from the MD to all workers setting out how we have done, what our objectives are for the next quarter, etc. We have a lot of notices up around the plant, covering general information such as giving employees times that new adverts will be flighted, announcing when Sarel van der Merwe is going to be racing the Audi Turbo and when it can be seen on TV. The aim is to get employees to identify with the product and the company. The aim is total communication and not only the 'must know' but the 'nice to know' things you should tell the whole family, the things we told only the managers in the old days.

6   Another activity is the *team talks in the morning* at the start of production. We tried it some time back and it did not work too well. We are re-introducing the idea of a team talk in the morning where the workers would report for the first ten minutes to the foreman's office, and review what has to be done for the day, what the target is and what had been achieved the previous day. It provides a chance for the foreman just to talk to the workers and sort out any work or domestic problems before the line starts.

7   Another interesting thing we introduced a few years ago, was the concept of a *year-end show*. It is really a big Christmas party. We clear out a huge warehouse and all 8 000

employees gather there, but rather than just a band, our marketing division have had a show developed with a cross-cultural theme. The theme of the show is that we need to live together and understand each other in South Africa and inside VW; the emphasis is on cross-cultural music, and usually a humorous show written around Volkswagen, with the emphasis on black/white mixing and the breaking down of racial barriers. The aim is to build the VW Family and to break down barriers between levels and races.

8   A vital issue in South Africa is that of the *black/white interface* and the cultural and political issues which arise at this level. We have started a series of workshops where black and white workers, supervisors and managers meet and discuss issues of concern, not only work issues but political issues as well, and try to build up better understanding and eliminate some of the prejudice and fear. It is early days but I think these groups are very important. We can no longer ignore white fears and black aspirations.

9   In recent years we have also done a lot of *research* into employee attitudes and concerns. Professor Kamfer from UPE has spent three months with us doing research into employee attitudes and employee understanding of our three core values. Coming out of that, every manager and supervisor will have an action plan to implement corrective action where problems were highlighted.

These are some the 'actions' we believe will build a strong VW Family, based on a philosophy of trust and respect. We believe this forms a part of our labour relations philosophy, and complements the pluralist labour relations philosophy.

To return to the industrial relations area, employee representation at Volkswagen is very much built on the shop steward system at the shop-floor level. At this level we have the two unions with two full-time shop stewards for Iron and

Steel, and six full-time shop stewards for NUMSA. They have a full-time shop steward for every 750 members. At plant level we have a number of joint union-management committees, which I will cover in some detail below. These committees are not negotiating forums, but there is detailed discussion on company strategy, philosophy and company policy and procedure. Traditionally we used to negotiate wages and conditions of service in a Regional Industrial Council. From this year, the direction is towards a national negotiation forum. So we see labour relations operating on the shop-floor, at plant level and at a regional level and possibly, in the future, at a national level.

To come back to the committee system. The major mechanism of joint union–management communications at a senior level is what we call the *Joint Union Management Executive Committee*, which meets quarterly. The chairmanship of the committee alternates between union and management. The committee consists of the Managing Director, Directors, key Production Management and the full-time Shop Stewards from both unions. The purpose of this committee is to discuss corporate strategic issues. The committee discusses, for instance, the company's five-year plan which is presented every year to the parent company in Germany. Our five-year model range planning is discussed with that committee. All major corporate issues are open for discussion. At the same time the company gets feedback from the union on their attitude to things like the Labour Relations Act, political developments and major corporate issues. We have had some very heated debates in that committee—no holds barred. These debates often range across company issues and national political issues and the company's attitude to these. It has been going for about two years, and we have found it a very positive development.

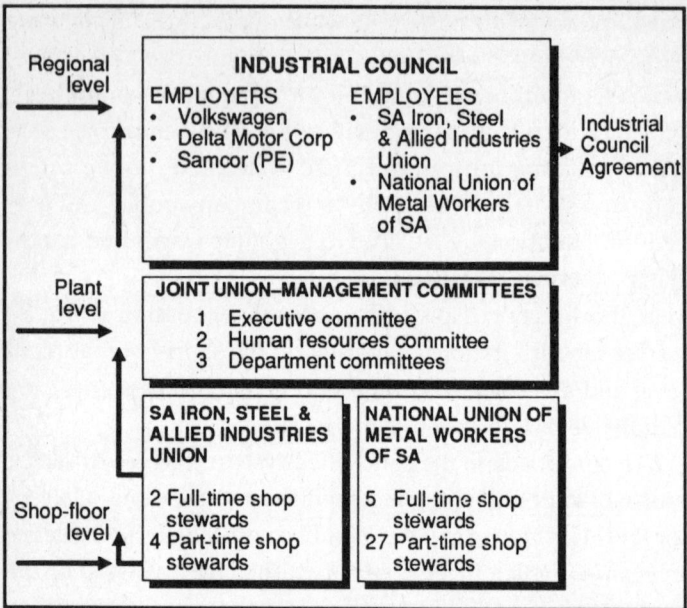

FIGURE 9.1
Employee representation at Volkswagen of South Africa

At the next level we have what is called a *Human Resources Committee* where all the department managers in the Human Resources Division, and the full-time shop stewards meet to discuss policy and procedure on all people issues. Issues such as training, advancement, recruitment, health and safety, are discussed, debated and agreed.

At the third level we have *Joint Union/Management Department Committees* for each major department such as the paint shop, assembly, etc, where all major production-related department managers, senior supervisors and shop stewards (full and part-time) for that area, meet to discuss all issues affecting the worker. In some areas these committees are working well. In other areas, where some of the shop stewards are not that effective, they are not working that well.

The idea is that these committees would discuss production targets, hours of work, production problems, training, people, facilities, relationships, etc. Some years ago we introduced a *quarterly Finance and Marketing Review*, attended by all shop stewards where the Finance and Marketing Director give a full financial and market presentation on how the company is doing. A full discussion on our financial position is entered into; our full balance-sheet is disclosed, as well as a full discussion on the market, where we stand and what our plans are.

	TABLE 9.1		
	JOINT UNION–MANAGEMENT COMMUNICATION STRUCTURES		
1.	Joint union/management executive committee (quarterly)	MD, directors and full-time shop stewards.	Corporate strategic issues.
2.	Human resources committee (quarterly)	HR department managers and full-time shop stewards.	Policy and procedure on all people issues.
3.	Department committees (monthly)	All major production related departments, management, senior supervision and shop stewards.	All issues affecting the workers.
4.	Finance/marketing review (quarterly)	All shop stewards.	Full financial and market disclosure.
5.	VW community trust.	Managers	Shop stewards and workers.

Last year we introduced the *VW Community Trust*. The company set aside some seven million rand to establish a trust, which is run by a limited number of managers, one shop steward representative from each union and representatives selected from the workforce. The unions put forward names of workers who are active in community affairs and they become trustees. The trustees have full responsibility for all community and social responsibility expenditure, and make all the decisions as to how that money should be spent and allocated. Our experience has been that a lot of those worker representatives, when spending R20 000, think about it a lot more responsibly than some of us managers who may think: 'Should we worry too much about R20 000?.' We were also concerned that this money might be channelled in political directions. Up to now the money has been used very responsibly on community projects in Uitenhage and Port Elizabeth, and the value has been that the people who serve on the Trust live in and are active in these communities, and know where and how the money should be spent. This is preferable to management agonising over these decisions, with hundreds of requests from different organisations and very little knowledge of who really needs help the most and, which is very important, which organisations have community legitimacy.

SOME CONCLUDING THOUGHTS

I have tried to share some of the things we are doing at Volkswagen. I must emphasise again—we are not doing everything right. We have not got all the answers—we certainly do not have an easy passage in the labour relations area, but we are committed to this process despite setbacks such as occasional industrial action, and we are determined to move forward with it. We have in fact indicated to the trade union that we would have no problem with some sort of system of worker representation at board level, which we would see as another step towards a system of co-determination based on a pluralist system of labour relations within the context of a

VW Family. In closing, I would like make certain very brief observations:

For real worker participation, or as the Germans call it, co-determination, to really work in South Africa and when I say really work, I mean to move beyond Quality Circles, Briefing Groups and Joint Union–Management Committees, to full participation, i e some type of industrial democracy, we need a total rethink on the part of management and trade union leadership.

Through genuine worker participation, we can build companies into non-racial democracies, based on equality, trust and respect; we can make our companies models of what most of us would like South Africa to be. But like building a new South Africa, this is going to require from both sides (black and white, management and union), leadership, discipline, vision and some risk-taking.

On the management side, we are going to have to enter the risky area of politics; we are going to have to address management prerogative and worker control. On the union side, we are going to have to start working with the 'bosses' and not blame them for all the problems in the company or the country. Unions are going to have to distinguish between progressive and repressive managements, they can no longer just lump all management together and blame all the problems on them.

Management can do only half the participating; there has got to be commitment from both sides for worker participation to work. If we are going to build an industrial democracy, we will need strong companies and strong trade unions that accept their mutual interdependence.

Without fear of co-option or the loss of management prerogative, management and labour have got to set joint objectives to ensure the success and growth of individual companies and the trade union movement. In the move to a new South Africa, business and the union movement is going to face certain threats and I believe both parties could ensure their long-term survival through a system of co-determination which produces companies run as a partnership between management and labour, who, while they have different short and medium-term goals, both have the long-term goal of strong and prosperous companies within a strong and growing economy. Management and labour cannot wish each other away but need to be very careful that they don't kill each other in their fight against apartheid. We might find we should have been fighting on the same side. Divide and rule has allowed apartheid to survive for over 40 years. I believe a strong union movement, together with strong companies committed to an industrial democracy within a new South Africa, could achieve much more than any armed struggle or boycott politics.

10

Steve Dewar

TOTAL WORKER INVOLVEMENT AT TOYOTA

THE MEANING OF WORKER PARTICIPATION

Worker participation is a phrase which has a buzz connotation at the moment and means different things to different people. There is a fashionable regard for worker participation with very wide variations of how it is perceived by a wide variety of people. Unfortunately many of that self-same spectrum of people fail to recognise the people element of worker participation. It is mistakenly regarded as a modern managerial technique of getting the highest possible productivity from workers and therefore it is removed from the involvement of the workforce. The object of these employers is to get more for less.

I have never liked the terms 'Worker Participation Programme' or 'Worker Involvement Programme' and prefer *Total Worker Involvement Programme*. There is a classical Japanese saying: 'Darkness reigns at the foot of the lighthouse'. No time shall be wasted explaining its meaning as it pertains to everyday Japanese life. The Toyota version of what the saying means is slightly different. The Japanese criticise Western management for a tendency to manage from the top down, forcing thinking, ideas, concepts and even prejudice down to the shop floor through managers and supervision. Therefore Toyota's definition of 'Darkness reigns at the foot of the lighthouse' is just that.

We see the lighthouse as a company and the light shining from the top as management, attracting the attention of shareholders, customers, financial institutions, the Press, and the public at large. The column of the lighthouse representing the organisational structure from senior management downward. As one descends the organisational ladder, so the darkness deepens until the shop floor is reached where darkness reigns supreme. The darkness of neglect, the darkness of poor communication, the darkness of ignorance. All this creates the now traditional mistrust of motive. As the bottom of the organisation is in the state of darkness as to management's thinking, equally so is management blinded by its own brilliance, unable to see the needs and aspirations of those condemned to the darkness.

In this paper some of the Toyota total involvement programmes in operation at present will be addressed before concentrating on two of these, namely Siyacabanga and Quality Circles. Total worker involvement programmes at Toyota have been generated by various systems used company-wide which encourage total involvement at all levels, ranging from the operator to director. These programs utilise both accepted practices and uniquely developed Toyota applications and have proved successful not only by quantifiable means but also by employee self-realisation and development. The aim of the programme is to create thinking people.

KEY ELEMENTS OF THE TOTAL WORKER INVOLVEMENT PROGRAMME AT TOYOTA

Eyakho (your own) is a quality programme whereby individuals investigate and resolve problems affecting their area caused by a preceding operation.

Kaizen (improvement) is a management-overseen group activity involved with the elimination of waste to achieve savings other than labour standard reduction.

Jishuken (by myself, investigate) is a management-driven group activity using basic method study techniques to reduce labour standards through the elimination of waste.

Quality circles is a group activity, using step by step problem-solving techniques. The problems selected are of the groups' own choice encompassing quality, cost reduction, safety, maintenance, and workplace improvements.

Siyacabanga (we think) is a quality of work life programme whereby individuals effect improvements within their area of responsibility to the advantage of their subordinates or themselves.

QUALITY CIRCLES

Toyota has never enjoyed dwelling on the past and has resolved to leave old memories alone. There is nothing to be gained from brooding over the past and we prefer instead to make a clean break and set our sights squarely on the road ahead. However, for purposes of this discussion, it is necessary to relate our experience several years ago before the light dawned. One of the objectives in the Management by Objectives programme was the establishment of Quality Circles. It is interesting to bear in mind that Quality Circles did not originate in Japan, nor at Toyota. During the 1930s there was an attempt to introduce the concept of worker involvement and Quality Circles into American industry. However, due to the total lack of management–worker involvement, it was an abysmal failure. In 1946 an American army lieutenant stationed in Japan attempted to introduce Quality Circles into Japanese manufacturing. The objectives and aims of the programme were explained and debated and on obtaining acceptance there was no looking back. There had been an immense amount of time spent in deliberation between management and workers.

Further attempts were made to introduce Quality Circles into American companies but the symptoms were familiar—the good QC strategy was not well executed. Costs rose out of all proportion to gains in productivity—high rates of absenteeism persisted—and a disaffected workforce, taking little pride or pleasure in what it did, retarded innovation and quality improvements. To those at the top of the corporate ladder, it seemed as if they were the captains of a ship in which the wheel is not connected to the rudder. Whatever decisions were made, little happened below. However, they had once again fallen into the trap of a top-heavy management with little communication with the workforce or employees.

In conjunction with our Japanese colleagues, we highlighted this shortcoming and attempted to avoid it in the South African context. We saw that for survival and success of a worker involvement programme, *the top manager* in the organisation or at the particular site of the organisation that is launching a total involvement programme had to be committed to the programme, including its philosophy, its intended multiple outcomes and its structure and process requirements. Even more, *senior management had to be personally involved* in the programme and its steering committee. This is the most important single factor in determining success in Toyota's experience. *Total worker involvement is a philosophy of management, a process and a set of outcomes.* It is a *philosophy of management* that believes that every employee has the ability and the right to offer intelligent and useful inputs into decisions at various levels of the organisation. Total worker involvement is a *process* to involve employees at every level of the organisation in decisions about their work and workplaces. It refers to the *intended outcomes* of practising this philosophy and process with improvements in working conditions, environment, and practices, and in the general climate or culture of the workplace. Total worker involvement also brings *organisational benefits* of cost reduction, quality improvements and personal development benefits which are also integral parts of the working life concept.

Accordingly, Toyota SA originally set about the introduction of Quality Circles with very little regard to the background, identity, and likes and dislikes of its employees in organisational makeup. The resolve was to get a group of guys together, sit them down in a room and get the foreman to lead the group, give them a list of quality defects and tell them to get on with the job. Then sit back and wait for the results. There were no results. We ascertained that there were a number of reasons for this failure. The education level was not high enough. There were cultural differences—Japanese versus Europe and Africa. Quality Circles would work well in other industries, but not in the automobile assembly industry as it was too complicated. In other words all the old excuses. We gave up. For 3 long years, we made an attempt— for 3 long years, we failed. Should Toyota be likened to the Japanese lighthouse, then there would have been many shipwrecks. However the production director attended a Quality Circle course at Toyota Japan, and there he saw the light. *The only path to enlightenment is education and training.*

In regard to education—what does it mean? We arrive in this world without any instruction manual. It is a good thing to be schooled in memory and authority-orientated subjects such as multiplication tables, history, science, reading, writing and arithmetic. But that is purely academic. Toyota sees that education actually means a leading out of mental darkness into enlightenment, training and thinking laterally, familiarity and certainty in doing, analysis rather than dogma. It also means preliminary training, actual training in and being able to demonstrate the basic simplicities upon which complexities are built so that one can return to these when necessary. Education is no sacred cow. It should go hand in hand with schooling and then continue to a definite finished product.

Toyota accelerated its literacy training programmes in order to ensure that all workers and employers were literate in at least one language, either English or Zulu. The intention is to enable the employee to become at least Zulu literate so that he or she could improve his or her total worker involvement and thereby quality of working life.

Given a high level of literacy at Toyota, we can learn through a step by step procedure. Toyota is beginning to let light pass from the bottom to top and top to bottom. A navigation expert would shudder at the waste—but what a magnificent beacon the lighthouse now is!

There is a saying that nothing succeeds like success. This is true of Quality Circles. Once people have seen a team give its presentation and solve its problem, they themselves are keen to go on to the next one, and other people want to get involved. The light of the enlightenment will attract people.

Without *senior management commitment*, Quality Circle programmes will never succeed. Every Friday at 10.30 at Toyota, we have Quality Circle presentations. Recently a senior director arrived late for such a presentation. As he approached the room where the presentations are made, the employees were leaving and one of them stopped the director and asked why he was late. It was explained that he had been busy in his office and he had not noticed the time. The group leader stated that this director should have made the presentation, and said that if the director was going to be late, he should have phoned and the presentation would have waited. In order to overcome his embarrassment, the director accompanied the employees into the plant and saw first-hand the improvement they had made. That was a telling off he welcomed. It showed that the group leaders were involved, that they enjoyed their involvement and wanted him to show his involvement. Dare it be said that they wanted their light to be seen.

The question frequently asked by visitors from other companies at Quality Circle presentations at Toyota is 'What are the returns that can be expected?' They believe that Quality Circles are a pure productivity exercise. This is totally incorrect. Quality Circles is an exercise in total worker involvement, mutual support and respect that will assist in paving the way towards a more productive quality-of-worklife, worker-participative, harmonious unit. Should you believe that all direction comes not from the top of the lighthouse; should you believe that quality of life is important, and should you believe that everyone in the organisation can contribute to quality working conditions, cost and maintenance, then adopt the quality circle route. It is a common misconception that Quality Circle activity is a productivity tool—it is and it isn't. *We at Toyota define productivity as an attitude of mind.* It is a mentality of progress, of the constant improvement of that which exists. It is a certainty of being able to do better than yesterday, and less well than tomorrow. It is the will to improve on the present situation, no matter how good it really may be. It is the constant adaption of economic and social life to changing conditions. It is the continuous effort to apply new techniques and new methods. Finally, it is the faith in human progress..

Worker participation contributes to improved quality of working life.

The best Quality Circle teams are not necessarily the ones that reduce cost. The best, irrespective of cost savings, are those that display a high degree of innovative thinking on the part of members of the team through the step-by-step approach, and those that display that an obvious solution has not been pounced upon, but that methodical thinking has prevailed to ensure that the latent cause of the problem has been highlighted. I have a fairly old Japanese write-up on Quality Circles given to me by Toyota Japan. This paper states the objective of a Quality Circle and total worker involvement programme. Please excuse my Japanese-English.

- Delightfulness in accomplishment of mission or target.
- Delightfulness in being recognised.
- Delightfulness in accomplishment of targets.
- Delightfulness in improvement of techniques, skills and advancement.

Most of the Toyota Circles are from the hourly rated workforce. Four years ago most of those workers would not have known what a percentage was. They would have been shy about standing up and talking and expressing their views. The delightfulness I mentioned a moment ago is attained through mutual development and repeated improvement activities by the Quality Circle group. Feeling such delightfulness, each member can themselves contribute to establishment of a bright and worthwhile workplace—that is the definition of Quality Circle activities in Toyota.

For those who have not yet started on the Quality Circle programme and total worker involvement, this message from Japanese wisdom—'Even a thousand mile road has a first step'.

SIYACABANGA

One of the production systems and total worker involvement programmes that we have at Toyota is the creation of thinking people. We said to ourselves after the successful introduction of Quality Circles that this really was clearly meant for a group activity. We saw, however, no reason why there should not be an interim stage for individual involvement in pursuit of a technique. One of the facts that we stumbled onto was that we knew a great deal about the wrong ways of doing things, wasteful ways, walking, bending, and stretching. Research established that employees were interested in, among other things, a degree of authority to exercise their own judgement, attain respect, and have management and supervisors willing to listen to them.

Pride is the biggest motivator of people and relates to a sense of responsibility, achievement and recognition. It was ascertained that the employee wished to improve the quality of his worklife.

To satisfy these needs, a new total worker involvement programme was designed. Bearing in mind that the word productivity does not translate into Zulu, the programme Siyacabanga was developed. Siyacabanga means 'we think'. It centres on a questionnaire which details all the wrong ways to produce a vehicle, both by man and machine. It is a basic method and study programme with the object of eliminating waste. It is produced in Zulu and English and acts as a catalyst to convert an ordinary worker into a motivated thinker. This in turn helps to cut across language, cultural and racial barriers which in many instances unintentionally isolate subordinates from management.

The Americans talk about Ergonomics—the relationship of the worker to his workplace. This is what we call Siyacabanga. The worker has a say about his work situation. The Ford Motor Company had the University of Michigan carry out a five-year investigation costing $2,2 million. We asked our workers what they felt. The answers were extremely similar to the answers furnished by the University of Michigan. The worker wanted a say in how and in which way the work should be done. He also wanted to talk about comfort at work in regard to tasks to be performed. Work is now comfortably performed at waist height at Toyota.

We developed a standard questionnaire for completion by operators and group leaders. Question 13 of the questionnaire concerns a torque wrench. The question asks whether the operator uses a torque wrench and if so, does he wind it more than twice. In one operator's situation and in connection with the Corolla front suspension, he felt he was working too hard at tightening bolts with a torque wrench and questioned the process. Together with his group leader, he calculated the number of applications or movements. There are two suspension arms, each one takes one bolt. Each time the man put the torque wrench on, he actually wound it 8 times with the left and then 8 times with the right. The fact that the worker was doing it 8 times appears to be insignificant, but then he was doing it 16 times per unit. That is not too impressive. However 2 600 times per day amounts to a horrendous 637 000 times per year. Plant management, at the operator's own request, tested the torque wrench, found that it was defective, and quickly replaced it.

The initial improvements are physical and relate to repositioning of stock to the advantage of a subordinate. The subordinate exercises judgement and earns respect. As confidence develops, simple production aids lead to quality improvements and the easing of physical work. The worker is given the opportunity to address Plant Management and say 'Look what I have done'. People are now listening. The Siyacabanga programme has the advantage of reaching many employees over a short period of time.

The biggest barrier to productivity is that people cannot see where improvements can be made. By nature, people are critical, so if someone points out something wrong, we have plenty of ideas on how it should be fixed. But the omission is that people cannot see where improvements can be made.

If there needs to be a facility change as a result of the workers suggestions, it is referred to one of the TPS workshops. These are totally separate from Maintenance and established to make production aids. These workshops are each staffed by an artisan, and various assistants. They will make the production aids as requested using predominantly scrap material and they turn them around in the region of about less than two days. Eighty percent of the materials used are scrap material. Once the production aid has been tried and tested, the employee makes a presentation to senior management. He gets a round of applause and then questions may be put to him. Most people think of productivity in big terms. However, which would you prefer, one employer making a million rands saving, or 1 000 individuals coming up with a thousand rands saving each. Small contributions are important.

In conclusion, I would like to suggest that a successful total worker involvement programme not only contributes to quality of worklife but also to a stable working environment, where the major players in the relationship will most certainly benefit.

11

Clive Fletcher

THE ANGLO AMERICAN GROUP'S EMPLOYEE SHAREHOLDING SCHEME

South Africa is a mixture of first- and third-world economies. It has the largest and most diversified economy in the southern African region and, indeed, on the continent of Africa. In some areas, such as banking and life assurance, there is a considerable degree of sophistication and there is a burgeoning informal sector. Share dealing started in Cape Town in 1820 and was given impetus by the discovery of copper in Namaqualand in 1850. The first stock exchange began in Kimberley in 1880 when diamonds were discovered and others followed after the discovery of gold in the Eastern Transvaal in 1884. The Johannesburg Stock Exchange, today the only one, opened for business in 1887. It boasts 781 listed companies with an equity capitalisation of some R400 billion. Daily turnover is presently around R70 million. Preference shares, gilts, debentures and Krugerrands are also traded.

102 years after the establishment of the Johannesburg Stock Exchange some 360 000 individuals and 20 000 corporate bodies now hold shares directly in listed companies and a very large number of individuals have indirect interests in equities through entities such as life assurance companies, pension, provident and mutual funds, all of which offer ways of capital formation by individuals. The total population of South Africa is 35,6 million of whom, according to the Department of Manpower, 10,7 million are economically active including 2,1 million members of registered trade unions.

Clearly there is a good deal of room for growth in private share ownership.

If we examine employee share ownership more closely, the picture becomes slightly blurred as statistics are not readily available. Whilst we have a fairly long history of executive share incentive plans, the notion of extending share ownership down through the ranks is a relatively new phenomenon, but it is one which is attracting increasing interest from management and workers alike. I am certain that significant progress will be achieved in this area in future years.

My estimate of the total number of employee shareholders in the whole country is about 200 000 or 6 % of the formal private-sector workforce excluding agriculture. This level of employee participation has been achieved in the last two years or so and the figure is not included in the 360 000 individuals owning equities directly as nearly all employee shares are held through trusts, at least initially, which are counted as single shareholders in company registers. The listing of the state-owned steel producer, Iscor, in November this year could boost the number of employee shareholders by up to 30 000 people.*

This statistical picture tells only a small part of the story so this seems to be an appropriate point to look at the environment in South Africa before examining how share ownership is being extended to employees.

Firstly, it needs to be said that the *tax legislation* in South Africa provides almost no incentive to encourage ownership of shares amongst employees. For instance:

1   The cost of shares given to employees can be deducted from the employer's income only by grossing up the amount of employees' tax and calling the resultant sum a

* Iscor was listed in November 1989 but figures for employee
  participation have not been published.

bonus which is immediately taxed in the hands of the employee.

2   The difference between market value and an option price is taxed when an option is exercised, whether or not the shares are actually sold.

3   Any interest differential between the rate charged on a loan granted to acquire shares and the so-called official rate, which is close to a market-related rate, is taxed in the hands of the individual.

4   There is no capital gains tax but taxpayers can be taxed on sharedealing profits if they trade frequently.

5   There are no provisions such as the use of pre-tax income to retire loans or which allow banks to grant soft loans to promote the use of ESOPs.

However, it seems to me that as the notion of employee share ownership gains ground, the pressure for changes in the tax laws will become irresistible.

Secondly, a comment on the *socio-political situation* in South Africa in so far as it concerns share ownership is required. The 1980s have witnessed the growth of the black trade union movement. In addition to their collective bargaining function in the workplace, trade unions represent one of the few ways in which black South Africans are able to express themselves politically. Generally, the unions are collectivist in their approach and their philosophy embraces socialist-style nationalisation and/or worker control. They tend to be ambivalent about share ownership in general and to reject individual ownership as tokenism and as a way of undermining their control over their membership.

On the other hand, the increasing influence of black South Africans on economic activity in both the formal and informal sectors needs to be noted. For example, a major growth area in the informal sector is that of savings associations—known

as 'stokvels'—which are resulting in an increased awareness
of the benefits of saving and capital formation.

Thirdly, alongside the growth of the union movement,
human resource management has been evolving new strategies
and embracing new policies. The emphasis is on individual
employees and the way in which people can use the system
to their advantage. Provident funds, providing lump sum
benefits on retirement, as opposed to pension funds, housing
programmes enabling employees to own their own homes,
education and training programmes to enhance individual
skills, and employee involvement in workplace decision-
making are all part of the current environment.

Since its establishment the Anglo American Corporation
has sought to demonstrate that the creation of wealth, if it is
to be sustained, must benefit the broader community and
employment practices have been directed towards this end.
In 1986 we felt that the time had come to introduce the notion
of *stakeholding* to our employees. To paraphrase our chairman,
Mr G W H Relly, we wanted to involve our employees in the
wealth-creation process and offer them an opportunity to
participate in the long-term growth and divident performance of the Anglo American Corporation. We conducted
world-wide research into stakeholding programmes.

Our experience and research into employee share schemes
locally and abroad demonstrated convincingly that successful share ownership was associated with a sense of employee
stakeholding in the enterprise in which they worked. At its
most elementary, stakeholding was simply a sense of 'being
part' of the enterprise, not only in respect of sharing in its
growth and dividend performance but also in participating
in the rule-making and decision-making affecting the worklife of employees in the enterprise.

In the development of our share scheme we gave very
particular attention to generating this sense of stakeholding.

While this paper focuses primarily on the share scheme itself, a few words on the complementary theme of employee participation may be appropriate.

The challenge of employee involvement lies in extending to each and every employee the opportunity to participate in workplace decisions effecting him or her. Much of the debate around employee involvement centres on how this involvement is structured in the day-to-day workplace. For our part we have tended towards the view that no one particular form or structure of employee involvement is suited to all workplaces at all times. We have tried rather to initiate a process in which the constraints on greater involvement are eliminated and opportunities continually created to allow employees and their supervisors to develop sustainable ways of reaching decisions together, which are particular to their workplace circumstances. As the concept of involvements in employee supervisory relations takes root it would inevitably develop new forms or structures; extending the scale of involvement in decision-making in both its level and scope.

It is integral to our approach to employee involvement and share-ownership, indeed to the stakeholder concept itself, that it is a process which will evolve over time. It is not a package that 'fits' or not into a particular workplace. As new relationships are defined in the workplace through financial participation and employee involvement, different opportunities will arise which will give further effect to the sense of stakeholding we set out to achieve. The scheme, which I define in more detail below, is the beginning of a process which we have cast in sufficiently broad brackets to adapt to continually changing dynamics both in and out of the workplace.

As a mining finance house, the Anglo American Corporation is the head of a family of subsidiary and associate companies and companies in which it has equity stakes and to which it provides technical and administrative services. The companies operate in areas such as gold, coal and diamond mining, steel and paper production, engineering, automobile manufacturing, agriculture, chemicals, banking and insurance. All companies are separately managed and most are quoted on the Johannesburg and other stock exchanges.

After much deliberation, we decided on a *single group scheme* to provide employees with at least two years' service with a modest number of Anglo American Corporation shares annually for at least five years and at no cost to themselves. Each issue of shares is held in trust for four years after which the shares are released to the employee. Shares are released immediately upon retirement, retrenchment or death but the vesting period continues upon resignation or dismissal. Dividends flow through the trust to the individual employee shareholders. Importantly, the scheme is universal in that it is available to all employees with two years' qualifying service and egalitarian in that all eligible employees within the same company receive the same number of shares. Participation in the scheme by employees is entirely voluntary.

We invited nineteen of our subsidiary and associate companies to participate in the scheme on the basis that they would bear the cost of providing the Anglo American Corporation shares to their own employees (figure 11.1), and all agreed to do so. Altogether these companies employ some 270 000 people, 192 000 of whom had the necessary two years' service required for participation in the scheme. The approval of the shareholders of all participating companies, including those of the Anglo American Corporation, was sought on the grounds that the scheme is an arrangement between shareholders and employees, as opposed to management and employees. The scheme is not a substitute for a wage income.

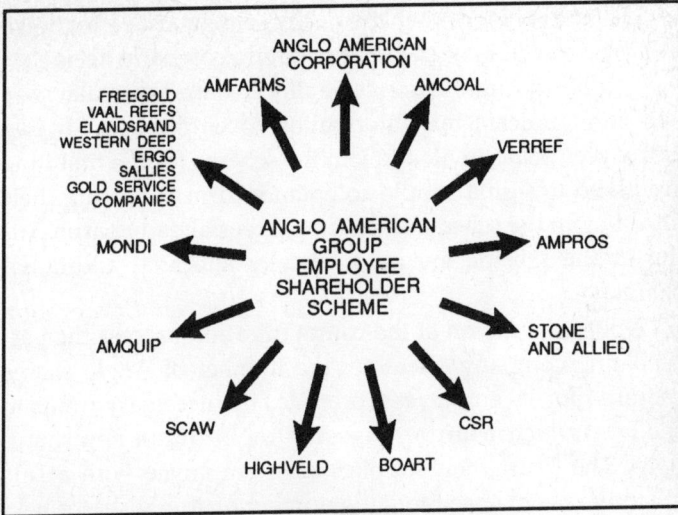

FIGURE 11.1
Participating companies in the Anglo American Group's
Employee Shareholder Scheme

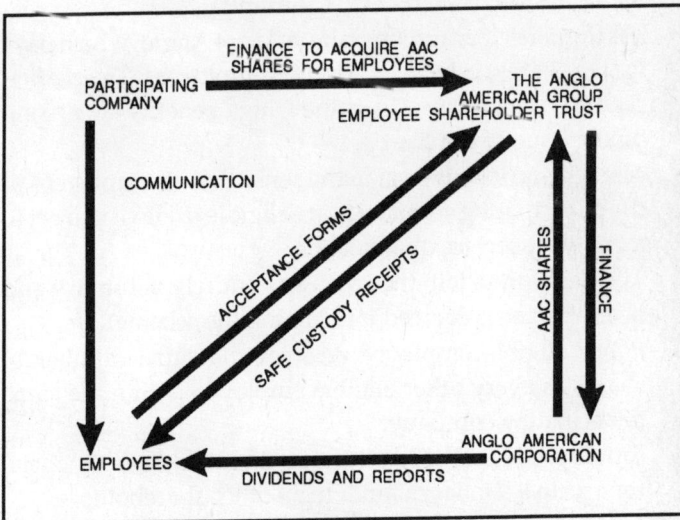

FIGURE 11.2
Mechanics of the Anglo American Group's
Employee Shareholder Scheme

The mechanics of the scheme are best described in figure 11.2. The directors of each participating company decide on the number of Anglo shares to be allocated in a particular year and communicate this information to employees. Eligible employees being invited to join the scheme for the first time are asked to sign a simple acceptance form indicating their wish to join the scheme while employees already participating in the scheme are automatically allocated additional shares.

Upon completion of the communication process the participating company calculates the number of Anglo shares required for its employees, provides the necessary funds to the Trust which in turn arranges for Anglo to issue new shares to it. The Trust then supplies each employee with a safe custody receipt specifying the number of Anglo shares held on his or her behalf.

The following points should be noted:

1   An allocation of shares is made annually.
2   It is the participating company, and not Anglo, which pays for the shares on behalf of its own employees. The participating company also pays the fringe benefits tax arising on the issue of the shares.
3   The scheme is universal in the sense that all employees of the participating companies are eligible to join it subject to a two-year service qualification.
4   The decision to join the scheme is entirely voluntary and no employee is coerced into joining the scheme.
5   Every eligible employee receives the same number of shares as every other eligible employee within the same participating company.
6   Employee shareholders receive dividends and financial reports in a similar manner to all other shareholders.

Prior to launching the scheme at the end of 1987 we conducted extensive research to establish levels of comprehension about share ownership and determined that an extensive *communications process* was required.

Between January and July 1988 some 192 000 eligible employees were briefed in groups of 20–30 about the scheme and 121 000 (63 %) accepted the invitation to join it. With one exception all employees were offered 5 Anglo shares having a total market value at that stage of about R250. Every eligible employee received a personal letter of invitation and a brochure about the scheme. For the most part both documents were in the employee's preferred language. In communicating the scheme extensive use was also made of small groups briefings, information sharing sessions, audio visual presentations, posters and house publications.

Each employee shareholder was provided with a copy of a specially prepared annual report and dividends totalling R11,63 were paid to all employees holding 5 shares during the financial year to 31 March 1989.

A similar process of communication was employed between January and May 1989 for the second allocation. Those who joined the scheme in 1988 were automatically allocated a further five shares while those who became eligible for the first time or who declined to join the scheme last year were invited to join the scheme in 1989 and receive 5 shares for the first time. At the completion of the 1989 allocation *145 000 employees or 73 % of the eligible population had become shareholders*. In addition, about 10 000 employee shareholders terminated their employment in 1988 and the vast majority of these have retained their shares.

For the record, at the time of writing 10 Anglo shares were worth R1 000 and paid dividends of R27 per annum.*

Having described the way in which the scheme works and dealt with some of its attributes including its universality, its

* As at February 1990 10 Anglo shares were worth about R1 550.

egalitarianism and its voluntary nature, attention can be turned to some of the *criticisms* which have been levelled against it. These include claims that the issue of control of Anglo was not addressed; workers want a living wage and not shares; the scheme was not negotiated with the unions; and that the scheme was introduced with the sole purpose of undermining the unions.

It seems to me that the criticims were based on a misinterpretation of the scheme and the manner in which it was implemented. In this respect I should like to quote some extracts from the letter which our chairman, Mr Gavin Relly, addressed to shareholders of Anglo in November 1987 when approval for the introduction of the scheme was sought:

> 'The future prosperity of the Corporation is inextricably linked with the future prosperity of South Africa. This in turn demands the participation of all South Africans in the creation of significant new wealth, in the context of a free and fair economy and society.
>
> The Anglo American and its associated companies are engaged in a number of initiatives to enhance the involvement of employees in wealth creation. Enhanced skills produced through training and education, home ownership, trade unionism and collective bargaining as well as new forms of involvement in workplace decision-making can all enhance the forces of wealth creation. The Employee Shareholder Scheme opens a new avenue of financial participation for employees.
>
> The scheme offers the employee the opportunity to become an investor in the Anglo American Corporation. As investors, participating employees, therefore, will have a stake in the long-term growth and dividend performance of the Corporation.
>
> South Africa is in a transition away from apartheid. In the new society now emerging South Africans need common goals, common experiences and common challenges. Your Board believes that this scheme can make a contribution to this purpose and I feel sure you will wish to support this investment in our future.'

Mr Relly further stated in his 1989 Chairman's Statement:

> 'The scheme is clearly succeeding in one of its core aims—to enable employees to acquire a tangible stake in the business—and research indicates that it is also having some success in achieving another, which is to promote a greater sense of belonging, and hence participation in and identification with our operations.'

The question of control of Anglo was simply never on the agenda nor was the scheme in any way intended to be a substitute for formal wage income. In regard to the latter, Anglo is committed to paying a fair rate for the job and the scheme is not linked to any programme of incentives or conditional reward.

Instead *the scheme has some fairly narrow and modest objectives*. We wanted to engender a sense of stakeholding amongst our employees and we wanted to expose them to the process of wealth creation in a modest way—specifically how a company operates, why it needs to earn profits and how its profits can be used to the benefit of shareholders as well as the community as a whole—shareholders benefiting from increases in dividends and share prices brought about by reinvestment of profits which have the effect of creating more jobs for the benefit of the community. We see skills development programmes, home ownership schemes and our contracting schemes with small business as part of the same process of encouraging employees and others to take part in wealth creating opportunities. Indeed the newly launched industrywide provident fund for black mine workers could also be seen in this context. Perhaps the major point on which the Corporation parted company with the unions was on the question of negotiation. Firstly, there was a practical reason for not negotiating the scheme with the unions. Some 19 of Anglo's subsidiary and associate companies participate in the scheme and many of their employees do not belong to unions while those that do, belong to about 36 different unions. It is unlikely that the scheme would have got off the ground had we attempted to negotiate it with all 36 unions. Secondly, we believe that there are some issues on which employees need to make *individual* decisions and our scheme is one of them.

Nevertheless, we remain committed to forging an industrial democracy with the unions as part of the wealth creation process. Indeed, as Mr Relly put it in his 1989 Chairman's Statement:

'It should go without saying that the scheme is not intended in any way to undermine our commitment to trade union rights and collective bargaining, and indeed it should be seen as an arrangement between shareholders and employees—not one between management and workers.'

Finally, the scheme as I have described it is a reality and will remain so in the sense that our employees will continue to be shareholders in Anglo American and will continue to benefit in a modest way from its future growth and prosperity.

The Anglo scheme is large by any standards and certainly the largest in Africa, but it is not the only form of employee shareholding in evidence.

1   Since the beginning of 1988 one of our major associate companies, De Beers Consolidated Mines Limited, has been operating a scheme similar to that of the Anglo American Corporation and now has some 9 000 employee shareholders.

2   Following on the disinvestment by Ford a trust was established to own 24% of South African Motor Corporation (Pty) Limited on behalf of the workforce. Samcor is not quoted and Anglo American and its associates own the other 76 % of the equity. Employees share equally in dividends received by the trust from Samcor.

3   A leading life assurance company offers its staff two or more years' service options to take up shares three years after the granting of the option.

4   A quoted supermarket chain offers employees with 5 or more years' service the opportunity to purchase its shares by way of a soft loan plan. The shares are released as soon as the load is repaid.

5   A quoted cement manufacturer operates a plan similar to that of the Anglo American Corporation for employees with ten years' service.

6   A quoted engineering company operates a unit trust scheme based on its own shares for employees with ten years' service.

7   A soft-drink manufacturing company offered employees the opportunity to acquire shares by way of soft loans some two years prior to its recent quotation on the Johannesburg Stock Exchange.

8   Iscor, a state-owned steel producer, is preparing for its privatisation and quotation in November and is in the process of offering some 10 % of its equity to its 55 000 employees in three parts, viz a free allocation of 100 shares to everyone; the opportunity to purchase, by way of a soft loan, a specified number of shares at a 20 % discount to the listing price; and a preferential allocation of a specified number of shares prior to the listing.

The Anglo scheme addresses some of the complex legal, tax and administrative issues surrounding share ownership and, I think, provides a platform from which other ideas consistent with the notion of wealth creation can be implemented including

1   providing a facility to enable employees to buy and sell small lots of shares;

2   providing a facility to enable employees to enter into savings plans for the purchase of shares; and

3   formalising the notion of profit participation and allowing employees a choice between cash or shares.

These, as well as measures designed to encourage employee buy-outs (which by the way are true ESOPs), are part of the business world in many other countries and will become part of South Africa's scene in the future. It seems that we should be engaging one another in debates about some of these issues at least at a practical rather than rhetorical level.

12

Rob Birt

WORKER PARTICIPATION IN THE AECI EMPLOYEES' PENSION FUND

INTRODUCTION

Although this chapter does not attempt to get into the debate on Pension vs Provident funds, it is appropriate to open it by referring to an article from the March 1987 edition of *Frontline*, 'Pensions and Justice', written by a prominent South African trade unionist, Taffy Adler. The article cites fundamental trade union concerns about pension funds which link it to the focus of this book namely 'Worker Participation'. The issues raised in the article include:

1   'The demand that "committees controlling these (Pension funds) should consist of an equal number of worker and company representatives".'
2   'Workers have a lifelong distrust of institutions dealing with their money, eg employers, burial societies, hire purchase corporations, etc . . .'
3   'The effort for pensioners to get their pensions is enormous, involving long queues, red tape and constant hassle.'
4   'The average mortality rate of a Black male is 60, whereas pensionable age is 65', ie they do not reap the benefits of providing for old age. (It must be pointed out that this figure is skewed by the incorporation of the high South African infant mortality rate).
5   'The vast majority of Black workers in South Africa have not contributed to a fund for a long time and don't have high salaries, with the result that returns are low (R92,00

per month in 1987) and in addition dismissal and retrenchment impacts on this problem.'
6   'Black pensioners want all their money in their hands as
      quickly as possible, and the Company's contribution
      when dismissed.'

These issues shall be returned to at the conclusion of this
paper because it can be illustrated that they are being addressed through the process of Worker Participation, certainly in the AECI Employees' Pension Fund.

This paper will address:
1   A brief *history* of the AECI Employees' Pension Fund.
      Thereafter some *comparisons* will be drawn between the
      traditional pension funds and the AECI Employees' Pen-
      sion Fund. The structure of the Employees' Fund and
      'worker participation' in the fund will be discussed.
2   The role and functions of the local committees.
3   The role and function of the Main Board of Trustees.

HISTORY OF AECI EMPLOYEES' PENSION FUND

It is important to preface a discussion of the history of the fund
by referring to a commitment which AECI espouses and
attempts to practise with regard to its Employees' Pension
Fund, namely:

> 'We are committed to the involvement and participation of employees
> in decision making processes at work and in other areas of mutual
> interest.'

These values are encapsulated in a document called 'Towards
2002', which resulted from a strategic exercise carried out by
senior AECI managers in 1986. Although this document was
put together 3 years ago, AECI has long practised these
values, albeit more so in the 1980s. The origin of the Employees' Pension Fund dates back to 1971 when the idea was
first conceptualised by the then Company Personnel Manager
proposing the replacement of the existing 'Gratuity Scheme'

by an Improved Pension Scheme. This idea was crystallised in January 1972 when the AECI Employees' Pension Fund was started in order to provide benefits to those employees who were not members of the AECI Pension Fund. The scheme, at its inauguration, was limited to black employees in the lower semi-skilled job classes as the cost of putting all employees into the fund at that stage was prohibitive. For that reason the majority of employees continued to receive gratuity awards upon retiring from the company. It was minuted in November 1972, at the Somerset West Factory, however, that there were 'complications of payment' to pensioners 'in the homelands'—the first indication that a need existed for worker participation. Although worker participation was not explicit at that time, a problem relating to communication with pensioners was beginning to manifest itself.

In 1973 it was emphasised by the group personnel manager that the existing gratuity scheme did not adequately provide for old age and low wages made the individual provision for old age, and sudden death, somewhat difficult and often impossible. He added that it was the intention of the company to introduce, over a period, pension benefits to all 'Bantu' and 'Asiatic' employees in recognition of 'the company's moral obligation to long-service employees'. Over time this happened and the fund's membership grew by phasing in membership for all employers over the next 4 years. By 1975 there were 14 AECI centres participating in the Scheme, and today there are 44.

In 1987 the establishment of a committee of trustees was mooted, on which Black representatives would serve and which would be set up to improve the contact between the fund's members and the company—views were called for on how the trustees would be elected and another fundamental of worker participation was established. During the period up to 1977, numerous liaison committee meetings had enquired about membership of the fund.

During the late 1970s various improvements to the fund were made, for example during 1977 employees employed by AECI prior to joining the fund had their pensionable service increased by 25% of the period between their date of engagement and date of joining the fund. In addition, the service fraction was reduced from $\frac{1}{80}$ to $\frac{1}{60}$ (33% improvement). During 1978 employer contributions were increased from 7,5 to 9,0%. Ultimately in 1979 a final commitment by the company secured pension rights for all Black employees and in October 1979 the biggest AECI factory, Modderfontein, placed all their employees in the fund—not only at company initiative but also in response to the employees' interests and in recognition of their needs. Employees over 55 years of age were entitled to join the Provident Fund.

Improvements were at this stage motivated largely by management upon evaluation of the *assets* of the fund. The early 1980s, however, saw the establishment of local committees due mainly to the reactions from employees to the proposed Preservation of Pensions Bill in 1982, including a major strike at Umbogintwini Factory. This was probably the most significant stage in the process towards worker participation. It was recognised at that time, primarily by Bokkie Botha (Group Human Resources Manager) that there appeared to be a considerable amount of misunderstanding and lack of information about the Pension Fund. Workers were largely ignorant of the philosophies tied to the concept of a pension fund and were certainly not at that stage part of its decision making processes. Unfortunately the strike resulted in the dismissal (by agreement with the union) of the workforce at Umbogintwini, in order to obtain the resultant payout of all pension benefits (little as they were, after such a short period of contributions). Those who were re-engaged (the majority) started as new employees with a zero balance for service calculations—much to their subsequent detriment.

The introduction of local committees was thereafter accelerated and in the major centres they were established along worker participation lines. Today there are 10 committees at sites with workforces of not less than 200 members, eg Modderfontein, Midland (Sasolburg), Somerset West, Umbogintwini, SANS, Vynide and Ballengeigh (Newcastle) amongst others. Since the introduction of the local committees, benefits and the revision of rules have been the focus of attention. In 1985 a further 25% pensionable service was added to the period between date of engagement and joining the fund; and a 15-year service requirement for ill-health retirees was removed. The employee contribution to the fund was increased from 5% to 5,75% to provide for an ill-health benefit.

The difference between the late 1970s and mid 1980s really lay in the participation by members of the fund (by now 10 600) in the improvement to these benefits. In 1988 there were an additional 6 improved benefits to the fund—a few of which will be described in discussing the activities of the local committees and Main Board of Trustees.

In summary then, the fund has, since its inception in January 1972, seen a remarkable growth in:

- Members;
- Total pensionable salaries;
- Total assets;
- Total pensioners;
- Total trust accounts;
- Compound annual performance against the inflation rate.

Much of this historical growth has had an impact on the Pension Fund's credibility in the eyes of its members. This information is shared with them in a regularly published and revised general information booklet.

However, of greater significance is the growth in the role local committees have played in developing the concept of worker participation.

LOCAL COMMITTEES

The 'Towards 2002' document referred to above espouses a commitment to democracy:

> We are committed to democratic principles, individual freedom and human rights, and a socially responsible free enterprise economy.'

Fundamental rights of freedom of association are embodied in the structure of local committees (and that of the Main Board of Trustees), namely the role of the ballot to elect trustees to serve on the committees and Main Board. Embodied in the constitution of local committees is the right which fund members have to nominate representatives to serve on those committees. Once nominations are received by the local secretary of the fund (usually a pensions officer) ballot forms are drawn up with a description of the credentials of each nominee and the 4 member representatives and an equivalent number of company representatives on each committee. It must be stressed that the right of members to elect who they wish is fundamental and this obviously includes the choices of union members or shop stewards as nominees. In reality, and in most committees, there is usually a strong trade union presence. This has caused a problem where more than one union is present on a site. To illustrate this, a minute of a particular local committee meeting in October 1988 is quoted:

> Before the meeting could start, a lengthy debate ensued because SACWU members who serve in the Pension Fund Committee objected to the presence of UWUSA members with whom they had 'no working relation'. After several caucus meetings by management on one side and SACWU and CWIU on the other side, it was eventually agreed to

continue with the meeting and that Trade Union differences should not
interfere with the administration of the Fund.'

It is suggested that this demonstrates a fundamental principle
of worker participation. In other words, the application of
democratic processes to ensure fair representation of all the
members.

These local committees meet on a regular basis (depending on the size of the site), once per month or less frequently.
The meetings are usually chaired by the local personnel manager and a secretary takes the minutes of the meetings. An
agenda forms the structure of the meeting and the standard
formalities relating to notice, welcome, apologies, matters
arising and new matters are dealt with.

The objectives of the local committees are mainly:
• to interview dependants and consider recommendations
  in connection with death-in service cases;
• to keep the Main Board of Trustees informed on local
  pension fund matters and administration problems;
• to assess the needs of the employees and to ensure that the
  pension fund benefits meets those needs;
• to recommend changes to the Rules if necessary;
• to act as a communication link between the Main Board of
  Trustees and members.
• to ensure appropriate training is conducted for representatives and members.
Some of these activities are illustrated as examples of viable
worker participation.

Interviewing dependants of death-in-service cases
This is usually carried out by a pensions officer together with
one of the member representatives in the event of a death. The
company operates a group life insurance scheme, an accident
insurance scheme and a travel insurance scheme.

Benefits resulting from membership must be allocated to
dependants in the event of death. Invariably it is the repre-

sentative who accompanies the widow and family to the pensions office for a confidential consultation of the personal circumstances of the dependants. Details acquired include age of spouse and children; degree of dependence on the deceased's income, current and future requirements of the family and other family considerations (eg is there another wife?). The benefits available to the spouse are also explained to her and she is required to indicate her financial needs. A discussion thereafter ensues between the pensions officer and representative, and a recommendation formulated on the allocation of benefits. This may be a monthly payment or could be a lump sum. Essential to this process is a balanced approach to the preservation of the benefit for as long a period as possible while maintaining payment levels which will meet the dependant's needs. Lump sum benefits could range from R20 000 to R50 000 depending on salary at the time of death and if the employee was a member of the group life insurance scheme. In the past there were numerous cases where widows were paid out lump sum benefits and a few years after the payout the widow would return to the company requesting assistance. This very sad state of affairs has however, decreased greatly owing to the formation of trust accounts. Local committees now consider how payments will be made and can ensure that dependants are catered for—especially children who until the age of at least 18 years need a guaranteed source of assistance. Each recommendation is considered at local committee level for a final decision. It may happen that lengthy discussions will occur at local committee level but the committee has the delegated authority (from the Main Board of Trustees) to take a final decision on how to apportion benefits. If there is no consensus and a dispute arises, which is very seldom, this is referred to the Main Board of Trustees for a final decision.

Worker participation therefore includes:

- deciding on the apportioning of benefits;
- interviewing spouses;
- making contact with the family members of the deceased.

A regular activity of the pensions officer, together with a member representative, is to travel to the homelands to visit pensioners, widows and family members to assess their needs, to establish any changed circumstances, to communicate any important changes to the benefits and to re-establish the link between the member and the company. Representatives play a very vital role not only in participating in this link but very often it is they who are able to geographically find the house of the pensioner. Naturally there is a cost factor to this allocation of time and travelling expenses but it is believed that visits of this nature are an investment in worker participation.

Changes to rules

Another important objective of the committee is to assess the needs of employees and recommend changes to the rules where necessary. This process can be illustrated by using an example of how this objective operates.

Prior to July 1988 funeral expenses in the event of a death of a member were largely confined to benefits provided for by the local factory, eg the provision of a coffin, transport of the body or in many cases a small cash assistance. The family members could also request an advance from the anticipated pension benefits but this negatively affected the benefits due to the spouse.

In addition to this, some employees joined independent burial societies and this may or may not have been beneficial—depending on the reliability of the society. With such a variety of benefits, or no benefits, members at the Umbogintwini factory put forward a proposal to their local committee to consider an improved benefit from the pension fund.

This was discussed at the local committee where a proposal was formulated and submitted to the Main Board of Trustees who meet on a quarterly basis. At that meeting an assessment was made by the trustees after requesting an evaluation from the actuaries (Old Mutual) on the effect of such a benefit on the value of the fund. After a positive report the trustees decided that the fund would be capable of paying out:

- R1 000 in the event of the death of a member or spouse or dependent child aged 14–21 years;
- R500 for a dependent child between 6 and 13 years;
- R250 for a dependent child under 6 years.

Obviously the trustees prescribed various requirements regarding certain controls before payment of the benefit.

As indicated before, this was one of 6 benefits improved in 1988 by utilising this process.

Withdrawal of benefits

A significant additional improvement was that related to withdrawal of benefits in the event of dismissal or retirement. Since 1988 a member receives his own contribution and interest plus 5% of the company contribution plus interest for each completed year of contributory service in excess of 5 years, subject to a maximum of twice contributions and interest.

This surely goes a long way toward addressing the earlier mentioned trade union concern about employees receiving the company's contribution if they resign or are dismissed. Again, the process assessing whether the pension fund could handle the financial implications was the key to the improved benefit. The financial implications were explained to trustees who then decided to implement the improved benefit.

These examples demonstrate the application in practice of worker participation. Improvements currently being contemplated from local level include: financial assistance to medically boarded retired employees with medical expenses, and a request that dependants of medically retired employees should, after the death of such a pensioner, continue receiving a pension up to the time he/she would have turned 65 years of age. A decision has yet to be taken on these benefits.

Trustees *are* responsible for taking decisions on these types of issues which will impact on their members. This is a significant and responsible position and affects the future of the 10 600 members of the fund, 834 pensioners and 574 trust accounts.

As an aside, it must be logical that any rules/benefits may be agreed and implemented, providing the funding of the fund provides for the continuing needs of the members. This perspective surely has relevance for the Pension vs Provident fund debate.

Having illustrated local committee process, I hope that an understanding of how the structure and objectives of the local committees demonstrates worker participation has been established.

MAIN BOARD OF TRUSTEES

Although touched on earlier, further aspects of the functions of the Main Board of Trustees require some expansion.

Company and employee representatives serve on the Main Board of Trustees. Members of the pension fund elect their representatives who once a quarter, meet management trustee representatives to carry out the following functions:

- consider all recommendations made by local committees as illustrated in the previous examples;

- decide on important issues such as benefit improvements;

- ensure effective communication on the activities of the fund to its members;

- review investments and consider the funding of the fund.

These activities clearly involve important levels of decision-making processes and again reflect the application of worker participation.

Essential to this whole process is the need to ensure that trustees have sufficient knowledge to make a meaningful contribution to its meetings. It has been recognised that managements who do not take care of this educational need run the risk of burning their fingers before introducing the process of co-determination. Essential to this process is the teaching that co-determination also means co-responsibility and that this conveys both privileges and duties.

To this end trustees introduced and now constantly review the following to ensure that their members also understand the activities of the fund:

- The General Information booklet, the purpose of which is to provide members with as much information as possible on the fund;
- Pension Fund Benefit Statements;
- Videos which are produced to demonstrate the funding activities of the pension fund;
- Briefs on improvements to the fund.

In addition, trustees go through training sessions on how the fund operates, and their roles. This also requires them to develop an understanding of fairly sophisticated concepts related to pension fund funding activities because once a year a presentation is made by the actuaries to the trustees on the financial status of the fund. To make this presentation meaningful, graphs are presented and figures reflecting performance are discussed. Trustees have the opportunity to question the investments of the funds from the information freely available to them. Every 3 years there is also an actuarial evaluation and a presentation is made by the actuaries. Should there be surplus funds these are declared to the trustees who then hold lengthy discussions on how the surpluses are to be utilised. Proposals are made and are then canvassed across all local committees who take the proposals to their members. Should members agree to these proposals, or suggest amendments, then implementation of the improved benefits results. In 1988 this was particularly evident by the number of improvements which were made. Processes are therefore top to bottom and vice-versa. Throughout the process, worker participation has played a major role.

There was an interesting request from trustees in 1987 when a company in which the fund had shares, had dismissed its employees who belonged to the same trade union. The trustees called for a sale of that company's shares. After lengthy discussion on the performance of the shares in question, it was finally understood, and agreed, that because disinvestment would materially affect the fund, no such sale should occur—a demonstration of the need for education and of the fact that trustees certainly have the right, within the requirements of the Pensions Act, to make recommendations on investments.

The resolution of disputes is another activity which gives meaning to the role of worker participation and co-determination in the fund. A case occurred in 1988 where the local committee was not able to resolve a dispute regarding the allocation of benefits to the dependants. The matter was referred to the Board of Trustees and a final decision taken.

A recent point raised by the trustees of the fund is the recognition of the credibility of their fund as compared with traditional pension funds. The discussion arose out of a shop-floor point raised by members of the fund stating that members of the Employees' Fund preferred the way it had been administered. At the meeting of the Main Board of Trustees it was suggested that the method of running the Employees' Pension Fund had developed to suit the needs and requirements of the members, and the fact that traditional pension funds had developed along different lines probably indicated a difference in the perception and requirements of its members.

This meeting highlighted three aspects:

1   The employees have developed a trust in the Employees' Pension Fund because it meets their needs;

2   Employee representatives have become involved by virtue of seeking solutions to those problems which affect the members.

3   There *are* differences between this fund's operation and that of traditional funds which reflect the role of worker participation in the Employees' Pension Fund.

DIFFERENCES BETWEEN TRADITIONAL AND THE AECI EMPLOYEES' PENSION FUND

1   Contribution rates are generally lower in the Employees' Pension Fund but it has been made known that workers are prepared to increase their contributions for greater benefits.

2   Certain benefits are less favourable in the Employees' pension Fund, eg:

2.1 Penalty for early retirement;

2.2 Pension at pensionable age;

2.3 Benefits in the event of a death of a pensioner;

2.4 Death-in-service benefits;

2.5 Deferred pension.

Depending on availability of funds and the contributions referred to above, benefits will, over time, improve.

3   Benefits that are currently more favourable in the Employees' Pension Fund include:

3.1 Return of contributions upon dismissal;

3.2 Funeral benefits.

These improved benefits reflect worker requests and really are in response to moving towards meeting the needs of the members, which might be totally different to those of members in more conventional funds.

However, the operations of these Funds are considerably different to the AECI Employees' Pension Fund, eg

- The local committees' function in the Employees' Pension Fund;
- the activities of the main Board of Trustees in the Employees' Pension Fund ensure that benefits are improved/changed in consultation with its members (there is therefore considerably more worker participation in this Pension Fund than in other funds—I have referred to the role of the ballot box, for example);
- benefit statements are issued to members of the Pension Fund.

Benefit statements which are issued to members each year are unique and reflect the recognition of the need to communicate with employees on the value of their membership. This process was also a response to trustee suggestions on the need for employees to know what benefits they are entitled to. A typical statement is reflected in the Appendix to this chapter.

However, despite the extent of worker participation reflected here, all is not rosy and comfortable. The company is *still* challenged on the need to provide for a provident fund. Not all factories have local committees. Members of the fund in smaller far-flung centres know little about the benefits of the fund. The major trade union still sees the fund as a 'company structure', and believes that this will need to be negotiated to meet the needs of its members. Despite these issues employee representatives continue to operate within the structure and *do* play a major and powerful role in its administration. The role of worker participation continues to operate despite these problems.

It is now possible to work through a few conclusions relating to worker participation in AECI Employees Pension Fund.

Numerous interpretations of the concept of worker participation are provided in this work. These cover a wide range of labour–management relations, and include decision-making at various levels. It takes the form of joint control and moves beyond consultation and collective bargaining which have traditionally been management's preserve. It involves new structures and responsibilities, and a shift in management styles and trade union roles. It raises issues of differing values, perceptions and goals due to the differing approach by employees and trade unions. Alternatively, it is employee self-management where major adjustments in economic and authority relations see a shift in ownership. It must therefore include processes wherein lower ranks of workers participate in decision-making.

It is proposed that the AECI Employees' Pension Fund fits all of these concepts of worker participation to a lesser or greater degree. I believe that it may be categorised as 'joint control within the enterprise at both high and workstation levels' but final conclusions are left to the reader.

What of *my* conclusions? Referring back to the introduction, trade union concerns about Pension Funds were listed. The issues were:

- Joint control of committees controlling pension funds—it is proposed that the AECI Pension Fund addresses this issue.

- The deep-seated distrust of institutions—it is suggested that this distrust is being eroded by a greater sense of ownership of the fund by its members.

- The effort for pensioners to get pensions—this is facilitated by decisions taken by local committees and visits to the homelands.

- The high mortality rate. The impact of the inclusion of the infant mortality rate on figures has already been referred to. However, the numbers of pensioners supported by the AECI Employees' Pension fund is increasing. The level is now at 7%. In 1984 it stood at 2% of total membership.
- Pensions are low (the figure quoted is R97,00 per month). In AECI the lowest paid employee who retires with 20 years' pensionable service (not uncommon in AECI) will receive approximately R300 per month. This is also adjusted each year and payments have increased significantly in the past. The trustees decide on the increases.
- The requirement that pensioners want all their money at retirement and the company's contribution when dismissed. In AECI one third can be taken in cash upon retirement. If dismissed, however, employees with 20 years' service would qualify for double their contributions plus interest. This is an issue which members would have to consider improving in relation to the availability of funds.

It is really up to the members to decide how to apportion their benefits based on the wealth and liquidity of the fund. Worker participation will, however, assist members to meet their own needs in the management of *their* fund—the AECI Employees' Pension Fund.

APPENDIX

AECI EMPLOYEES FUND
It is important to us that you know what membership of the AECI Employees Pension Fund is worth to you, which is why this benefit statement has been prepared for you personally and confidentially. Should you want to know anything more about your benefits or the Pension Fund, please ask your local Secretary or Personnel Manager.

CONFIDENTIAL TO:

YOUR PERSONAL BENEFIT STATEMENT
Improvements to the benefits were recently made from
1 July 1988 and they will be shown on next year's statement

1 Pensionable Service
   (a) Your pensionable service (for retirement purposes
       only) began: 1976/02/01
   (b) Your pensionable service (for all other purposes)
       began: 1972/11/01
2 Your normal retirement date at the age of 65 is: 2006/02/01
3 Your benefits have been worked out at: 1988/03/01
4 Your pension at your normal retirement date if your pensionable earnings do not increase will be: R4767 p.a.
5 If you are medically boarded at the date in 3 above your
   benefit will be: R4767 p.a.
6 On voluntary early retirement your pension will be reduced by your unearned service and by 4,5 percent for
   each year by which you retire before the age of 65.
7 Benefits for your dependants if you die before retirement.
   (a) Lump sum benefit: R19068
   (b) Your contributions to the fund up to the date shown in
       3 above (without interest) totalling: R2330.02
8 A pension for your widow if you die after retiring is not provided for, but you can arrange for such a pension with the
   company at the time of your retirement.
9 If you have completed 12 or more months of pensionable
   service and you are retrenched, you will be paid twice the
   amount of your own contributions to the fund — plus interest

13

Gopalang Sekobe

WORKER PARTICIPATION IN HEALTH AND SAFETY MATTERS

Introduction

Occupational Health, or Health and Safety, has been defined by both the World Health Organisation (WHO) and the ILO as all those activities that aim to preserve, protect, and promote the health and safety of workers.

If we add the meaning attached to 'health' by the WHO, viz: the physical, mental and social well-being of the individual, the total explanation covers a very wide area including

- safety (accident prevention),
- occupational hygiene,
- occupational medicine,
- ergonomics,
- anthropometry,
- ecology,
- occupational mental health, and
- supportive social services such as care of the aged and child care.

As industrial production sophistication increases, so will the list.

If we accept that workers must participate in health and safety matters as it is *their* lives at stake, then perhaps Michael Salamon states the position best when he describes worker participation as a

'philosophy or style of organisational management which recognises both the *need* and the *right* of workers, individually or collectively to be involved with management in areas of the organisation's decision making beyond that normally covered by collective bargaining'.

Owing to the fact that the work situation is inherently conflict-ridden, I suggest that for worker participation to be successful it needs to have constitutional guarantees.

In this essay I will discuss this subject in terms of:

1   the role of (government) legislation;
2   appropriate workplace structures, viz:
    (a) procedural agreements;
    (b) health and safety agreements;
    (c) workplace surveys;
    (d) safety representatives;
    (e) safety Committees;
    (f) safety policy; and
    (g) occupational health services.
3   other arguments and issues, viz:
    (a) arguments of costs;
    (b) 'cultural' issues.

THE ROLE OF LEGISLATION

Felice Morgenstern (1982) has listed the statutory duties placed on both employers and workers in almost all countries, with regard to health and safety matters.

Employers, as they have control over the work environment, are held to have overall responsibility for its safety. 'Strict duties' of compliance, and liability for breach, are laid upon employers. This is the situation in countries such as the United Kingdom, and raises a lot of questions, e g Who in the company is responsible? Must there be collective responsibility *or* should the Chief Executive Officer *or* the responsible agent carry sole responsibility?

In terms of section 5 of the General Administrative Regulations to the Machinery and Occupational Safety Act of 1983 (MOSA), employers have a duty to inform workers of the hazards and potential hazards existing in the workplace. It must be noted here that this provision in no way opens the way for 'co-determination' rights for workers. It took the Industrial Court ruling in *MAWU v Tvl Pressed Nuts, Bolts and Rivets* (Durban 1988) to determine a company's refusal to negotiate health and safety matters as an unfair labour practice.

It is common knowledge that the 'Right to Information' in the USA, Canada, Australia and Japan does not automatically make information accessible to workers. Battles had to be fought before this 'right' could benefit workers.

In countries such as the Netherlands, West Germany and Luxembourg, decisions on health and safety matters must be agreed to by the workers' representatives, in line with the co-determination provisions. In Belgium, workers have to agree to the hiring and firing of medical officers.

Other legislative provisions deal with Safety Representatives and Safety Committees, which will be discussed later.

In the light of these observations the following questions need answers:

1   Does legislation provide adequate deterrents and does it improve standards?

The UK with its civil liability practice employs the 'objectivisation' of negligence principle without reference to the defendant's capacities as these are expected to be insured.

In South Africa this question has not been answered.

Ian Macum (1988) has observed that although MOSA increased employers' health and safety awareness, this awareness is not thorough-going, as in most cases there is a lot of emphasis on the provision of safety equipment rather than on addressing the basic issues (causes of the problem).

2 *Should workers have the right to sue for negligence in addition to compensation awards?*

If so, where must this action concentrate: loss suffered by the victim *or* degree of fault by the accused? In other words, should the emphasis be on improving compensation or health and safety standards?

Which cases should be handled in which way?

3 *What role will the courts have in relation to the law?*

Will it be confirmed to that of interpreting obligations?

Is there any extra value of the courts other than that relating to interpreting the law?

What authority must inspectors' decisions have?

4 *What must be the purpose of law enforcement?*

Certain principles seem to be emerging strongly from the European Community legislation that has been passed so far, viz:

(*a*) Compliance must be obtained

(*b*) Dangers must be prevented

(*c*) Employers must apply their minds to ways and means of reducing work-related injuries.

Georges Spyropoulos (1984) suggests strongly that legislation be combined with promotional activities.

Unfortunately, MOSA completely ignores the value of worker collectivities and the important contribution they could make towards the setting of standards and compliance at shop-floor level. Macun (1988) reports that 47 % of the companies he surveyed were unhappy with MOSA regarding training of Safety Representatives (inadequate) and their authority and responsibility (insufficient); as well as the lack of employee involvement, and the Act being too manage-ment-orientated. Also many employers remain suspicious of Trade Union involvement in health and safety matters as being politically motivated.

APPROPRIATE WORKPLACE STRUCTURES: WORKER PARTICIPATION

Collective bargaining in South Africa remains the main form of worker participation.

The Health and Safety 'general duty' clauses in Procedural Agreements can and have been widely used to open the way for workers' activity in health and safety. The other clauses used are those which outline what areas are to be covered by negotiations, and 'declaration of intent' clauses.

Depending on the approach of the trade union, the abovementioned clauses may be used to negotiate a full *health and safety agreement*. Provisions may include:

- election of safety shop-stewards;
- functions of shop-stewards;
- access; inspections and investigations; information; factory inspector;
- right to bring in Trade Union health and safety advisors;
- composition and function of the Safety Committee;
- continuing fora for handling issues.

Workplace surveys may be carried out by service groups (as is mainly the case in this country) and to some extent by the Trade Union's own health and safety units (e g the NUM).

Reports of workplace surveys, such as those by the Urban Training Projects Health and Safety Unit, which could be followed by full medical screenings if necessary, form the basis for specific demands for corrective action.

The safety representative or safety shop-steward's duties will be *established in negotiations*, though MOSA lists some of these. Effectiveness depends on, among other things, the authority and extent of access provided. Generally, these duties include those listed in Annexure A.

Effectiveness of *safety committees* depends on factors such as size, composition, authority, frequency of meetings, and level of education provided, amongst other factors. The role of occupational health practitioners needs to be carefully outlined by both parties. Annexure B is a list of important questions pertaining to Health and Safety Committees.

Company safety policies are other tools that can be used to clarify the understanding employers must have of their responsibilities.

There is a debate as to whether these policies must be subject to collective bargaining. For a safety policy to be useful, some of its provisions need to cover:

- what the responsibility is (and its extent);
- what the objective is;
- responsibility of different managers in the effort to achieve this objective;
- the manager with overall responsibility;
- who will take over this responsibility in the absence of those with overall responsibility;
- who is to sign the policy;
- how often it will be reviewed;
- how it will be communicated to workers.

The effectiveness of a safety policy is its *usability*.

Annexure C is a checklist that can be used in determining the effectiveness of the policy.

Occupational health services are also being debated with the following identified as the challenges:

- How must they be provided?
- What is the role of the professionals?
- What education have these professionals?
- Who are the professionals responsible to?

In France, the employer runs the service under the supervision of the Works Council. In Denmark, the codetermination rights of workers over this and similar issues are extensive. The Belgian and West German situations have already been referred to.

In the United Kingdom, the Royal College of Nurses suggested that employers donate the expenses of running these services without a demand for control over them.

In South Africa workers have no statutory influence over these services nor are there agreements allowing for this. Several obstacles may be identified: Firstly, the professionals are against this, viewing it as a challenge to them. That is not the issue of course. It is not the role of those in the workplace to tell them how to perform physical examinations, but it certainly is part of their role to advise them what and where to investigate (e g use of chemical or material Y in department X could be responsible for so many headaches, coughs, etc. in that department), as in the Belgian approach. Secondly, there is the question of confidentiality of medical information. This is accepted as valid—though the refusal to provide this information to the person to whom it pertains, even on written request, defies any logic.

OTHER ISSUES AND ARGUMENTS

The 'cost–benefit' argument generates an intensity of emotion which sometimes clouds rationality.

It is true that in adopting safety and preventive measures, the company balances their *costs* against the *benefits* of such measures. Indeed, it is ideal to select a least-cost method to reduce injury and disease. However, rigid adherence to this position leads to the snare of seeking an easily demonstrable close accounting relationship between cost and benefits.

1 Identifying and quantifying costs

Whatever approach is selected, it is difficult to enumerate and quantify all the indirect effects of hazardous working conditions. Heinrich (1989) has suggested 'direct costs multiplied four times' as a near enough estimation of the true picture.

There are also problems of *latency* and a *synergistic effect*, making it difficult to estimate total accident and damage costs.

2 *Social costs and benefits*

It is not only the *individual* (the victim) who suffers loss, i e decreased income, loss of fringe benefits and potential decrease in income and associated benefits, vulnerability in times of high unemployment or during introduction of new technology, less job security because of handicap, the handicap affecting social status thus effecting personal social relationships. The *family* of the victim also become disadvantaged through: loss of income from a disabled breadwinner; the need for someone to take care of disabled member leading to loss of the income of the caring member; the need to modify life style to fit in with the condition of the disabled member; extra money needed for the disabled member (not ordinarily provided by the compensation received or being received).

Society has also to provide social security, rehabilitation and social welfare services, costs of which are diffused throughout the population in the form of taxes.

There are no beneftis at all.

3 *Valuation problems*

What is life worth? This is a very difficult question to answer, with the possiblity of loosing a flood of moral judgements.

4 *Efficiency versus equity*

If investment in health and safety is to be increased to a point where it becomes too expensive to prevent accidents and health risks, the concern is then about *efficiency*. The celebrated 'reasonably practicable" statements are a manifestation of this concern.

It is a tragedy for policy makers to concern themselves only with the 'amount of money spent' and not also with question of 'Who pays the price in terms of lost lives and who reaps the benefits?' These are issues of equity.

5 Efficiency, equity and risk premiums

The distribution of risks amongst workers is unequal in terms of
1 industry differences; and
2 certain job categories.

It is therefore clear that the conflict between efficiency and equity challenges society to make a trade-off of some efficiency if a more equitable distribution of the burden and costs of accidents is to be achieved.

6 'Cultural' factors

True or false, depending on which side of the 'fence' onc is, there are certain cultural beliefs that are important. A 'relationships by objectives' exercise the author once participated in, raised issues of cultural differences and how to handle them.

Some examples of the relevance of cultural factors in health and safety are:
1 the 'cleansing ceremony' that has to follow fatal accidents (workers carry this out in line with the traditional practices of the deceased); and
2 the importance of compassionate leave as an opportunity for the next of kin (extended as the family may be) to pay their last respectsto the deceased, and participate in the rites that have to be carried out. There is great cultural importance to this in black communities.

CONCLUSION

It is fitting, in this forum, for me to refrain from laying down guidelines, for consideration, except by way of sharing ideas as I have done. Suffice it to say that, even though the courts may have developed the understanding of 'right to negotiate',

and MOSA has provided the 'right to be informed', it is the
outcome details of joint agreements, arrived at through effective methods, that will set, improve and ensure application of
health and safety standards. South African management and
labour have taken only cautious steps towards getting to grips
with issues of health and safety in the workplace, in properly
debating issues of responsibility, risk, efficiency, equity and
culture, and their implications for industry and the wider
society in a future South Africa.

BIBLIOGRAPHY

Eva, D and Oswald, R *Health and Safety at Work*. Pan Books, London, 1981.

Heinrich, H W *Industrial Accident Prevention* 4th Edition, McGraw Hill Book Co., London, 1959.

Macum, I 'Safety Management, Yes Sir, MOSA, No Sir' *Indicator* vol 5 no 3, Autumn/Winter 1988, Durban p 67.

Morgenstern, F 'Some reflections on legal liability as a factor in the promotion of Occupational safety and health' *International Labour Review* vol 121 no 4 ILO, Geneva, Switzerland, July-August 1982, p 397.

Spyropoulos, G 'Working conditions in the industrial nations: What lies ahead?' *International Labour Review* vol 123 no 4, July-August 1984, p 391.

ANNEXURE A
SUMMARY OF FUNCTIONS OF SAFETY SHOP
STEWARDS

1   To represent the membership on health and safety issues.
2   To investigate:
    (a) potential hazards
    (b) dangerous occurrences
    (c) causes of accidents
    (d) complaints by employees.
3   To make representations to management.
4   To accompany and consult with the Inspector/s.
5   To receive information from Inspectors.
6   To inspect the workplace:
    (a) regularly
    (b) if there are any changes in working conditions
    (c) if new information about plant design, working process and materials used come to light
    (d) in cases of accidents/near misses
    (e) in cases if a disease is suspected to be caused by work.
7   To receive information from the employer
8   To consult with company Health and Safety practitioners.
9   Regular reports to Shop-Stewards Committee, members and Union Office.
10 Advise and educate members on:
    (a) Workman's Compensation procedures
    (b) Unemployment Insurance Fund (especially exptectant mothers)
11 To help the union isolate and safety issues at the workplace.
12 To lead the union members in monitoring implementation of the Health and Safety matters.
13 To attend Health and Safety courses, meetings and workshops run by the Union and pass information on to members.

ANNEXURE B
CHECKLIST ON JOINT UNION/MANAGEMENT
SAFETY COMMITTEES

To address the effectiveness of such Committees, these questions must be asked:

- How will the Committee meet?
- How big is the Committee and how is the size controlled?
- Who will chair the meetings?
- Are joint Secretaries required?
- Who will draw up and issue agendas?
- When will agendas be issued?
- Who will issue the minutes?
- Will all Safety Representatives and Shop Stewards receive copies of minutes?
- Will the minutes be put on notice boards for all members to see?
- What education is there for members of the Committee?
- What decision-making powers does the Committee have? (i e who will sit, especially on Management's side, on this Committee?)
- Will the Committee accept that Safety Representatives are not accountable to it?
- Will it be accepted that the existence of the Committee does *not reduce employer's primary responsibility for Health and Safety*?
- What investigative powers (*particularly access*) will the Committee have?
- What role does the Safety Officer, Nurse, etc, play?
- If there is more than one Trade Union, is representation in proportion to membership or equal?
- How is the attendance of meeting?

ANNEXURE C
SAFETY POLICIES: CHECKLIST

Obtain a copy of your workplace's Safety Policy and check:

1 Does it give details of policy of employer on providing information and training to workers and supervisors?

2 Are procedures laid down for recording accidents, near misses and ill-health at work?

   How does it define 'near misses'

3 Does it say if Management will always be on the look-out for new information (on materials, machinery and work process)?

4 Does it say how such information will be given to workers?

5 Does it identify the main dangers and rules and methods required to deal with them?

6 Does it give details of arrangements for and on:

   (*a*) senior managers responsible for Health and Safety?

   (*b*) duties of other managers and supervisors?

   (*c*) managers who will relieve those with responsibilities for Health and Safety?

   (*d*) duties of employer in collecting and circulating information?

7 Is the policy readily available to all workers?

8 In what ways will the policy be brought to the attention of workers?

9 Is there a provision for the revision of policy?

10 In what ways and after how long will the policy be revised?

11 Who signed the policy?

12 How old is the policy? (look at the date below the signature).

INDEX

INDUSTRIAL RELATIONS TITLES FROM JUTA

INDUSTRIAL RELATIONS HANDBOOK
Policies, Procedures and Practices for South African Managers
ANDREW PONS

This loose-leaf publication assists the management team to promote successful relationships with employees in order to continue to develop in the medium to long term. It has been designed to take cognisance of developments both in labour law and the current practice of industrial relations in South Africa. Practical guidelines are set out in detail ensuring the value of this book as a "hands-on" text suitable for all levels of management.

INDUSTRIAL RELATIONS IN SOUTH AFRICA
SONIA BENDIX

In some 600 concise and informative pages, frequently punctuated by tables, figures and charts, Sonia Bendix skilfully analyses international industrial relations principles and specifically gives in-depth insight into our own. It includes the 1988 Amendments to the Labour Relations Act and a chapter is devoted solely to dispute settlement machinery in South Africa dealing with the question of fairness, unfair labour practice and the Industrial Court.

PERSONNEL MANAGEMENT: THE BUSINESS OWNER'S HANDBOOK FOR SMALL AND MEDIUM SIZED COMPANIES
JULIA HOLDEN

Written specifically for any business that is operating without in-house personnel management staff, this easy-to-read, subscription publication provides a working system that is quick to implement and provides the procedural 'knowledge' required to deal with employees. It is the only publication available that provides vital working documents that the subscriber is free to copy and to use. The only entrepreneur who can afford to be without this handbook is the specialist who consults and works alone.

NEGOTIATION—THEORY, STRATEGIES AND SKILLS
PROFESSORS M SPOELSTRA & W PIENAAR

Although various approaches and theories of negotiation are acknowledged, the authors of this test clearly view negotiation as a process wherein the development of alternatives to strongly emphasised. Verbal and non-verbal strategies and skills in negotiation receive detailed attention. The book explains how power can be deployed during negotiation and how attitudes and behaviours can be changed through the use of a few step-by-step recipes.

CONFLICT MANAGEMENT
PROFESSOR D DE VILLIERS

This is a pathbreaking text on one of the most important aspects of industrial relations written by one of South Africa's leading academics from the School of Business Leadership at UNISA. It is of value to anyone affected in any way by employer–employee relationships and, indeed interpersonal relationships in every sphere of their lives.

THE McGREGOR LIBRARY

McGREGOR'S WHO OWNS WHOM—The Investors' Handbook

A thorough, exhaustive and easy-to-use analysis of relevant data on over 700 companies listed on the JSE. The most comprehensive work on any stock exchange in the world.

"Few publications relating to Diagonal Street provide more valuable references than Robin McGregor's annual offering."
FINANCE WEEK June 1987.

McGREGOR'S QUICK REFERENCE TO THE JSE

This six-monthly publication provides a detailed summary of listed companies' annual reports. Graphic reflections of performance over fifteen months and performance relative to each company's sector are included to give the subscriber an instant appreciation of the relevant share's trend.

McGREGOR'S TAKEOVER TALK

A companion volume to WHO OWNS WHOM—THE INVESTORS' HANDBOOK, this loose-leaf publication keeps you up to date on a monthly basis on a whole range of related and pertinent topics, takeovers, mergers and other important company changes.

McGREGOR'S PRIVATISATION IN SOUTH AFRICA

Including schedules of State owned bodies the book pinpoints where privatisation and de-regulation can assist in regeneration and revitalisation. Of value to all decision-makers in both the public and the private sector, and for the academic.

McGREGOR'S THE MECHANICS OF THE JOHANNESBURG STOCK EXCHANGE

Not only does this volume provide the reader with a detailed account of exactly how the Johannesburg Stock Exchange works, its history, who it belongs to and where it is going, but it also gives authoritative opinions on such subjects as the various investment philosophies, the merits and demerits of unit trusts, debentures, gilts etc and the value and usage of indicators. There is also a chapter on the concentration of control of the JSE explaining in full the methodology and rationale behind this concept. It is an essential reference work for the big and small investor, the student and the businessman.

McGREGOR'S CYNIC'S GUIDE TO THE STOCK EXCHANGE

Although related in a relaxed, witty and droll style, Dr Jannie Hofmeyr's on-going tryst with the stock exchange reveals a set of incisive strategies of use to the serious investor, the dabbler or for those who merely dream of tilting at the JSE. A wealth of research data, historical precedent and anecdote all serve to address the basic questions, fears and forebodings of every investor, especially after the Great Crash.

McGREGOR'S DICTIONARY OF STOCK MARKET TERMS

The main problem in learning any subject is its nomenclature. As more private investors start to learn about shares and the stock market, the greater the room for misunderstanding. Yet, with the greater specialisation of the financial markets, the greater is the need for a specialised language and a dedicated glossary of terms. This dictionary by Ciaran Ryan will help in the understanding of these markets, and their peculiar languages.

THE FREE MARKET SERIES
FROM JUTA & COMPANY, LTD

SOUTH AFRICA'S WAR AGAINST CAPITALISM *Walter Williams*

Williams analyses the negative economic impact made by apartheid and he illustrates how discriminatory legislation (of any kind) militates against the development of a free market economy. He shows how costly this legislation has proved itself to be and why it was deemed necessary in the first place. He also warns that its perpetuation in a changing society is not only possible, but probable. A vital work for students of labour relations, policy makers, industrial relations practitioners and the informed layman.

LIBERTY AND PROSPERITY *Vorhies & Grant*
Essays in Limiting Government and Freeing Enterprise in South Africa

This collection of essays advocates a market-based economy and a decentralized, non-racial and democratic system of government for South Africa. Issues addressed include: sanctions; monopolies; privatisation; the distribution of wealth; conscription; education; the role of a free press, etc. These essays show how liberal reforms and institutions can be used to the benefit of our society. This book will prove invaluable to anybody, inside or outside of government, connected in any way to the emerging process of negotiated change.

CONSUMER POWER IN A FREE MARKET *Seijas & Vorhies*

South African consumers have long been accused of being among the most apathetic in the world. The message that emerges from these essays is that economic freedom and the threat of competition give consumers – not government or big business – the ability to decide the goods, the services and the prices in an economy. This book provides the South African consumer with a clear and comprehensive introduction to consumer issues in South Africa and the importance of a market economy to protect consumer interests.

COMPREHENDING KARL MARX *Vorhies*

The ideas of Karl Marx are introduced from a non-Marxist, individualistic perspective in this concise and non-technical book. It presents his theories in an objective and balanced fashion and, because this is the case, the serious flaws in Marx's approach to social development begin to become apparent to the reader. It is crucial that educators, industrial relations practitioners, negotiators and the informed public in favour of a free market have a source which provides them with a clear and straightforward introduction to Marxism.

THESE BOOKS ARE AVAILABLE FROM JUTA BOOKSHOPS OR LEADING BOOKSELLERS COUNTRYWIDE